THE OLIVER WENDELL HOLMES DEVISE
HISTORY OF THE SUPREME COURT
OF THE UNITED STATES

General Editors: PAUL A. FREUND and STANLEY N. KATZ

THE
Oliver Wendell Holmes
DEVISE

HISTORY OF
THE SUPREME COURT
OF THE UNITED STATES

SUPPLEMENT TO VOLUME VII

THE OLIVER WENDELL HOLMES DEVISE

History of the
SUPREME COURT
of the United States

Supplement to Volume VII

Five Justices and the Electoral Commission of 1877

By Charles Fairman

NEW YORK

Macmillan Publishing Company

Collier Macmillan Publishers

LONDON

Macmillan Publishing Company
866 Third Avenue, New York, N.Y. 10022
Collier Macmillan Canada, Inc.

Library of Congress Cataloging-in-Publication Data
(Revised for volume 7)

Fairman, Charles, 1897–
Reconstruction and reunion, 1864–88.

(History of the Supreme Court of the United States, v. 6–7)
Half title: The Oliver Wendell Holmes Devise.
Includes bibliographical footnotes.
1. United States.   Supreme Court—History.   I. Title.
KF8742.A45H55   vol. 6   KF8742   347'.73'26   70–169254
ISBN 0–02–536920–2

10 9 8 7 6 5 4 3 2 1

Printed in the United States of America

Contents

Illustrations

ix

Foreword

THE *History of the Supreme Court of the United States* is being pre-
pared under the auspices of the Permanent Committee for the Oliver
Wendell Holmes Devise with the aid of the estate left by Mr. Justice
Oliver Wendell Holmes, Jr. Mr. Justice Holmes died in 1935 and the
Permanent Committee for the Devise was created by Act of Congress in
1955. Members of the Committee are appointed by the President of the
United States, with the Librarian of Congress, an *ex officio* member, as
Chairman. The present volume is a supplement to the seventh volume in
the series. The Committee hopes to complete the history expeditiously
while maintaining the high quality of the scholarship. The volumes in the
Holmes Devise *History of the Supreme Court of the United States* bring
to this subject some of the best legal scholarship of the decades since Mr.
Justice Holmes' death. They will also have such advantages (not anticipated at the time of the Justice's death) as can be secured from a more
than ample measure of judicious deliberation. We hope that, when completed, the series will widen and deepen our understanding of the Supreme
Court and bring honor to the memory of one of its great Justices.

Daniel J. Boorstin
LIBRARIAN OF CONGRESS

xi

PERMANENT COMMITTEE FOR
THE OLIVER WENDELL HOLMES DEVISE

(TERMS OF EIGHT YEARS EXCEPT FOR INITIAL APPOINTMENTS)

Charles T. McCormick	1956–58	(two-year term)
Edward S. Corwin	1956–60	(four-year term)
George L. Haskins	1956–58	(six-year term, but resigned 10/7/58)
Virgil M. Hancher	1956–64	
Frederick D. G. Ribble	1958–66	
Ethan A. H. Shepley	1959–67	
Nicholas Kelley	7/8/60–7/22/60	
Jefferson B. Fordham	1961–69	
Harry H. Ransom	1964–72	
Herbert Wechsler	1966–74	
Robert G. McCloskey	1967–69	
J. A. C. Grant	1970–78	
Alfred H. Kelly	1970–78	
Philip B. Kurland	1975–83	
Charles A. Wright	1975–83	
Stanley N. Katz	1976–84	
Paul J. Mishkin	1979–87	
Gerhard Casper	1984–92	
Richard B. Morris	1985–93	

xii

Editor's Foreword

Since secession and civil war there have been three major constitutional crises in our history. In two of them, the Court reorganization plan of 1937 and the presidential tapes controversy of 1973, the Supreme Court found itself at the center of the storm. In the third, and possibly the most acute, the disputed presidential election of 1876, the Court was involved in a different and unique way. It was involved not as an institution but through the appointment of five Justices to the Commission of fifteen created by Congress to resolve the stalemate arising from the political division between the Senate and the House. Not until a few days before the date fixed for the inauguration did the Commission's eight-to-seven decision conclude the contest, in accordance with its congressional Charter, through its acceptance by the Republican Senate, notwithstanding rejection by the Democratic House. Divided seven to seven on recognized party lines, the decisive vote and opinion was that of the member appointed for judicial impartiality, Justice Joseph P. Bradley.

The place of this episode in a history of the Supreme Court presented a question. Since it fell outside the mainstream of the Court's business it might have been treated in passing as simply a peripheral duty imposed on certain of its members. The significance of this episode for the reputation and proper role of the Court, however, makes it impossible to divorce it from the Court's history. When the Commission first met, Representative James Garfield noted in his diary that Justice William Strong told him that "all the judges except one were very sorry to be called to the Commission." (The exception was presumably Justice Stephen J. Field, an indefatigable Democrat.) More particularly, obloquy has been heaped on Justice Bradley for what has been depicted as a last-minute change of position under covert political pressure.

Fortunately for this History, Professor Fairman has had a long-standing scholarly interest in this affair. His characteristically scrupulous and thoroughgoing study throws new light on the controversy which vindicates Justice Bradley against his detractors. Professor Fairman is able to show how the congressional critics had themselves taken Bradley's legal position when the question arose before partisan interests were engaged; how inherently incredible representations were made about Bradley's preparation of his opinion and delivery of it in an executive session of the Commission; and how malice and perhaps even hallucination have fed the assault.

This is a work that should give rise to a revision of historical understanding, a work that combines intensive research with all the fascination of a detective story.

The volume does not pursue the story beyond the labors of the Electoral Commission and into the politics of what is known as the Compromise of 1877. Justice Samuel Miller, returning from the inaugural ceremony, wrote that "the cannon are peacefully playing the last part in that drama. It is to me a great relief."

Paul A. Freund

Preface

THE AUTUMN PRESIDENTIAL ELECTION of 1876 brought the nation to the brink of peril. It appeared that Samuel J. Tilden of New York, the Democratic candidate, would have a small majority of the electoral votes, but that Florida, Louisiana, and South Carolina were in political disorder and might make conflicting returns. The outcome might be a bare majority for Rutherford B. Hayes of Ohio, the Republican candidate. Neither the Constitution nor the statutes provided for such a situation.

The Second Session of the 44th Congress, convening on December 4, 1876, recognized the urgent need for a solution to permit the peaceful inauguration of a President on March 4, 1877. The House of Representatives (under Democratic control) and the Senate (with a Republican majority) each named a committee which, working in conjunction, would report a proper mode of counting the electoral votes.

In aid of that mandate on December 23 an order was made a compilation of the proceedings and debates of Congress relating to the counting of electoral votes from the first election to the present time. That was executed while Congress was in recess over the holidays.

When Congress returned the committees busied themselves in finding accord on a report. On January 8, 1877, they laid before the Houses a measure to create an Electoral Commission to which disputed returns would be submitted for decision. That became law on January 29. The Commission would be composed of five Senators, five Representatives, and five Associate Justices of the Supreme Court. Four of the Justices were designated as being assigned to the First, Third, Eighth, and Ninth Circuits; by them the fifth Justice would be chosen.

The resulting body would include Senators Edmunds, Frelinghuysen, and Morton, Republicans; and Thurman and Bayard, Democrats. From the House came Payne, Hunton, and Abbott, Democrats; and Hoar and Garfield, Republicans. The Justices would be Clifford and Field, known to be Democrats, and Miller and Strong, Republicans. The fifth Justice was Bradley, a Republican. The senior Justice, Clifford, would be President of the Commission. All the Commissioners took an oath impartially to examine and consider all questions and true judgment give, according to the Constitution and laws.

The Commission convened on January 31 and in the ensuing month decided conflicts from Florida, Louisiana, Oregon, and South Carolina. All decisions were by the eight Republican members, the Democrats all dissenting. The result was that there were 185 electoral votes for Hayes and 184 for Tilden.

Historians have generally treated the episode of the Electoral Commission as a shabby affair. For example, one wrote ''There could be no question of the decision . . . since there were eight Republicans and seven Democrats. The commission was, in reality, no tribunal at all. . . . It was a comedy.''

To another, ''The careful studies . . . long after the heat of the battle had passed indicate that Tilden was deprived of his rightful claim as President.'' Reference was made to ''the magnitude of the fraud.''

A third wrote, ''even with the disputed states counted as Republican, Tilden had a plurality of 250,000 votes over Hayes. There is no longer any doubt that the election was 'stolen.' ''

One wrote in disbelief, ''Bradley always claimed that his work on the Electoral Commission was as pure as the driven snow.''

It is high time that a much better-informed account be presented to the public.

Recall the order of December 23, 1876, for the compilation of proceedings and debates since the first election. *Counting Electoral Votes*, House Miscellaneous Document No. 13, 44th Congress, Second Session, is a document of 807 pages, produced by January 4, 1877. Of great significance is the little-known report of debates in the Senate in February 1875, near the close of the Second Session of the 43d Congress, renewed in March 1876 at the First Session of the 44th Congress. The Senate was searching for a prescription for the mode of counting electoral votes in advance of any awkward situation. No Senator could foresee where partisan advantage might lie if a controversy arose. Many solutions were proposed. A number of Southern Democrats insisted that counting of electoral votes should be decided by the President of the Senate, although that office then and for some years to come would be filled by a Republican. Near the close of the debate Senator Thurman said

There was not an allusion on any side that could be considered in any sense partisan. . . .

xvi

The sincerity and disinterestedness of what was said in the debates of 1875–76 give them a unique credibility. The most thoughtful and understanding participants were Thurman and Bayard, Democrats, and Frelinghuysen and Edmunds, Republicans.

Unfortunately it proved impossible to agree upon a measure to be sent to the House, and on August 15, 1876, the session came to an end.

The ensuing autumn election showed to each party where its immediate interest lay. On November 15, 1876, Abram S. Hewitt, Democratic National Chairman, stated what would be the party's position:

> Congress [should] go behind the [governor's] certificate and open the same to get into the merits of all cases. . . .

That was precisely what Thurman, Bayard, and other Democrats, and Frelinghuysen and other thoughtful Republicans, had been insisting *must not be done*.

Only one Senator in the debates had taken the view Hewitt established for the Democratic party: that was Boutwell of Massachusetts, a Republican.

If commentators had been sufficiently penetrating to study the Senate debates of 1875–76 they might have learned that the position seized by the Democrats after the election was in contradiction to the thoughtful opinion recently approved by their leaders. Also they might have discovered Democratic statements precisely in accord with what became Justice Bradley's judgment in the Commission.

Hewitt went on to become a reform mayor of New York City in 1887–88. His devoted service to Columbia College, his alma mater, caused President Nicholas Murray Butler to seek the production of an appreciative biography. Professor Allan Nevins, whose seven-league marches had covered wide areas of American history, undertook the writing of the book. No question is here raised as to the high quality of *Abram S. Hewitt, with Some Account of Peter Cooper* until it comes to Hewitt's account of the election of 1876 and the Electoral Commission. When Democratic submission to arbitration ended in the defeat of Tilden, some of his followers in their bitterness turned upon Hewitt for his management of the campaign. Henry Watterson denounced him as "a falsifier and charlatan." Hewitt himself took pride in securing acceptance of the Commission as "one of his chief public services."

In self-vindication in 1878 he wrote an account of the episode. This he revised in 1895 as the "Secret History" and left to be published only when all participants were gone.

When Nevins' biography appeared in 1935 this account was presented at length as true and reliable. So confident was he in the story that he failed to test it. Rather he went on to supply elaboration.

After painstaking study I became convinced that Hewitt's account was not reliable, and that Nevins in his infatuation with his subject had led historians astray. This I have undertaken to establish in the account that follows.

This brings to a close my *History of the Supreme Court, 1864–88*. I have been privileged to walk in my thoughts with great judges, notably Miller, Waite, and Bradley, magistrates ever mindful of the Constitution's cardinal purpose "to establish Justice," generous in spirit, and faithful to the end. They remain with me.

My file of correspondence with my friend and counselor, Paul A. Freund, Editor-in-Chief of the *Holmes Devise History of the Supreme Court*, is three inches thick, and our conversations by telephone are too numerous to record. I have relied upon his wisdon, and am grateful for his never-failing helpfulness, especially in his assumption of the task of proofreading. Now that the work is finished there abides our bond of affection and respect.

CHARLES FAIRMAN

*Five Justices
and the Electoral Commission*

PROLOGUE

"There is now no law, and there has never been a law, providing what shall be done in case of a contested election of presidential electors."

Representative James A. Garfield, March 24, 1868

I N APPROACHING THE DISPUTED Presidential election of 1876 one should bear in mind certain basic constitutional provisions.

By Section 1 of Article II,

Each State shall appoint, in such Manner as the Legislature thereof may direct, a Number of Electors, equal to the whole Number of Senators and Representatives to which the State may be entitled in the Congress: but no Senator or Representative, or Person holding an Office of Trust or Profit under the United States, shall be appointed an Elector.

Then by the language of the Twelfth Amendment, adopted in 1804,

The Electors shall meet in their respective states, and vote by ballot for President and Vice-President, . . . ; they shall name in their ballots the person voted for as President, and in distinct lists of all persons voted for as President, and of all persons voted for as Vice-President, and of the number of votes for each, which lists they shall sign and certify, and transmit sealed to the seat of the government of the United States, directed to the President of the Senate. . . .

Here it becomes relevant to quote from Article I, on the organization of Congress, that

The Vice President of the United States shall be President of the Senate, but shall have no Vote, unless they be equally divided.
The Senate shall chuse their other Officers, and also a President pro tempore, in the Absence of the Vice President. . . .

Resuming quotation from the Twelfth Amendment,

> The President of the Senate shall, in the presence of the Senate and House of Representatives, open all the certificates, and the votes shall then be counted. . . .

Counted by whom? Inferentially by the President of the Senate? But he would be a prominent politician, perhaps himself a candidate for the Presidency, or for reelection as Vice President. Was that an acceptable answer?

The Twelfth Amendment continues, establishing the possibility of election by the House:

> The person having the greatest number of votes for President, shall be the President, if such number be a majority of the whole number of electors appointed; and if no person have such majority, then from the persons having the highest numbers not exceeding three on the list of those voted for as President, the House of Representatives shall choose immediately, by ballot, the President. But in choosing the President, the votes shall be taken by States, the representation from each State having one vote; a quorum for this purpose shall consist of a member or members from two-thirds of the States, and a majority of all the States shall be necessary to a choice. . . .

Under this provision in 1824 the election had been by the House. Jackson had received 99 electoral votes; John Q. Adams, 84; W. H. Crawford, 41, and Henry Clay, 37. On resort to the House, Adams received the votes of 13 States to 7 for Jackson.

If electoral proceedings were ever again brought to this extremity, conceivably a majority of the States, dominated by one party, though woefully misrepresentative of the nation as a whole, might elect the President. A far more worrisome possibility was that conflicting certificates might be sent up from a State in disorder.

On March 24, 1868, Garfield offered a resolution in the House of Representatives:

> That the Committee on the Judiciary be directed to inquire into the expediency of providing by law for the settlement of contested elections for electors of the President and Vice President of the United States, and that they report by bill or otherwise.

He explained,

> It seems to me it would be a great calamity should the time ever come when one State of the Union, perhaps holding the balance of power,

2

should appear in the Electoral College by two sets of electors, and there was no provision to settle the question.[1]

The resolution was adopted, but no such measure was reported.

The likelihood was that if such a deadlock occurred in the course of the next few Presidential elections it would be in one or more of the Southern States restored to representation, and that hostility to blacks would be at the root of the difficulty.

When Garfield spoke it was not quite three years since Lee's surrender, Lincoln's death, and the accession of Andrew Johnson to the Presidency. Under Provisional Governors the rebel States had enacted black codes and maintained pre-war institutions for white rule, minus "slavery." When the 39th Congress convened on December 4, 1865, the President's message had announced that "gradually and quietly" he had brought the insurrectionary States to the point where they were prepared "to resume their places in the two branches of the national Legislature, and thereby complete the work of restoration."[2]

At that moment ratification of the Thirteenth Amendment had been completed:

> Section 1. Neither slavery nor involuntary servitude, except as a punishment for crime whereof the party shall have been duly convicted, shall exist within the United States, or any place subject to their jurisdiction.
> Section 2. Congress shall have power to enforce this article by appropriate legislation.

Eight of the States not yet restored to representation had been counted for ratification.

If Johnson's prescription had been followed by Congress the errant States would have been subject to no additional restraint beyond the abolition of "slavery." They would have joined their friends the Northern Democrats, with the prospect that in the reapportionment following the Census of 1870 the former "Slave States" would gain in relative strength over the "Free States" in the House of Representatives and the Electoral College, inasmuch as former slaves would be counted as "free persons," no longer at three-fifths of their number.[3] It would have seemed possible soon to elect a Democratic President, well disposed to claims by the South. For a people defeated in their rebellion, what more could be asked?

Congress, each House dominated by Unionists, determined first to establish additional guaranties to secure the results of the war. A Joint

---

[1] Cong. Globe, 40–2, 2083.

[2] Cong. Globe, 39–1, App. 1, 2.
[3] Constitution, Art. I, Sec. 1, cl. 3.

Committee on Reconstruction set about framing a Fourteenth Amendment. Meanwhile the Civil Rights Act of April 9, 1866, carried over a veto, declared persons born in the United States to be citizens, with equal right to contract, sue, give testimony, and to have equal benefit of laws for the security of person and property.[4] Also over a veto, a Freedmen's Bureau Bill had extended military jurisdiction to protect the civil rights of citizens in the South.[5]

On June 13, 1866, the Fourteenth Amendment was submitted to the States. It made clear that blacks born in the United States were citizens thereof; no State should deprive any person of life, liberty, or property without due process of law, or deny equal protection of the laws. It did not secure black suffrage, but Section 2 sought to reduce the representation of any State in proportion to the number of adult males it excluded. Section 3 would bar from holding office, but not from voting, all persons who had given aid to the rebellion *after having taken an official oath to support the Constitution.*

Tennessee, under Republican control, made haste to ratify, and on July 24 was restored to representation under a joint resolution reciting that the consent of Congress was requisite to readmission.[6]

The line had been drawn for the autumn election of Members to the 40th Congress: would the voters in the loyal States endorse the work of the 39th Congress—or would they support President Johnson and the Democratic party? The President went on an electioneering trip to Chicago and St. Louis, with stops along the railroad line. He reverted to his unguarded acrimony—mortifying his well-wishers and alienating the voters.

The election in November 1866 was an unprecedented triumph for the Republican party, which in the 40th Congress would have a preponderance of nearly 3 to 1 in the House and nearly 4 to 1 in the Senate.[7]

When the 39th Congress returned for its Second Session it found the unreconstructed States rejecting the Fourteenth Amendment as degrading: they supposed that if they held together the Amendment must fail for want of ratification by three-fourths of the thirty-seven States. Kentucky, Maryland, and Delaware were also rejecting.

Congress was not going to allow itself to be frustrated so easily. Proceeding from measures considered at the First Session, it settled on a bill "to provide for a more efficient Government of the Rebel States," which being carried over a veto became the Act of March 2, 1867.[8] When a State had by impartial suffrage framed a constitution in conformity with

---

[4] 14 Stat. 27.
[5] 14 Stat. 173.
[6] 14 Stat. 364.
[7] *Oliver Wendell Holmes Devise His-tory of the Supreme Court of the United States,* VI, 117–33, 182.
[8] 14 Stat. 428.

the Constitution of the United States, and had ratified the Fourteenth Amendment, it would be entitled to representation in Congress. Meanwhile the States were divided into five military districts, each under a general officer. Any civil government then existing would be subject to the paramount authority of the United States in all respects.

The 40th Congress met on March 4, 1867, and on March 23 passed a Supplementary Act providing detailed steps whereby a State might be readmitted to representation.[9] An impartial registration would be held of adult males qualified to vote. Then the commanding general would call an election for delegates. Those in favor would vote *for a convention,* those opposed would vote *against a convention;*

> Provided, That such convention shall not be held *unless a majority of all such registered voters shall have voted on the question* of holding a convention. [Emphasis supplied.]

Thus if obstructionists registered, and then stayed away from the election in a number amounting to a majority of those registered, they would defeat the Congressional plan and cause the State to remain under the control of the commanding general—a result they considered highly desirable: black suffrage would be averted, and time would have been gained for a Democratic victory at the polls, or perhaps the Supreme Court would hold the Reconstruction measures unconstitutional. But if they failed in their obstruction, they would have surrendered constitution-making to white Radicals and blacks—a result Congress had not intended.

The experience in Georgia was typical: The returns from registration were

$$
\begin{array}{r}
96,333 \text{ whites} \\
\underline{95,168 \text{ colored}} \\
191,501 \text{ total}
\end{array}
$$

Of those registered, only 106,410 came to the polls. They voted as follows on calling a convention:

For: 32,000 whites   Against: 4,000 whites
       70,283 colored   127 colored
     102,283 total   4,127 total

Of the whites registered, 37 percent came to vote; of the colored, 74 percent. The great mass of conservative whites had spurned the proceedings.

---

[9] 15 Stat. 2. A reasoned discussion of the various solutions considered in reaching the two statutes is set out in VI, 333–43.

The convention called by General Meade met at Atlanta on December 9, 1867. The constitution it framed was submitted to the people on March 11, 1868, and was ratified by 89,007 votes against 71,309 opposed.[10]

Proceeding under the Congressional plan, seven States had by the end of July 1868 ratified the Fourteenth Amendment and been declared by Congress to be readmitted to representation: Arkansas, North Carolina, South Carolina, Louisiana, Alabama, Florida, and Georgia. In June and July their Representatives had been seated and (except for Georgia) so too had their Senators.

Virginia and Mississippi had run into difficulties,[11] and Texas had been coming along slowly. Those States—and Georgia—would not be restored until 1870.

CONTRETEMPS IN GEORGIA (1868)

PERVERSE ACTION IN GEORGIA now gave early warning of commotion that could arise between House and Senate over the counting of a State's electoral vote.

The legislature chosen under the State's new constitution met on July 4, 1868. On the twenty-first it ratified the Fourteenth Amendment. All seemed to be in order for Georgia to resume its place in the Union. Six Representatives—two Democrats and four Republicans—had been seated. A seventh seat had been contested, and remained vacant.

On September 15, however, the lower house of the legislature expelled its twenty-five black members by vote of 83 to 23. The Senate followed suit. The vacancies were to be filled by those who had stood next in the polls. "The [white] Radicals and Democrats seem to be united on this question," the *Augusta Chronicle & Sentinel* reported, "for without the aid of the former it would have been impossible. . . ." "WELL DONE," said the *Atlanta Constitution;* "we congratulate the people of Georgia on their return to a 'white man's government.' . . ."

When the 40th Congress met on December 7, 1868, for its third and short session that must end by March 3, there was indignation over the action in Georgia but uncertainty what to do about it. One reaction was that there should be a constitutional amendment to secure *the right to hold office,* as well as the right to vote, against denial on account of race. This concern would loom large when in a few days debate began on a Fifteenth Amendment.

Quite aside from that, should Congress now declare that Georgia,

---

[10] VI, 412–13.　　　[11] VI, 406–32.

6

by reason of the action of its legislature, was not entitled to readmission to representation? For want of time, that matter was deferred.

One question, however, demanded instant attention: when the result of the recent Presidential election was announced, should Georgia's nine electoral votes be included? In December 1868 all the world knew that Grant and Colfax, the Republican candidates for President and Vice President, had been elected and would be so declared with 214 electoral votes. The Democratic candidates, Seymour and Blair, would have 80 or 71 votes, depending on whether Georgia's votes were included or excluded.

On February 6, 1869, Senator George F. Edmunds introduced a concurrent resolution to meet the situation:

> Whereas the question whether the State of Georgia . . . is entitled to representation is now pending and undetermined, [if the counting or omitting of the electoral votes from Georgia] shall not essentially change the result, the Presiding Officer would announce what the result would be in the one case and in the other, but that in either case _____ is elected President. . . .[12]

The Senate adopted this proposal and the House concurred.[13]

On February 10, 1869, at a joint convention, the President pro tem. of the Senate, Benjamin F. Wade of Ohio, began opening the certificates, which were then announced by one of the tellers. When, last of all, Georgia was reached, Representative Benjamin F. Butler of Massachusetts objected on four grounds: first, that the electors had not met and voted on the day fixed by law; other objections were that Georgia had not been readmitted; that it had not fulfilled the requirements of the Reconstruction Acts; and that the election in Georgia in November had not been free and fair. Edmunds addressed the chair: the objection was out of order, since in regard to Georgia the concurrent resolution had changed the rules. Representative Butler: "the votes must be counted or rejected by the convention of the two Houses," notwithstanding any prior concurrent resolution; "this is a matter of constitutional law and in other times may make great trouble. . . ." The President pro tem.: "Objection being made, the Senate will retire to their Chamber to deliberate. . . ."[14]

What was the question to be decided? Butler's first objection, that the electors had not voted on the day fixed by law, was something quite aside from the status of Georgia. Hence, in his view, it fell outside the scope of the concurrent resolution. Edmunds' contention was that the

---

[12] Cong. Globe, 40–3, 934. Edmunds used a form that had been adopted in certain other instances where the decision of a difficult question would make no substantial difference.
[13] Ibid., 978, 971–72.
[14] Ibid., 1049–58.

concurrent resolution governed the entire matter: the announcement should be that Georgia's vote, counted or not, would make no difference. If the House were to vote to sustain Butler's objection and say "No" to counting the votes, and the Senate were to sustain Edmunds' position, there would be a variance between the decisive "No" and the evasive "No matter."

And so it happened. In the House, the question was put, Shall the vote of Georgia be counted? The response was 41 yeas (almost all from Democrats) to 150 nays. In the Senate, Edmunds proposed "that under the special order . . . the objections . . . are not in order." On that resolution the vote was 32 yeas to 27 nays.

When the Senators returned to the Hall of the House, Wade resumed the chair and announced,

> The objections of the gentleman from Massachusetts are over-
> ruled by the Senate, and the result of the vote will be stated . . . under
> the concurrent resolution. . . .

The difference between the two Houses would have been awkward enough, but the statement that the Representative's objections were *overruled by the Senate* proved to be fighting words.

Butler precipitated what soon became a disgraceful commotion. "I do not understand that we are to be overruled by the Senate in that way. . . . I know I speak the sentiment of the House. Do I not?" There were cries of Yes!, Yes!, also of Order! Order! while the President reiterated that "The tellers will perform their duty under the concurrent resolution as directed." The reporter interjected "great confusion," "laughter," "great uproar"; "Renewed shouts of 'Order!' " Butler: "I move that this convention now be dissolved, and that the Senate have leave to retire." The President: "The tellers will now declare the result." Senator Conkling, a teller, "amid great noise and disorder" then announced the result, that Grant had received 214 votes, Seymour 80 or 71, etc.

As soon as the Senate had withdrawn and the Speaker had resumed the chair, Butler was on his feet with a resolution, that what the President pro tem. had done "was a gross act of oppression and an invasion of the rights and privileges of the House." Debate followed until adjournment that day (Wednesday, February 10), and was continued on Thursday and Friday.

The discussion ranged widely. Shellabarger of Ohio, Republican, inferred from the text of the Constitution that "in the absence of legislation," the counting of electoral votes would be *by the President of the Senate;* "the opening and counting together" seemed to be one act. Surely, replied Thomas of Maryland, a Democrat, "It cannot be that

[Representatives and Senators] should sit by here and permit the President of the Senate to make a false count . . . thus, perhaps, throwing the country into confusion." He concluded that "Congress had the power, by law or by joint resolution, not only to prescribe the manner in which the vote should be counted, but to inquire into the validity, the sufficiency, the actuality of the votes that might be presented to the Vice President to be counted. . . ."

Garfield recalled that there was need to provide by law for the settlement of contested elections for electors of the President: a year before he had raised that matter in a resolution still before the Judiciary Committee. On the immediate question, however, it was his view that the concurrent resolution on Georgia governed "to the exclusion of all other rules." The language of Wade's announcement was not strictly correct, but it was not "worth while to dispute about the mere form of words." Butler, he said, had displayed "a manner and bearing of unparalleled insolence." If the President pro tem. had faltered before the "unseemly clamor," we might have "found ourselves in chaos after the 4th of March next, with no President-elect. . . ."

During the debate Butler became less audacious. He modified his motion to omit the censure. "I have never believed . . . that Ben Wade meant to do . . . a wrong act."

Logan of Illinois brought a cessation by an appeal "to reflect, as cool, honorable, just men who would not knowingly wrong anybody"; he moved "to lay this whole subject on the table," and so it was ordered by vote of 130 to 55.

If such a storm could be raised by one Congressman against a Senator of his own party, where the difference was over a nice question of no practical consequence, how intense would be the controversy eight years later when the Presidency was at stake after an election viewed as decisive for the future and the Houses were controlled by opposing parties!

THE SENATE IN SEARCH OF A RULE, 1875–76

ACCOUNTS OF THE DISPUTED ELECTION have ignored the effort of Senators in February 1875, renewed in March 1876, to frame a proper measure to regulate the counting of electoral votes, including cases where conflicting returns were sent up from a State. It was an exercise in innocence and truth, in patriotism and faith. Wisdom, however, had to wait on dilatory Time, and when the crisis arose there still was no regulation, and the interest of party became paramount. We shall be enlightened to learn Members' sincere views as disclosed before the test came.

(When in December 1876 it became evident that the election had produced a controversy, House and Senate each appointed a committee to seek a mode of resolving the difference. Henry B. Payne of Ohio was chairman of the select committee of the House. He caused a volume of precedents to be compiled, a book of 807 pages, *Counting Electoral Votes. Proceedings and Debates in Congress relating to the Counting of Electoral Votes,* including proceedings in the constitutional convention of 1787 [House Document No. 13 Miscellaneous Documents, 44th Cong. 2d Sess.] In addition to citing the *Congressional Record* we shall cite also to the equivalent place in *Counting.*)

Back in February 1865 when the counting of electoral votes was at hand the two Houses resolved that the States in rebellion were ineligible to join in the voting; accordingly it was declared by the 22d Joint Rule that "no vote objected to shall be counted except by the concurring vote of the two Houses."[15]

Ten years later, on February 4, 1875, the Southern States being restored to the Union, but with some internal disorder, the Senate near the close of the Second Session of the 43d Congress took up a concurrent resolution reported by Morton from the Committee on Privileges and Elections:

> That the twenty-second joint rule . . . is hereby repealed.

But then Morton said that in the light of consultation with other members he offered a substitute:

> That the twenty-second joint rule . . . be so amended that no objection to the reception and counting of any electoral vote or votes from any State shall be valid unless such objection is sustained by the affirmative vote of the two Houses.[16]

Bayard of Delaware, Democrat, spoke at once, "without having given the examination or consideration to this subject that its importance demands. . . ."

> I confess that I do not see where the power can possibly be found which is assumed by the joint rule, either as it now stands or as it is proposed to be amended, giving the two Houses of Congress right to say whether votes shall be counted or not be counted. The Constitution declares that the electors of the States, chosen in such manner as the people in those States shall see fit to direct by law, shall have their certificates of election signed and certified *by themselves;* and when they have been

---

[15] Cong. Globe, 38–2, 505, 608.

[16] Cong. Rec., 43–2, 969; *Counting,* 444.

so signed and certified shall then be sealed and transmitted to certain officials of the Federal Government. The duty of the President of the Senate is simply ministerial. He is not vested with discretionary or judicial functions. . . .

He cannot even inspect [the certificates], except in the incidental and casual manner that is implied by the fact that his hand shall open the sealed envelope which contains the list of the electoral vote. Then the votes "shall be counted" in the presence of the two Houses.

Morton asked, "counted by whom?"
Bayard responded:

There is no distinct provision as to that. They shall be simply counted in the presence of the two Houses; but I apprehend . . . that the members of each House are simply witnesses to the count and tally of that vote. That you could not delegate that power to another body I cannot doubt.[17]

Anthony of Rhode Island, Republican, said, Suppose there are two packages from the same State?

Bayard replied that he could understand the difficulty of dealing with such a question. He spoke only to deprecate haste. He was trying to find a solution, "and the truth is that all my theories of government come just about to this: That if they are not to be honorably, honestly, and fairly administered, any laws that you make will be perfectly worthless to procure . . . justice and certainty. . . ."

Bayard had been a Senator since 1869, when he succeeded his father; now he is a leader in his party. He is clear that the choosing and certification of Presidential electors is exclusively a concern of the State: the President of the Senate does no more than open the envelope; Members of Senate and House sit as witnesses; and in the space between them, somehow, the counting is made. He has no answer to the possibility that there might be more than one certificate from a State. He has been unable to think of an appropriate rule, and rather disparages the effort: "I apprehend that there is no rule which you can frame that will not be open to defeat by some supposititious case." Any scheme designed to aid the fortunes of one party "will only return to plague the inventor. . . ."

Thurman of Ohio, Democrat, had sat on that State's supreme court; in 1867 he had lost the Governorship to Hayes by a narrow margin, and thereupon had been elected to the Senate. He was judicial in temperament and clear in his analysis of a problem. Neither Morton's original resolution nor his substitute had had the benefit of study in committee. Merely to repeal the 22d Joint Rule was subject to an insuperable objection:

---

[17] Ibid., 970; *Counting,* 445–46.

there would be nothing at all to determine how the votes should be counted; . . . we would proceed to the Hall of the House of Representatives in February, 1877, without any rule whatsoever or any statute whatsoever to prescribe what should be done after we got into that assembly. That would never do, Mr. President.

Whereas by the 22d Joint Rule no return should be *counted* unless the two Houses concurred, under Morton's substitute no vote would be *rejected* unless the two agreed to do so. Then if two returns, each one supported by one House, came from a State, "you would have to count both returns." It was necessary to go beyond the substitute and provide for the situation where more than one return came up from a State.

The country, Thurman said, had never gone on the theory that it pertained to the President of the Senate to determine what returns were valid: "otherwise the twenty-second joint rule never would have come into existence."

Some provision ought to be made for that case [of more than one return]. It ought to be provided that where that is the case the Houses shall decide between those returns, and how they shall decide, and such a provision as that requires great care in draughting it.

Under the joint rule, when objection was made to any certificate the Senate withdrew, each House voted, and then they "immediately reassembled"; "and upon any such question there shall be no debate in either House." It was, said Thurman, "so unsatisfactory, so unreasonable," to be required to decide what might be an important question without a full knowledge of the facts and an opportunity for argument. The rule, however, should be so drawn as to preclude that a "factious minority might . . . speak out the whole time up to the 4th of March."

The framing of a rule called for "great care in the use of language and great reflection," such as was possible only in "the privacy of a committee room or of a library or of a closet." Thurman moved that Morton's resolution and substitute be referred to the Committee on Privileges and Elections; he did not doubt that they could propose a rule that would pass both Houses at the present session.[18]

Frelinghuysen, Republican of New Jersey, agreed in the main with Thurman, yet on this matter one should keep an open mind. Questions of various sorts might arise in determining the electoral vote for the President: since the duty of the President of the Senate was at an end when the certificates were opened, it must be the Senate and House that carried out the counting.

---

[18] Ibid., 971–73; *Counting*, 448–51.

Bayard interrupted to inquire, Did the Senator consider that the two Houses, or either of them, had any discretion to say that the vote of a State should not be counted? Would that not be an act of revolution?

Frelinghuysen replied that if, for instance, a State sent more electoral votes than it was entitled to, the Houses must determine what votes were to be counted. He would amend the present rule to provide that no electoral vote should be rejected except by the concurrent vote of the two Houses. And in accord with the thought of Senator Thurman he would provide that when the Houses were in separate consultation "no person shall speak more than twice, or more than ten minutes in all."

For the case where *two* sets of electoral votes came from one state, a specific provision should be made, one that did not tempt the House of Representatives, by disagreeing with the Senate, to throw the election into the House.[19]

Here Morton entered into the discussion. All the Senators, he said, agreed that the 22d Joint Rule was dangerous and absurd in allowing one House to exclude the electoral vote of a State. "Let us therefore relieve it of its danger. It is much safer for this country—and that is the ground on which I put the whole thing—to say that the vote of a State shall be rejected only by both Houses and not by one House; and you take from one party, where the Houses are divided in politics, the power to change the result by rejecting the vote of a State. . . ."

"There is another great danger lying behind all that which we cannot provide for except by a constitutional amendment. The electors in a State may be elected by fraud or by violence, but if they come up here properly certified there is no power here to examine the vote in the State below. . . . It was not the intention that Congress should have that power. That was placed with the States; and it was the theory that the election of President should be left to the States and taken away from Congress. You cannot provide for that except by amending the Constitution. . . .

"Upon the question of the power of Congress to adopt this rule I entertain very great doubts. I do not believe myself the power exists; but there is a divided sentiment here. We cannot act upon any other position except that the power does exist. . . ."[20]

Senator Edmunds was "rather surprised" at Morton's denial of Congressional power to regulate the counting of electoral votes. The Constitution declared that "the votes shall then be counted"; it also authorized Congress by legislation to enforce its provisions.

Thurman supplied the exact text:

To make all Laws which shall be necessary and proper for carrying into Execution the foregoing Powers, and all other Powers vested by

---

[19] Ibid., 973; *Counting*, 451–52.   [20] Ibid., 973–74; *Counting*, 452–55.

this Constitution in the Government of the United States, or in any Department or officer thereof.

Edmunds said that Morton's view would lead to the conclusion that Congress could not do by statute what the two Houses could do by concurrent rule, which seemed untenable.

He agreed with Thurman that the resolution and the substitute should be referred to the Committee on Privileges and Elections; action should be taken before the 43d Congress came to an end in a month.

The matter was so referred.[21]

On February 6, 1875, Morton reported from the committee: He asked that it be discharged from consideration of the resolution, and presented S. 1251, a bill to provide for and regulate the counting of electoral votes.[22]

By Section 1, three tellers would be appointed, one from the Senate and two from the House, to whom the President of the Senate would hand the certificates as he opened them; the tellers would read the certificates to the two Houses; and if upon the reading of a certificate a question arose on counting the votes therein certified, the Senate would withdraw. Each House would consider and vote on the question; "and no electoral vote or votes from any State" to which objection had been made "shall be rejected except by the affirmative vote of the two Houses."

That dealt with the situation where there was a question over the certificate sent up from a State: but it was foreseen that there would be greater difficulty if two parties within a State each sent up a return. To meet that problem Section 2 would enact:

> That if more than one return shall be received . . . from a State, . . . all such returns shall be opened . . . in the presence of the two Houses when assembled to count the votes; and that return from such State shall be counted which the two Houses acting separately shall decide to be the true and valid return.

By Section 3, when the Houses had separated upon an objection, no Member should speak more than ten minutes, and after two hours of debate a majority could require that the question be put to a vote.

On February 25 the Senate in Committee of the Whole considered the bill.[23] On Thurman's motion there would be *two* tellers on the part of the Senate. Also, certificates from the several States would be presented in the alphabetical order of the States, starting with A.

---

[21] Cong. Rec., 43–2, 974–76; *Counting*, 455–58.
[22] Ibid., 1020. The text of S. 1251 is at p. 459 in *Counting*.

[23] Debate on February 25, 1875, lies in pages 1759–86; *Counting*, 458–519.

Bayard spoke at length. Prior to 1865 Congress had made no regulation to supplement what the Constitution itself provided;

> And nowhere is power given to either House of Congress to pass upon the election, either the manner or the fact, of electors for President and Vice-President; and if the Congress. . . , either one or both Houses, shall assume, under the guise or pretext of telling or counting a vote, to decide the fact of the election of electors who are to form the college. . . , then they will have taken upon themselves an authority for which I, for one, can find no warrant in this charter of limited powers. . . .

Again,

> There is nothing in this language [of the Constitution] that authorizes either House of Congress, or both Houses. . . , to interfere with the decision which has been made by the electors themselves and certified by them and sent to the President of the Senate. There is no pretext that for any cause whatever Congress has any power, or all the other departments of the Government have any power, to refuse to receive and count the result of the action of the voters in the States in that election as certified by the electors whom they have chosen. That questions may arise whether that choice was made, . . . whether that election was properly held or whether it was a free and fair election, is undoubtedly true; but there is no machinery provided for contest and no contest seems to have been anticipated on this subject. It is *casus omissus,* . . . and if there be necessity for amendment [of the Constitution], for its supplement, that must be the action of the American people in accordance with the Constitution itself; and I am free to say that some amendment on this subject should be had. . . .

But it would be unjustifiable for Congress to assume power to make such a rule.

Bayard could not accept Section 2, which purported to deal with the case of multiple returns from a State.

> It declares that all of these returns, the false as well as the true, shall be opened, and I can construe the language of the bill in no other way than that they shall be counted unless there is a concurrent . . . vote of both Houses rejecting them. . . .
>
> I shall be glad to be instructed to the contrary. I have read the section many times; I have submitted it to the judgment of others whose opinions I value more than my own, and have found a concurrence in the belief that this section is an opportunity, if not an invitation, for the annihilation of the electoral votes of States by having the false vote made equal in weight with the true, and forbidding the rejection of either except by the concurrent vote of both Houses of Congress.

Frelinghuysen spoke out to say that "I understand that by this second section if there be two sets of votes sent up from any State, the concurrence of both Houses as to which shall be counted is required, and that is the rule at the present time."

Bayard responded that if that was the meaning there should be inserted at the end of Section 2,

> And in such case the validity of any return shall be agreed to by both Houses, or the same shall not be counted.

But, he continued, something more was needed to meet the danger:

> there should be, as there is not now, some tribunal in whom a deposit of power to determine such contests should be lodged. How shall that be reached? Only by an amendment to the Constitution . . . in which all men, without respect to party results must join. . . .
>
> There is ample time for the settlement. No use for such a law can arise for two years to come. It cannot be until the winter of 1876–'77 . . . when the machinery we seek to provide can be called into requisition. . . . Why not then let this subject rest . . . until you can have assured . . . a non-partisan decision in regard to a subject that should be for the safety of this whole nation, lifted high above the atmosphere and heat of party? . . .

That was, wait until the coming in of the 44th Congress in December 1875, when the House would be in Democratic hands.

Senator Thurman followed. He agreed that there should be no haste, and would prefer that the problem be acted upon by the next Congress.

> But a majority of the Senate have determined otherwise. . . . I find the opinions of the Senator from Delaware . . . and my own on an important section of this bill very far opposed. . . . I think that the point upon which he mainly relies in opposition to that section [2] is not well taken, that the difficulty he supposes can never by any possibility exist. . . .

Inasmuch as Bayard had objected to Section 2, Thurman sought by repeated explanations to show what would be the effect of retaining Section 1 without Section 2 to govern the case of multiple returns from a State:

> Suppose we are in January, 1877, and this second section is not a part of the law, but the first section alone is the law. Suppose the State of Alabama, the first on the list, is called, and there are two returns from

16

Alabama, returns from two bodies claiming to be electors. . . . Is there any law that says which of those returns shall be first presented by the President of the Senate? No, sir. . . . It is therefore within his discretion which one he will present first, . . . and hand to the tellers first; and [certainly he] will know which one of those two returns is the return of the republican electors [and he will hand that one to the tellers]. Then if the House may vote to reject it and the Senate to receive it, under this first section . . . it is received. Then the vote of that State has been counted, and there is no question upon any other return, and cannot be.

Such a scheme was surely wrong. Hence the need for Section 2:

what can you do but require the two Houses to consider each of those returns and then determine which of them shall be received? They can make no decision to receive one unless both Houses concur. One House has no superiority over the other. If the two Houses differ . . . and are inflexible, of course there can be no decision; but when there are two or more returns from a State, of necessity there must be a concurrence of the two Houses in order to receive one of them. . . .

The effect of Section 2 remained in doubt, and presently Senator George G. Wright of Iowa put a question to Senator Morton as author of the bill: by implication, if the two Houses could not agree upon one of multiple returns the vote of the State was lost. Should not that implication be made specific? Morton had no objection, and on Wright's motion Section 2 was amended by adding

And that return only from such State shall be counted which the two Houses, each acting separately, shall decide to be the true and valid return.

(Later in the debate Gordon of Georgia raised the same point; Morton recalled the amendment and confirmed, if the Houses could not agree upon one of two or more returns, "neither is counted.")

Edmunds made a long speech in which he seemed to be fumbling for a solution. "You must in some way, under the Constitution and the law, have a means of deciding, once and for all, what the true law of the case is." One possibility was a committee from the two Houses, chosen from "among the purest and best and most skillful in law and politics," who would render a sworn judgment upon which of disputed returns should be counted. By submission to such a body "is there not a greater probability that you reach the true and lawful result than there is if you leave it at large to three hundred men at the other end of the Capitol and to seventy-four at this end?''

Another possibility, Edmunds suggested, was that a contest be submitted to a federal Circuit Court, with appeal to the Supreme Court.

Thurman responded that he would want time to reflect on the idea of a select committee. As to the suggestion of reference to the judiciary, ''I entirely dissent.'' He gave numerous objections, based on Article III of the Constitution and on the Judiciary Act. ''It never was intended that the President should be in the exercise *de facto,* in virtue of the count made before the two Houses, of the Office of President. . . , and at the same time that his right to that office should be a subject of contest in the courts.'' ''I do not think that the framers of the Constitution intended that the title of the person declared in the joint assembly of the two Houses to be President should remain in doubt for a single moment. . . .''

Frelinghuysen added that ''The whole frame-work of the Constitution is repugnant to the idea of its being settled by the judiciary.'' The proposition ''to have a committee appointed who shall *instanter,* if the thing is possible . . . consider the votes, and if they report favorably on a vote it shall be accepted unless both Houses reject it, and if they report unfavorably it shall only be accepted on both houses voting for it; the only effect of that committee being not to take the jurisdiction away from Congress but to change the rule of evidence, it strikes me that it may be a precautionary measure of some value. . . .''

Senator Morton replied that the idea of reference to a joint committee had been considered but rejected by his Committee on Privileges and Elections.

Senator William T. Hamilton of Maryland, a Democrat, said ''My trouble is not in regard so much to this bill. . . ; it goes to the question of our constitutional power to pass any measure at all upon the subject. . . . As soon as we begin to legislate we get into trouble. . . .''

He referred to Edmunds' proposal of a joint committee:

> What is to be the reach of their power? Are they to inquire simply as to what arises on the face of the certificate only? How far is the inquiry to extend. . . ? Is it merely . . . to look at the certificates to see whether they are properly executed and have been duly attested? Is that the limit of the power, I ask, or can other questions, as to the appointment of electors, or in case of the return of two or more votes of electors to ascertain the rightful set, and then considering this to go back and behind all for that purpose? There is no such authority given. . . . The duty of the President of the Senate and of the two Houses is as simple as words can make it. And can we upon those words ingraft a whole system for contest and ascertainment?

He reiterated that the Constitution contemplated no inquiry behind the certificate from the State. Can we go back and inquire into the manner in which the electoral votes were cast—into the manner in which the electors were appointed—whether they were legally appointed or elected by the people? There was no authority to do so.

His hope was that the Senate would recommit this measure; that right would be done at the next Presidential election; and that in the meantime a constitutional amendment could be framed that would prevent any future trouble.

Presently Edmunds offered a text to enact his idea of a joint committee, four from each House; the concurrence of a majority of its members would be requisite to any action. There would be an oath "faithfully and impartially" to discharge the duties imposed. When the certificates of electoral votes were opened by the President of the Senate in the presence of the two Houses, the votes would be delivered to the committee, which would forthwith examine them, count the votes that appeared "to have been legally given and duly certified and returned," and make a report. Then if a Senator or Representative raised a question on any vote, the Senate would withdraw and each House would consider the question. The report of the committee would stand unless both Houses held to the contrary. In the event that the committee was equally divided on a vote, it would be counted unless both Houses concurred in rejecting it.

Edmunds moved that this text be submitted for Morton's. That was rejected without debate and without a record vote.

Augustus S. Merrimon of North Carolina, prominent at the bar and in Democratic politics, had come to the Senate in 1873. In later life he sat on the State's supreme court. In the debate on Morton's bill he took a stand on several significant points.

> The vote must be counted by the Congress in joint assemblage; it must be the act of this joint assemblage; and I maintain that, touching the counting of the vote, every question that shall arise must be decided by the Congress, not as two separate bodies, but as the Congress sitting in joint assembly.

In support he said, "It is done after the manner in which United States Senators are elected in the several State legislatures. . . . The two houses of the legislature vote on the first day separately. On the second day the two houses go into joint assemblage, and as a whole, as a joint body, they ballot for a United States Senator, and continue to ballot until one shall be elected." He called on Senators "to show me any constitutional authority" to the contrary.

(Upon further study, in the next Congress he abandoned his theory of Congress acting in a joint assembly.)

Merrimon repeated such propositions as these:

I do not believe that Congress or any national authority has any right to contest the election of President and Vice-President. . . . The whole matter is within the jurisdiction of the States, each for itself.

It has been asked, suppose there are great frauds practiced in the States in an election of President. . . . There is no power conferred in the Constitution on the national authority to contest the election in that behalf. The authority remains in the State to provide for that. . . .

. . . I admit that the States have not heretofore provided a tribunal for such contests, but that does not prove that they might not have so provided. . . . I believe that it is important that . . . every State should pass a statute regulating the manner and the election of electors of President . . . [just as they have done for contesting the elections for State officers].

The only question that ever can arise before Congress must arise before it in joint session, and [that body] can only determine whether a vote that is sent to the President of the Senate is the vote that was ascertained by the authorities of the State. . . . If the certification of election was so informal that it did not show that there was an election, Congress would have the power to say "It does not appear that any election was held in North Carolina," but Congress has no power to say that the election held for electors of President and Vice-President in North Carolina was fraudulent, that democratic electors ought to have been elected whereas the returns show that republican electors were elected, or *vice versa*. When the State authorities have determined the matter, there is the end of the controversy and Congress cannot inquire into it. . . .

Logan of Illinois, Republican, interrupted with a question based on the counting of the electoral vote in the Third Session of the 42d Congress in February 1873. Horace Greeley, the Democratic candidate for President, had died on November 29, 1872—after his defeat in the national election, but before the meeting of the electors in each State "upon the first Wednesday in December."

Representative Hoar of Massachusetts had objected to counting Georgia's electoral votes for Greeley on the ground that he did not exist. On retiring the Senate disagreed with the objection, while the House sustained it. There being a noncurrence between the two Houses, under the 22d Joint Rule Georgia's vote was not counted.

Senator Rice of Arkansas, Republican, had objected on two grounds to the counting of the electoral vote from that State. The Senate voted against counting; the House voted to count. Under the joint rule, Arkansas's vote was not counted.

Prologue

Several objections had been made to counting the electoral vote of Louisiana: Senate and House concurred in rejecting.[24]

Recalling these circumstances, Logan asked Merrimon, If the votes of Georgia, Arkansas, and Louisiana had "been sufficient to turn the election on either side," did he "believe we could have got through without a revolution?"

Merrimon:

> Yes, sir; I do. I think the republican party would have decided that General Grant was elected and I have too much confidence in the patriotism of the democratic party and the democratic people of this country to believe of them that they would revolutionize the country and destroy the whole system of government because that decision had been made by a power authorized to do it.

Logan:

> Now I will ask the Senator suppose it had been decided on the other side, what does he think the result would have been?

Merrimon:

> I think the republican people of the Union would have submitted to it.

He went on to say that

> I believe it is a characteristic of the American people that they submit to a decision properly made by the proper authority however much they may condemn its justice, however erroneous it may be, just as they submit to a decision made by a court having competent jurisdiction. . . . If the Supreme Court having jurisdiction of a question . . . were to make a decision that was distasteful to four-fifths or nine-tenths of the American people, I believe they would submit . . . because the proper constitutional tribunal had made the decision. . . .

The entire debate on S. 1251 had been crowded into the afternoon and early evening of February 25, 1875. Morton had sought a recess for dinner, to which Edmunds objected: he was pressing for the enactment

---

[24] The circumstances of the Louisiana and Arkansas contests of 1872 are recounted more fully infra, p. 80, n. 33.

of the Civil Rights Bill before the 43d Congress came to an end on March 3. Eaton of Connecticut moved to postpone consideration indefinitely: that received only 18 votes to 31 opposing. On the final passage by the Senate there were 28 votes of yea, all from Republicans. Voting nay were 13 Democrats and 7 Republicans; among the latter were Edmunds, Carpenter, and Conkling of the Judiciary Committee. Thurman was among the 25 absentees.[25] For the end in view that bill was a patent failure.

As the *New York Times* reported next morning, "few Senators seemed to be wholly pleased with the bill." The problem was left for the incoming Congress.

S. 1 IN THE NEW CONGRESS

WHEN ON DECEMBER 6, 1875, the 44th Congress first convened, the Representatives elected in the autumn of 1874 cast 173 votes for Michael C. Kerr, Democrat, to be Speaker, against 106 cast for James G. Blaine, who had held that office since March 1869. While the Senate remained under Republican control, there were new Democratic Members replacing Republicans from five Southern and Border States as well as one each from Pennsylvania and New York; against this was ex-Governor Booth of California, who replaced a Democrat.

On December 8 Senator Morton introduced S. 1 to provide for and regulate the counting of votes for President and Vice President. It contained "nothing affecting the substantial features" of the bill debated in February 1875.[26]

Concurrently, on January 20, 1876, the 22d Joint Rule was abrogated by action of the Senate. No one spoke in its favor, but Senator Bayard desired concurrent action of the House in disposing of it.[27]

Debate on S. 1 began on March 13[28] and consumed three times as much space as that of the previous year. Many more Senators participated, offering numerous proposals aimed at assuring a final determination of a conflict over plural returns from a State.

---

[25] Cong. Rec., 43–2, 1786; *Counting,* 519.

[26] As Morton said, Cong. Rec., 44–1, 1662–63; *Counting,* 520.

[27] Cong. Rec., 44–1, 517; *Counting,* Annex at 786–87.

[28] Debate on March 13 ran in Cong. Rec., 44–1, 1662–75; *Counting,* 519–47.

In the outcome, no measure was sent to the House of Representatives. Much was said, however, highly pertinent to the dispute that developed over the election of 1876.

Bayard sought concurrent study by a committee in each chamber, an idea that was not accepted. He still was uncertain over "the grave question whether the two Houses have the power to constitute themselves a tribunal for the acceptance or rejection of the vote of a State. . . ."

Morton said of the problem of plural returns from a State, the subject of Section 2 of the bill:

> You cannot read both sets, . . . and therefore read that set which both Houses of Congress, supposing men to be patriotic and to be honest and acting under the obligations of the Constitution and their oaths, shall decide to be the true and valid return. I think that is the fairest way.

That was no more than a confession of *non possumus*.

William A. Wallace of Pennsylvania, a Democratic newcomer, proposed an amendment to the effect that when the Houses acting separately disagreed as to which is the valid return from a State,

> the joint meeting shall finally determine the same by a vote by States, the representation from each State, including the Senators therefrom, having one vote; but if such representation shall be equally divided, the vote of such State shall not be counted.

Robert E. Withers, Virginia Democrat, was not prepared to accept Morton's solution that only if the two Houses agreed would either of disputed returns from a State be counted: he preferred Wallace's proposal, or even decision by the President of the Senate acting with full knowledge of his responsibility.

Samuel E. Maxey of Texas, another Democrat, asked,

> Can there not be some means devised whereby a sovereign State will have a right to have her vote counted [when the two houses disagree]? . . . I ask would it not be within the spirit of the Constitution to let the Vice President decide?

Senator George S. Boutwell of Massachusetts had when a Representative in 1869 urged that Congress by statute forbid racial discrimination in voting, in order that blacks would be able to ratify a constitutional amendment banning racial discrimination in voting. His strength lay in politics rather than in constitutional development.

Now he said that his study had convinced him that "the framers of the Constitution . . . did substantially all that was necessary to provide for the eventuality of conflicting electoral certificates. "The power and the duty are in Congress. . . . There can be . . . no tribunal to decide . . . any . . . question arising in the course of counting the votes, [because it is a] duty imposed upon the two Houses of Congress." And "in the very nature of the case, there is power under the Constitution . . . if the occasion demands it, to go behind the certificate and inquire into the facts . . . to ascertain the truth in regard to an election."

Boutwell's assertion went in the teeth of the repeated declaration by Democratic Senators and others that Congress could not inquire behind the State's certificate of the election of electors.

Next Thurman of Ohio: "This is not a new subject to me." Since the last election, when the votes of three States were rejected, he had recognized that the country might be "plunged into civil war upon the question who had been elected President. . . ."

He came at once to Section 2 of the bill, dealing with the case of conflicting certificates; some of his friends objected, because it might result that the vote of a State was not counted. He believed it was generally agreed that "the duty of the President of the Senate is simply ministerial; that he is not constituted the judge to decide whether a return is valid. . . ." The fact that on several occasions that officer "was himself a candidate either for . . . President or Vice President would seem to be quite sufficient to show" the impropriety of his judging the election.

"How are [the votes] to be counted?" Thurman answered his own query: "I believe that the law is the proper mode" of providing an answer; he referred to the Necessary and Proper Clause. By Section 1 of the bill, where there was objection to the return from a State, if either House was in favor of counting it, it would be counted. But provision must be made for conflicting returns, and as Section 2 was drawn, the result might be to "cast out the vote of a State because the two Houses cannot agree which is the correct return." He would "hail with joy any reasonable and constitutional mode that shall be proposed," but was not prepared to offer a solution.

He would say that submission to the Supreme Court was impermissible; and it was no solution to say that jurisdiction could be conferred upon the nine Justices as individuals. "Then we shall perhaps be brought" to consider giving a preponderance to one House of Congress. He hoped the discussion would produce a solution; otherwise he would vote for the bill.

Senator William Pinkney Whyte of Maryland differed from most of his colleagues in holding that "the Vice President . . . is the proper person to state which vote shall be counted, because the Constitution has put it in his hands," "in plain and unmistakeable words." It was safer to leave the responsibility to one man rather than in the hands of many. (A week later he spoke again to document his contention.)

Henry Cooper of Tennessee, a minority member of the Committee on Privileges and Elections, would add to Section 2:

> and if the two Houses do not agree on which return shall be counted, the House of Representatives, voting by States in the manner provided by the Constitution when the election devolves upon the House, shall decide which shall be the true and valid return.

Bayard hailed that at once. It "seems to run in the current of the constitutional provision." It "has the effect of proceeding to an ultimate arbitration, constitutional, fair, and just, one which cannot be alleged to be in the interest of any party. . . ." (Bayard would defend that solution to the end of the debate.)

Francis Kernan, Democrat of New York, did not accept Whyte's view, and recognized that some other mode of disposing of a disagreement between the Houses must be found. "My objection to the amendment of [Senator Cooper]—and I only suggest it to see if we cannot remedy it— is that, while it does not disfranchise a State, it certainly does or may annul the will of the people; because, voting in that way, a State which has . . . population only for a single Representative, will have a vote on that important question equivalent to the vote of four millions of people in another State." He urged further thought.

Justin S. Morrill of Vermont and Morton pointed out that submission to a vote in the House would be to a House elected two years earlier, which might have a result contrary to the later wishes of a majority of the people.

Bayard repeated his endorsement of the Cooper amendment: it invoked the principle with which the Constitution was replete, "the recognition of State sovereignty . . . upon important occasions. . . ." The situation was similar to that where there was no majority of votes for a President, and "the power is complete in the States meeting as States, . . . with equal voice proceeding to represent the people and elect a President for them." It was "all-important that the States should not be disfranchised, that we should have a decision . . . in a way that shall give satisfaction to all parties. . . ."

That led Morton to elaborate on the proposition that this "is a Government of the people, and is not a Government of States." The Union "is not a compact of States. The Constitution was formed by the people . . . and rests upon the broad shoulders of the nation."

These contrapuntal themes were in the air throughout the debate.

25

Morton added that "The idea of Congress having a right by a bill to provide an umpire in case the two Houses disagree, it seems to me is so utterly foreign to our system . . . that I can hardly regard it seriously. . . ."

To this Frelinghuysen responded that "it seems to me that, where the Constitution commits a subject to Congress and yet leaves it so undefined, so general, we have a power according to our discretion by law to carry out the authority committed to us. . . ."

On Morton's motion the Senate turned to executive business, and so ended the first day of debate on S. 1. For Senator Whyte, the Constitution had already designated the President of the Senate and there was no room for legislation. Bayard called for a statute that recognized State sovereignty. Thurman and Frelinghuysen claimed for Congress a discretion to find a solution. And Morton would not go beyond the responsibility of the two Houses to decide a conflict over votes by agreement reached through patriotism and a sense of justice.

If the Senators could not agree on principles to govern decision of a possible dispute, what was the prospect for meeting the actuality?

On the morrow, March 14, 1876,[29] the Senate in Committee of the Whole accepted without debate an amendment of Section 3 by Sherman of Ohio: it would cut off debate after two hours in the respective Houses over conflicting returns. That recognized the necessity of reaching a decision on the election of a President before March 4. As a practical matter such expedition would preclude any extensive inquiry behind the certificate to search for the truth such as Boutwell had contemplated.

Then John W. Johnston of Virginia, a Conservative, proposed an amendment of Cooper's amendment; he would give a different conclusion to Section 2:

> If the Senate should vote for counting one certificate and the House of Representatives another, the joint meeting of the two Houses shall finally determine which shall be counted, by a vote by States, the representation from each State (including the Senators therefrom) having one vote; but if the representation of any State shall be equally divided its vote shall not be counted.

That was rationalized by the reminder that by the Twelfth Amendment, the House chose the President where no person had a majority of elector votes, "the representation from each State having one vote."

Frelinghuysen proposed to modify Cooper's amendment to provide a still different solution:

---

[29] Proceedings on March 14 were in | Cong. Rec., 44–1, 1693–95; *Counting*, 547–51.

26

If the two Houses shall not agree, the difference shall be immediately referred to the Chief Justice of the Supreme Court, the presiding
officer of the Senate, and the Speaker of the House, whose decision
shall be final. If the Chief Justice is absent or unable to attend, the
senior associate justice of the Supreme Court present in the Capitol or
other place of meeting shall act in his place.

The question to be decided, he said, was both judicial and political. He
thought this was an appropriate solution, and one that would make sure
that the vote of no State would be lost.

When debate resumed on March 16,[30] Thurman surveyed the field.
"I think that the spirit of the Constitution requires that these votes shall
be counted in some mode by Congress, or the convention of the two
Houses." He opposed involvement of the judiciary. Cooper's amendment
tempted the House to disagree with the Senate, thereby throwing the
decision to the House. After reflection he had concluded that Johnston's
amendment came nearest to the spirit of the Constitution. "I see no other
solution that is likely to be as satisfactory to the people, to the country,
to the States, and to the requirements of justice and truth."

Morton defended his bill as it stood. But, "if we have power. . . ,
which I do not think we have, to create an umpire to decide where the
two Houses disagree," then Frelinghuysens' amendment was "much
the best."

On March 20[31] Whyte returned to his contention that the counting
of electoral votes was vested in the President of the Senate; if that was
true, it was idle to debate over legislation. By a detailed exposition from
the journals of Senate and House he argued that "in the beginning the
eye of Congress was turned to this very question and they recognized that
the President of the Senate . . . was the proper person to discharge the
duty of making the count and announcing it to the two Houses. . . ."

The Convention of 1787, he said, would not leave it to Congress
to elect the President: now Congress proposed to decide upon electors,
which was like deciding who was to be President.

Thurman inquired,

Does the Senator think that the question before the Senate is whether
we can go back of a return admitted to be genuine and regular upon
its face? . . . I certainly do not admit that you can go back and go into
a contest of the election at all. . . .

Henry L. Dawes of Massachusetts had come to the Senate in 1875
after nine terms in the House, where he had been chairman of the Com-

---

[30] On March 16, Cong. Rec.,
1749–57; *Counting,* 551–69.

[31] On March 20, Cong. Rec.,
1802–10; *Counting,* 569–88.

mittee on Elections. He had reflected on the subject under debate, and thought that S. 1 if enacted would create only "a fancied security." It addressed a contingency that was beyond the belief of the Framers.

> It was the State, and not the nation, that was to appoint [the electors]; and the State was to take good care . . . that its act, whatever it was, was to be verified by the State and not by the nation. . . .

The Framers "kept up the idea of the States all through, until, as they supposed, they had secured beyond peradventure the election of a President."

Now Section 2 contemplated an entirely different situation, where more than one return had come from a State, and that return should be counted which the two Houses acting separately held to be valid. Section 3 required each House to reach a summary decision within two hours. That, said Dawes, was "a poor cobweb attempt to smother a volcano." The country would not acquiesce in a decision so reached.

He concluded, "bring forward some measure for the amendment of the Constitution. . . . But while such an amendment is pending. . . . I shall vote for this bill; but I shall vote for it believing that . . . it is vain for us to tell the people that we have met the peril. . . ."

On Thursday, March 21, the debate continued without interruption from the close of "morning hour" until 4 P.M.[32]

Maxey of Texas held that the Constitution fastened upon the two Houses a duty in the nature of a personal trust, which could not be delegated: thus he disagreed with the proposed amendments that would submit a dispute to an outside body. If the two Houses failed to agree, it fell to the President of the Senate to decide. That seemed "the true solution."

Charles W. Jones of Florida, Democrat, found the bill "a plain departure from the Constitution." It belonged to the States to provide for the manner in which electors were to be chosen, and they might provide also for the decision of a contest between claimants. Yet the bill, as he saw it, would take this power from the States and vest it in Congress. With as much reason might it provide for a federal investigation of elections for Governor.

At the close of Jones' speech the Committee of the Whole began to vote on the pending amendments. First, that by Frelinghuysen whereby a difference between the Houses would be submitted to the Chief Justice, the Presiding Officer of the Senate, and the Speaker; the result was 20 yeas, all from Republicans, to 29 nays, all but five from Democrats.

---

[32] Cong. Rec., 1830–43; *Counting*, 588–615.

The question then recurred to Johnston's proposal: final determination by a vote by the State delegations (Senators joining with Representatives), each State having one vote.

At this point John W. Stevenson of Kentucky entered into the discussion to reinforce the argument of Senator Whyte that the power to count electoral votes was vested in the President of the Senate. Stevenson concluded that

> the safest and wisest course . . . is to adhere to the precedents which for sixty years guided our fathers in the election of [the] Chief Magistrate. Let us guard the States from encroachments of arbitrary Federal power over the suffrage. I am an old-school democrat; and I shall vote with the Senator from Maryland. . . .

Thurman responded at once, with what Whyte later called a "judicial broadside":

> How it could come into the head of any man looking at the Constitution alone . . . to suppose that the power of counting the votes is conferred upon the President of the Senate, is almost past my comprehension. . . .

He went over the old ground. The electoral votes were to be counted: but as the Constitution did not declare by whom, this called for legislation under the Necessary and Proper Clause.

Whyte and Stevenson feared that a State might lose its vote through disagreement between Senate and House: but if the President of the Senate had the power he too might exclude the vote of a State. Moreover the Senate had earlier in that session adopted a resolution "That the office of President pro tempore of the Senate is held at the pleasure of the Senate." That should give pause to those who would leave the counting of the votes to the President of the Senate.

Once again Thurman repelled the idea that the judiciary might be invoked to settle a contest over electoral votes:

> Certainly the Constitution requires the count . . . to be concluded without delay; and the President is inaugurated . . . Are you to proceed through one year, two years, three years, in some circuit court of the United States or in the Supreme Court . . . to find whether the President of the Senate correctly counted the vote, and then have a decree. . . , and then . . . how are you going to turn the incumbent out? . . .

Thurman now was anxious to settle upon the least objectionable measure that would serve the needs of the moment:

29

I feel as strongly as any Senator . . . that the Constitution needs amendment in regard to the choice of President. I feel that the idea of electors of President entertained by our forefathers has in practice wholly failed. Their idea was that these electors were to make the choice . . . according to their own good judgment and will. That idea has wholly failed. . . . I believe that some mode, clear and specific, free from doubt, ought to be constitutionally adopted. . . . But, sir, . . . we cannot amend the Constitution in a day. The necessity for action . . . is upon us now, and the question is, shall we exercise that power which the Constitution does confer upon us . . . ?

He foresaw "danger unless we settle this matter."

The question pending was on Johnston's amendment. Morton said that voting by States, whether Senators were included or not, was "the most objectionable plan that could be adopted." Delaware with one Representative and two Senators would have one vote, and so would New York with thirty-three Representatives and two Senators. If a delegation were equally divided the vote of that State would be lost. There would soon be thirty-eight States with the admission of Colorado, and if the votes of the States should be evenly divided, there could be no decision.

If we can thus depute a legislative power to be exercised by a joint convention, a body unknown to the Constitution . . . and voting by States, a matter which the Constitution never contemplated, we can depute that power to the Supreme Court. . . . I say that, if we have the power to create an umpire or to call in a new tribunal, then I think the safest umpire, the one most satisfactory to the people of this nation, would be the Supreme Court. . . , simply requiring that body to be in session when we come to count the votes, and in case of disagreement requiring it to decide it somewhere.

However, Morton repeated that he did not think that Congress had power to submit the question to any tribunal.

When consideration was resumed on March 22,[33] Morton asked that Senators "remain here to-day until this bill is disposed of." The response showed that that was not to be. It was a day for disposing of amendments. That offered by Johnston to submit disagreements to the State delegations in Congress, each State having one vote, received only 11 yeas (two from Republicans and the rest from Democrats, including Thurman) to 39 nays (slightly more from Republicans than from Democrats).

Then the question was on Cooper's amendment:

---

[33] Cong. Rec., 1874–84; *Counting,* 615–36.

And if the two houses do not agree as to which return shall be counted, then that vote shall be counted which the House of Representatives, voting by States in the manner provided by the Constitution when the election devolves upon the House, shall decide to be the true and valid return.

The vote on that proposal was 13 yeas (all Democrats) to 35 nays.

Maxey of Texas then moved his amendment, to add at the end of Section 2,

But if the two Houses fail to agree as to which of the returns shall be counted, then the President of the Senate, as presiding officer of the two Houses, shall decide which is the true and valid return, and the same shall then be counted.

Edmunds objected to referring to the President of the Senate as "presiding officer of the two Houses": it suggested that they acted "in a consolidated way," whereas they assembled as two bodies for a single purpose.

A substantial objection was that it was likely that the President of the Senate would often be himself a candidate for election as President or Vice President, and it was wrong in principle that he should decide where he had an interest.

Senator Merrimon no longer held to the view he had expressed at the last Congress that the two Houses when they came together acted as one body. But, be that as it may, he thought that "we have no power to delegate to the President of the Senate, or to the Supreme Court, or to commissioners, or to any tribunal whatsoever the right to decide any controverted question arising upon the count of the votes." He could not support this amendment.

Burnside of Rhode Island gave notice that he would offer an amendment to submit contested cases to the Supreme Court.

Eli Saulsbury of Delaware held that Maxey's amendment would be "very dangerous in practice if it should be adopted." Morton's bill made no provision for a contingency of "great difficulty and embarrassment"; he had favored Johnston's amendment for meeting it; but rather than see the Presiding Officer invested with "such fearful power" he would prefer to let the bill pass without amendment.

Frelinghuysen was impressed with the likelihood that the President of the Senate would himself be a candidate for the Presidency or the Vice Presidency, which made Maxey's proposal objectionable. His own amendment, though rejected, had received more votes than any other, and if no other were adopted he was inclined to renew his own when the bill had gone from the Committee of the Whole to the Senate.

Aaron A. Sargent of California, a Republican, supported Maxey's amendment. He said that "any man occupying the position of Presiding Officer . . . who should wrongfully . . . decide, whereby he became a gainer," would fall into a class with Benedict Arnold.

Edmunds was surprised: this seemed to say "that, if a man were to judge erroneously, wrongly, . . . to gain the election, . . . he would be so followed by obloquy and moral perdition in this world that he would be restrained from doing it."

Sargent: "I spoke of corruption; not of error in judgment. Errors of judgment we are all liable to make; and so is any human tribunal."

Edmunds replied "that no man in his own case can generally be considered as impartial, that his mind is biased, and his intellect, therefore, is unable . . . to hold evenly and fairly the balance between opposing considerations and opposing facts. . . ."

George G. Wright of Iowa, an experienced and upright judge, observed "that we know less of the strength of our own prejudices than of anything else on earth; and there is no one thing upon which we are such unsafe judges as when we come to determine how strong our prejudices or feelings or interests may be on a given question. If self in any instance this wavering balance shakes, it is rarely, if ever, right adjusted."

After much reflection Wright had concluded to vote for Section 2 as it stood. "I think the two Houses ought to count the vote, and if they are unable to agree where there are two returns, then if it occurs that the vote of the State is lost, it results after the most faithful, deliberate, and conscientious action, as I am bound to suppose, on the part of the two bodies." That would be a situation "that we cannot safely provide for perhaps as the Constitution now stands."

In closing the debate on his amendment Maxey said: "I believe that the two Houses of Congress will want to do right; but, when the question comes before them, honest men may differ. One of the two Houses may decide this question in one way and the other House in the other way." In that situation "I am willing to trust the man that the Constitution trusts." Such a man would not "so far forget himself, his oath, his honor, the confidence which the people had placed in him," that he would decide wrongfully.

The amendment received only 7 votes (four from Republicans, three from Democrats) to 38 nays.

Maxey and Sargent were practical politicians; they were also lawyers, presumably acquainted with the ethics of their profession. From either viewpoint their thought was shallow. Senators and Representatives might differ "honestly" over which vote should be counted: yet that one Senator who had been elected President of the Senate by colleagues of his own party, must decide between them—which perhaps would make a President, but surely would make himself seem "steeped in moral iniquity" to half the nation. One so beset might allow his own sober judgment to be overcome by a preoccupation to appear impartial. No man should be a judge in a case where he has a personal interest: that maxim is just, to protect him who must decide as well as those upon whom the decision must fall.

It was often commented in the course of this debate that Senators were sincerely seeking a sound solution with little calculation for partisan advantage. Here Maxey was promoting a rule that would have submitted a disagreement between the Houses to a Republican in the office of President of the Senate. Not until the 46th Congress met in the spring of 1879 would there be a Democrat in that office—most appropriately, Allen G. Thurman.

When the Senate, still in Committee of the Whole, met on March 23,[34] Merrimon of North Carolina offered an amendment whereby Section 2 would conclude by providing that if conflicting returns were received from factions in a State,

> that return from such State shall be counted which shall be duly authenticated by the State authorities recognized by, and in harmony with, the United States, as provided by the Constitution.

Suppose that neither faction had been recognized by the President or by Congress:

> My answer . . . is this: In the first place, it is not probable, it is only remotely possible, that such a case could ever arise. In the next place, it is not probable that the two branches of Congress, in the discharge of their high duty, would divide, one House against the other, upon a question of that sort.

At that point the following colloquy occurred:

> MR. JOHNSTON. Suppose one House recognizes one and the other House the other?

> MR. MERRIMON. In that case I think they would be bound to count the one recognized by the President, unless Congress should overrule his action.

---

[34] Cong. Rec., 1900–10; *Counting,* 636–57.

MR. JOHNSTON. Would a State government in harmony with the President, but not with Congress, be in harmony with the United States?

MR. MERRIMON. Most assuredly not; the Congress is the supreme authority in such a case. But that is to say the President is corrupt and has prostituted his office. We cannot proceed upon such a supposition. Laws are passed on the supposition that the authorities of the Government will do their duty as they understand it and faithfully.

That was no better than Senator Morton's defense of Section 2 as he had framed it:

I am not willing to believe that there is in either party . . . such an absence of patriotism as to do great violence to the rights of the people . . . and to the Constitution in a case like that. . . .

Indeed in attempting to improve, Merrimon had confused by drawing the President into the argument: the President had nothing to do with counting the electoral votes; in speaking of "recognition" Merrimon had quoted from *Luther v. Borden*[35] on the authority of Congress and of the President in respect of the constitutional guarantee to preserve to each State "a republican form of government." That was a wholly different matter.

The labored exposition did not generate any debate. After a few questions had been raised, a vote was taken and the amendment was rejected. No one called for a record vote.

What Merrimon dismissed as "only remotely possible" would soon come to pass, and the points on which he had made his pronouncements would become matters of desperately serious contention.

In short order after his proposal was rejected, minor amendments were made, and the Committee of the Whole reported S. 1 to the Senate. Motions to amend were in order.

On March 24[36] Burnside of Rhode Island offered an amendment whereby conflicting returns would be submitted to the adjudication of the Supreme Court. "I think in an emergency like this, if it is possible for Congress to give the Constitution a liberal construction . . . we ought to do it." [But would the Court display a like liberality in accepting jurisdiction?] He felt certain that the people "would bow to a decision of that kind without complaint."

---

[35] 7 How. 1 (1849).

[36] Cong. Rec., 1936–45; *Counting,* 657–76.

Burnside was a man of integrity, a soldier of uneven accomplishment, but not an adept in federal jurisdiction.

Then Bayard offered another amendment, a resubmission of the Cooper proposal. He thought it "the best solution thus far submitted."

Senator Morton spoke in despair: "I submit . . . that this discussion has demonstrated the absolute necessity of the adoption of a law upon this subject. . . . The 4th of March is close at hand. An utter diversity of opinion exists as to where the power is. . . . What is to be done?" What to one group seemed the true solution to others would seem a usurpation, thus increasing "the confusion and danger of the hour." "I exhort Senators to avoid this danger by agreeing upon some method. It is not so important what that method is as that there shall be some plan agreed upon that will avoid these dangers which are right before us."

Bayard said "I concur most earnestly," and immediately pressed for the acceptance of the Cooper amendment. "What objection can there be . . . in adopting this proposition now . . . ?"

The vote on Bayard's (that is, Cooper's) amendment was 18 yeas (all from Democrats) to 34 nays (which included Eaton, Whyte, and two other Democrats).

Then Burnside's amendment to send conflicts to the Supreme Court was rejected without record vote.

The President pro tem. put the question: shall the bill pass? There were 32 yeas, cast by Republicans joined by Thurman, Merrimon, and David M. Key of Tennessee. The 26 votes against the bill were cast by Democrats joined by Conkling, Edmunds, and Howe.

Thurman moved for a reconsideration. He was disappointed that so many Democrats had voted against the bill; he could not see that it gave advantage to one party over the other. He believed that the fact that Section 2 might not lead to an ultimate decision had counted against the bill. He hoped that with more effort the Senate would reach a harmonious result.

That was on March 24, 1876. The motion to reconsider remained pending.

On April 19[37] Thurman moved to resume consideration. He still hoped to pass a bill with substantial unanimity, and

I think I have never heard a discussion in the Senate on any great public measure that was freer from anything like party than was the discussion of this bill. There was not an allusion on any side that could be considered in any sense partisan. . . .

---

[37] Cong. Rec., 2582; *Counting,* 677–86.

Morton opposed further consideration: if the House "does not like this bill, it can amend it," and in a conference "the matter can be adjusted." That Section 2 would lead to an unresolved conflict was a "very remote contingency." He had faith in the "final integrity and patriotism of all parties" to give the true and lawful decision to such a question if it arose.

"It seems on the part of a majority of our friends on one side of the chamber there is but one arbitrament that they would accept," which was to make the House of Representatives, voting by States, the umpire in deciding upon a question of this kind. "It is simply going back a hundred years . . . to the confederation, . . . each State having one vote. This proposition . . . is a retrogression. . . ."

Bayard shot back:

> I regret that the Senator . . . should be so thoroughly possessed at all times, as it seems to me, with an idea of distrust, and almost of dislike, for the very name of State existence or the exercise of State power or the recognition of State individuality. . . .
>
> I . . . am afraid that he is over-sanguine in supposing that that day of political millennium has arrived in which he and his party friends, and I and mine, shall be able to look at facts imbued with all the color of party feeling, yet decide them as though we were entirely indifferent to the result of our decision.

Apparently the spirit of disinterested search to avert an apprehended danger to the republic was becoming somewhat strained. Morton was a formidable politician and an uncompromising defender of national authority in war and in peace. Bayard was devoted to the interests of the minority party; in his insistence on Cooper's amendment he supported an expedient which the nation had outgrown and which, as his colleague Kernan had said, was likely to "annul the will of the people."

Maxey said that in rejecting his amendment the Senate had strained at a gnat and swallowed a camel.

Merrimon declared "I am very sure I never could vote for an amendment which would provide an umpire"; the duty "devolves upon Congress exclusively."

Burnside repeated that a decision by the Supreme Court would be the most impartial and most acceptable solution.

Then 31 voted for reconsideration (Democrats joined by Conkling, Edmunds, and three other Republicans); 23 Republicans voted nay.

Further consideration was postponed by common consent.

The postponement lasted from April 19 to August 5,[38] when Thur-

---

[38] Cong. Rec., 5193.

man proposed that the bill be acted upon without delay "in order that it may go to the House of Representatives to see whether an agreement can be arrived at."

Frelinghuysen thought that it would be better to adopt some amendment before sending the bill to the House, and recalled his proposal that if two returns came up from a State the question be determined by the Chief Justice, the President of the Senate, and the Speaker. Thurman agreed; he would vote for Frelinhuysen's amendment if he could get nothing better.

Frelinghuysen suggested that the bill be passed over until he could prepare his amendment. Anthony of Rhode Island hoped that by general understanding the bill could then be taken up.

So the matter was laid aside informally—and that was the last that was heard of S. 1 to regulate the counting of the electoral vote. Ten days later the First Session of the 44th Congress came to an end.

Bayard regretted the small attendance during the debate. Of the then actual membership of seventy-three, only twenty-seven had spoken. On a vote, scarcely two-thirds on an average would be counted. For the majority of the Senators, apparently, the manner of counting the electoral votes in the future did not seem a matter of consuming interest.

Judging by the New York newspapers, the press virtually ignored the debates, except for the *World,* the Democratic organ. The headlines of the moment were concerned with the misdoings of prominent individuals.

At the Second Session of the 44th Congress, on December 5, 1876, Merrimon introduced S. 1049 to change the time for choosing electors. "I believe that the election of electors of President and Vice President is a State election, and experience has proven that the several States ought to provide some means for contesting such elections. The time which intervenes between the election of electors and the day when the electoral colleges meet is so short that no regular contest can be made. The purpose of my bill is to so alter the law that the election shall take place on the first Tuesday of October and the electoral college meet on the first Wednesday in January, so as to give reasonable time to make contest if one should be deemed proper in any State."

The bill was left on the table, without reference to a committee.[39]

Thoughtful members of the Senate, mindful of a danger to the republic, had aimed at establishing a consensus on counting electoral votes. The result, however, was a kaleidoscope of opinions. Then *click,* the election of 1876 reduced options to two: for Tilden, or for Hayes. The

---

[39] Cong. Rec., 44–2, 40.

result was close; perhaps one electoral vote in Oregon would be decisive. Abram S. Hewitt, chairman of the Democratic National Committee, telegraphed to the Governor of Oregon, Lafayette Grover, a Democrat, to certify a Democrat as an elector. "This will force Congress to go behind the certificates, and open the same to get into the merits of all cases."

That as we know (but as historians generally did not) was precisely what Thurman, Bayard, and other Democrats, as well as Frelinghuysen and other Republicans, had in the debates of 1875 and 1876 insisted *could not* be done.

The Electoral Commission was created to give judgment according to the Constitution and the laws. It comprised five Senators, five Representatives, and four Justices of the Supreme Court, carefully balanced as to party, and a fifth Justice to be selected by the four. Justice Bradley was their choice, and in fact upon his judgment depended the designation of the next President. So much will be narrated in Part One of the account that follows.

Part Two will report in somewhat full summary the *Proceedings* of the Commission, enabling the reader to judge on the merits. In the outcome Bradley casts his vote for Hayes and gives his reasons for so doing.

Part Three will tell of Democratic disappointment, leading to disparagement and abuse, based largely on rumor, visited upon Justice Bradley.

Part Four brings the denouement. About 1878 Hewitt wrote a "Secret History" of the disputed election. This he revised in 1895, directing that it should not be published until all parties named were dead.

Publication came in 1935 with Allan Nevins' biography, *Abram S. Hewitt, with Some Account of Peter Cooper.*[40] Professor Nevins presented the "Secret History" as trustworthy, and added some supports to bolster the story. *Allegedly* an emissary, John G. Stevens, went to Justice Bradley's home and was shown the Judge's opinion in favor of counting the votes of Florida's electors for Tilden. This news Stevens brought back to Hewitt. Between that night and the following morning, according to the story, Republican friends visited Bradley and, with his wife's assistance, persuaded the Justice to change his opinion so as to support Hayes. Perhaps, Nevins wrote, the change was made to secure "a lucrative job for Justice Bradley's son in the New York Customs House." Perhaps, Nevins continued, Bradley had bowed to the Texas & Pacific Railroad lobby.

At the very close of the biography Professor Nevins told how in Hewitt's old age exaggeration "sometimes crept into even a public speech."

---

[40] New York: Harper & Brothers.

38

Once in particular . . . some over-drawn statements about his "secret mission" from Minister Dayton [in Paris] to Minister Adams [in London] in 1862, which Charles Francis Adams, Jr., at once disproved, caused [Hewitt] much vexation. . . .[41]

In fact Adams did more than "disprove" an "exaggeration": he found that the story "was a pure figment of the imagination,—'such stuff as dreams are made on.' " He declared that "analysis yields positively nothing, no residuum whatever of historical facts."[42]

If such is the judgment on Hewitt's "Secret Mission," it may prove true of his "Secret History" of the disputed election as well. We shall see.

---

[41] Page 543.

[42]*Proc. Mass. Hist. Soc.* 2d Series, XXVI at 448 (Oct. 1903).

PART ONE

The Election
of Tuesday, November 7, 1876,
and the Electoral Commission Act
of January 29, 1877

"The patience, self-control, and admirable political sense
of the people have prevented the crisis from being more
than grave, but they have not by any means removed all
cause for anxiety."

The Nation, November 16, 1876

THE FIRST REPORTS of the Presidential election were that the Democratic candidate had been elected. The *New York Tribune*, which identified itself in *Pettingill's Newspaper Directory* of 1877 as "independent Democratic," on Wednesday morning, November 8, carried the headline, "TILDEN ELECTED." Apparently he would have 185 electoral votes, just enough to make a majority. Hayes, it seemed, had secured 149. Five States with 35 votes were listed as doubtful. A postscript at 4:30 A.M. reported Republican majorities in California, Nevada, and Oregon; Florida remained doubtful. Next morning it reported "HAYES POSSIBLY ELECTED." The outcome depended on the Southern States. By Saturday, November 11, the headline was "THE ELECTION OF HAYES ALMOST ASSURED." By Monday the thirteenth, it seemed that the Democrats had abandoned hope for Florida and South Carolina: "THE CONTEST NARROWING DOWN TO LOUISIANA."

Manton Marble's *New York World* justly claimed to be the "acknowledged leader in Democratic journalism in the United States." On the morrow of the election it declared "TILDEN TRIUMPHANT!" At 2:30 A.M. it seemed that he would have 206 electoral votes. On Wednesday morning the forecast was down to 188 votes. On Sunday the twelfth it reported "All Eyes Fixed on Louisiana." On the sixteenth it was "All Still in Suspense."

40

Part One: *The Election of 1876*

Charles A. Dana's lively and inconstant *New York Sun* described itself as "independent." At the moment it was utterly devoted to Tilden. On Monday before the election it had had "LAST WORDS FOR RE-FORM. The Iron Heel upon Louisiana and South Carolina." Tuesday was "THE DAY OF OUR VICTORY. NO POSSIBLE DOUBT LEFT OF THE ELECTION OF TILDEN." On Wednesday after the election he was "THE PRESIDENT ELECT. THE NATION REDEEMED." By Thursday the ninth it asserted that "HAYES CONCEDES TILDEN'S ELECTION." But by Monday, November 13, the *Sun* was cautious: "NOW FOR AN HONEST COUNT. Shall Partisan Returning Boards Reverse the People's Will?"

The *New York Times* was Republican without qualification. On the morrow of the election it reported "Results Still Uncertain." At the moment it appeared that Hayes had 181 votes and Tilden 184. But on Thursday it reported "The BATTLE WON. Gov. Hayes Elected President." On November 15 it affirmed a "CONTINUED ASSURANCE OF RE-PUBLICAN SUCCESS."

The *Cincinnati Enquirer* was unrestrained in its devotion to the Democratic party. On November 8 it announced "VICTORY! THE TIDAL WAVE OF DEMOCRACY. THE PEOPLE RISE UP FOR RE-FORM." On the ninth the headline was somewhat qualified: "THE CON-TEST STILL UNDECIDED." Next day, "TILDEN'S ELECTION AL-MOST CERTAIN." Sunday morning, the twelfth, brought "THE DAWN; Ending of Sixteen Years of Darkness." It hailed "Florida, Louisiana, and South Carolina, The Three Democratic Graces."

At Columbus, the State capital, Governor Hayes kept a diary. On Saturday, November 11, he looked back upon the week:

> The election has resulted in the defeat of the Republicans after a very close contest. . . . [From the returns that came in on Tuesday night] I never supposed there was a chance for Republican success. . . . But I took my way to my office as usual, Wed morning, and was master of myself and contented and cheerful. . . . From that time the news has fluctuated just enough to prolong the suspense and enhance the interest. At this time the Republicans are claiming the election by one Electoral vote. With La S.C. and Fla we have carried 185. This creates great uneasiness. Both sides are sending to Louisiana prominent men to watch the canvassing of the votes. All thoughtful people are brought to consider the imperfect machinery provided for electing the President. No doubt we shall, warned by this danger, provide by amendments of the Constitution, or by proper legislation against a recurrence of the danger.[1]

---

[1] T. Harry Williams, ed., *Hayes: The Diary of a President, 1875–1881* (New York: David McKay Co., 1964), 47–51.

On Sunday, November 12, he reflected:

> The news this morning is not conclusive. . . . But to my mind the figures indicate that Florida has been carried by the Democrats. No doubt both fraud and violence intervened to produce the result. But the same is true in many Southern States. We shall—the fair minded men of the country will—history will hold that the Republicans were by fraud violence and intimidation, by a nullification of the *15th* amendment, deprived of the victory which they fairly won. But we must, I now think, prepare ourselves for the inevitable. I do it with composure and cheerfulness. To me the result is no personal calamity. I would like the opportunity to improve the Civil Service. It seems to me I could do more than any Democrat to put Southern affairs on a sound basis. I do not apprehend any great or permanent injury to the Financial affairs of the country by the victory of the Democrats. The hard money wing of the party is at the helm. Supported as they should be, and will be in all wise measures by the great body of the Republican party, nothing can be done to impair the national credit or debase the National currency. On this as on all important subjects the Republicans will still hold a commanding position. We are in a minority in the electoral Colleges—we lose the Administration. But in the former free States— the States that were always loyal we are still in a majority. . . . In the old slave States, if the recent amendments were cheerfully obeyed, if there had been neither violence nor intimidation, nor other improper interference with the rights of the colored people, we should have carried enough Southern States to have held the country, and to have secured a decided popular majority in the Nation. . . .

Hayes attended church, and on returning home found a dispatch from Governor William Dennison, "a prudent and cautious gentleman" who had been Governor of Ohio, 1860–62.

Washington D.C. Nov 12, 1876

To Gov. R. B. Hayes

You are undoubtedly elected next President of the U.S. Desperate attempts are being made to defeat you in Louisiana, South Carolina & Florida but they will not succeed.

From that point all was uncertainty—in each of those States, what were the returns; had the election been honest; what would the returning boards do? On November 30, Thanksgiving Day, Hayes wrote:

> The Presidential question is still undecided. For more than two weeks it has seemed almost certain that the three doubtful States would be carried by the Republicans. South Carolina is surely Republican. Florida is in nearly the same condition—both States being for the Re-

publicans on the face of the returns, with the probability of increased majorities by corrections. Louisiana is the State which will decide. There is no doubt that a very large majority of the lawful voters are Republicans. But the Democrats have endeavored to defeat the will of the lawful voters by the perpetration of crimes whose magnitude and atrocity have no parallel in our history. By murder, and hellish cruelties they at many polls drove the colored people away, or forced them to vote the Democratic ticket. It now seems probable that the Returning Board will have before them evidence which will justify the throwing out of enough to secure the State to those who are lawfully entitled to it.

Such were the honest opinions of the Republican candidate, whose interest in victory was becoming more keen just when the race came to the muddiest ground of the course. At this time the Democrats, whose excitement was the greater for their having lost the last four elections, felt no less certain that the Republicans were engaging in fraud and corruption to defeat the will of the people. What Hayes termed a ''correction'' by a returning board was to them ''a steal.''

At this point it appeared that a matter of one elector in Oregon might gain for Tilden a 185th elector or, still better, cause inquiry to ''go behind the returns'' to the detriment of the Republicans. On November 15 the *New York Tribune* published a dispatch of the fourteenth from Washington to the effect that the Postmaster General had received from John W. Watts of Lafayette City, Oregon, his resignation of the office of postmaster, and that it had been accepted by telegraph and a special agent had been placed in charge.

Watts had been elected on November 7 as one of Oregon's three Republican electors.

On November 15 Abram S. Hewitt, chairman of the Democratic National Committee, sent a telegram to Governor Grover of Oregon, a Democrat:

> Upon careful investigation, the legal opinion is that votes cast for a Federal office-holder are void, and that the person receiving the next highest number of votes should receive the certificate of appointment. The canvassing officers should act upon this, and the governor's certificate of appointment be given to the elector accordingly, and the subsequent certificate of the votes of the electors be duly made specifying how they voted. This will force Congress to go behind the certificate, and open the same to go into the merits of all cases, which is not only just, but which will relieve the embarrassment of the situation.[2]

---

[2] Allan Nevins, *Abram S. Hewitt, with Some Account of Peter Cooper* (New York: Harper & Brothers, 1935), 327.

We have been hearing Democratic Senators insist that there is nothing in the Constitution that empowers Congress to interfere with a decision made by the electors themselves and certified by them. Yet now to secure an electoral vote that might make Tilden President we find the Democratic National Chairman anxious to force Congress to go behind the certificate and pass upon the merits in all cases. We are entering upon country where the compass swings wildly.

Samuel Bowles (1826–78), the second and most distinguished of the three of that name who edited the *Springfield Republican,* had a fierce pride in the independence and authority of his newspaper, whose circulation was greater than that of any other in Massachusetts, save for two Boston journals, and whose influence was nation-wide. When the electoral contest of 1876 opened he favored Hayes on the basis of his letter of acceptance and not from any devotion to the Republican party.

On November 11 the *Republican*'s first item on the editorial page was this note:

> Giving all the evidence, one side and the other, we must still report the votes of Florida, South Carolina and Louisiana as stoutly disputed, and, therefore, doubtful. The democrats are very generally feeling that these states, and particularly Louisiana, are to be counted against them fraudulently. The suggestion is so alarming . . . , the whole question is so grave, that original measures are being taken to secure a fair count, and obtain a result that will command the acquiescence of the American people.

The "original measures" to which the note referred were that President Grant asked John Sherman, Garfield, E. W. Stoughton of the New York bar, Cortlandt Parker of the New Jersey bar, and other outstanding Republicans to proceed to New Orleans and witness the canvass by the returning board. Hewitt, for the Democratic party, requested John M. Palmer of Illinois, Lyman Trumbull, Henry Watterson, George W. Julian, and others to attend the same board. Down to the time the board came to the final business of acting on the claims to exclude votes, the members of the two delegations were free to observe the board and actually to ask questions.

On Monday, November 13, generalizing from a mass of reports, the *Republican* said editorially that

> it seems more certain that the democrats have carried South Carolina for governor and perhaps the Legislature, but by a small majority that Hayes has probably received the presidential vote. The testimony as to Florida appears to strengthen the democratic claim, though the repub-

44

licans do not yet concede it. In Louisiana it seems more and more evident that Tilden has received a large majority of the votes cast—so large, indeed, that it will be difficult, if not impossible, for the state returning board to correct it to such a degree as to reverse the result.

On the sixteenth,

> The latest news gives assurance of these facts: That Mr Hayes has the electoral vote of South Carolina without dispute, and that Wade Hampton is elected its governor; that the democrats have carried Florida on the local returns for all their candidates by from 500 to 1200 majority; and also Louisiana by from 7000 to 10,000 majority. The republican hope of defeating Mr. Tilden's election . . . rests on the action of the state canvassers or returning boards of the two latter states. A great mass of charges of fraud, intimidation and irregularity in the local voting is presented on both sides. Some of it is, unquestionably, fictitious and exaggerated; much of it is doubtless zeal; and, if it could be sifted and adjudicated by a competent and impartial tribunal, that had the confidence of both parties and the country it would be the interest of justice that it should be done. The state canvassers of Florida have a good reputation; whether it will stand the test of the work put before them is doubtful. In Louisiana, the board is discredited by its own character and history. . . .

This sentiment is plucked from the editorial page of November 21: "the republicans deserved to lose the country, and the democrats didn't deserve to get it."

When the canvassing boards in Florida and Louisiana decided in favor of the Hayes electors, the *Republican* on December 7 reacted with indignation: "nobody expects this result is to be accepted by the democratic party. Moreover, it is not accepted by a large portion of those citizens who supported Hayes and Wheeler. There is no doubt that it is held by a great majority of the voters of the country as unjustly, and, in the true sense, illegally obtained, by proceedings morally violent and revolutionary, and justifying . . . for the cause of justice, for the sake of the country and for the safety of our republican institutions, an appeal to Congress for review and reversal. . . ." (Of course the editor had not had time to learn what might be the reaction of the mass of people for whom he purported to speak; neither did he know how the Congress might "review and reverse" the result of the election.)

One turns to William Cullen Bryant's *New York Evening Post* for reasoned judgments on public questions. On December 7 its leading editorial was entitled "A Legal and not a Moral Question." In Oregon Governor Grover [as advised by Abram S. Hewitt] had certified one Democrat as an elector in place of Postmaster Watts, Republican.

It is doubtful whether the doings in South Carolina, Florida and Louisiana combined have aroused a deeper feeling than will be aroused by the proceedings in Oregon. It will be said by the Republicans . . . that withholding a certificate from Watts was taking a sharp technical advantage . . . . If it should turn out that the Democrats have secured their needed elector by a trick . . . they will lose the sympathy of a good many persons who have been dissatisfied with the course of affairs in doubtful states.

. . . The case is important because it confirms the opinion which has been gaining strength lately—perhaps we ought to say the opinion which has been held from the beginning by all but heated partisans—that the Presidential question must be settled not on moral but on legal grounds. It is clear now, if it was not clear before, that between the two parties . . . "morals are easy." If Hayes and the Republicans would be compromised by securing the election by sharp practice in Louisiana, Tilden and the Democrats would be compromised by securing the election by sharp practice in Oregon. What now concerns citizens who care less for parties and persons than for the peace and prosperity of the country is a legal decision of the Presidential question.

. . . If, as we have inclined to believe, the appointment of electors is a purely state matter, and if there is no power to go behind the authentic certificates of state officers, that rule must be impartially applied. . . . If a wrong has been done in the appointment of electors there ought to be some way of righting it in the state, but we are not prepared to say there is any. In South Carolina the Democrats have suggested a precedent by calling upon the Supreme Court of the state for relief. But if there is no remedy for such a wrong within a state, is there a remedy anywhere else, upon the theory that the appointment of electors is a state matter?

We say nothing of the moral aspects of the Oregon case. If the controversy turns upon moral considerations it will remain undecided. The question is, What is the legal decision and how shall it be reached?

Edwin L. Godkin as editor of *The Nation* had been treating the two parties with complete impartiality. His appreciation of Tilden was restrained, while he regretted that Hayes had allowed such stalwarts as Zach Chandler, Blaine, and Morton to set the tone of the campaign, to the disappointment of reformers. Hayes unfortunately needed to carry the three contested Southern States: the canvassing board of Louisiana was suspect; that of South Carolina was "more respectable"; "the Florida board is, we believe, entirely respectable."[3] On December 14 *The Nation* carried an article on "Appointment of Presidential Electors" by John Norton Pomeroy, whose authority on legal subjects was coming to be recognized. It resulted from his discussion

---

[3] 23:291. Nov. 16, 1876.

that the power not only to choose, but to determine in every individual case the validity of their appointment, belongs wholly and exclusively to the several States. This must be taken as the fundamental principle which determines the nature and extent of the legislative authority possessed by Congress, and which restricts the functions of the national legislature and of either House simply to the *identification* and *registration* of the official acts performed by the States in pursuance of their own laws. . . .[4]

A fortnight later an article on "Congress and the Electoral Vote" made the point that all certificates and votes sent up from a State "must purport to be regular and in conformity with the State laws, and Congress may inquire . . . whether such regularity and conformity exist." "If two certificates should be transmitted from the same State having the color of lawful authority" it would be for Congress to pass upon the controversy.[5]

THE ELECTORAL COMMISSION IS CREATED

THE 44TH CONGRESS met in its Second Session on December 4, 1876. The Clerk called the House to order, Speaker Michael C. Kerr having died since the last session. Representative S. S. Cox nominated Samuel J. Randall, Democrat of Pennsylvania, for the succession, and he received 162 votes to 82 cast for Garfield of Ohio. The figures reflect the relative strengths of the two parties.[6]

Abram S. Hewitt of New York, chairman of the Democratic National Committee, moved that committees be sent to Florida, Louisiana, and South Carolina to investigate the recent elections and the work of the canvassing boards, and to report the facts. The rules were suspended and the motion was carried by vote of 156 to 78.[7]

More will be heard about these committees.

On December 7 Representative George W. McCrary of Iowa, Republican, offered a resolution reciting that there were great differences of opinion as to the proper mode of counting the electoral votes, and recognizing that it was of the utmost importance that uncertainties be removed by a tribunal "whose decision all will accept as final": therefore be it resolved that a committee of five be appointed, to act in conjunction with any similar committee apppointed by the Senate, to prepare a report without delay.[8] As reported back by the Judiciary Committee and passed on the fourteenth, the committee would consist of seven members.[9] The Speaker appointed Henry B. Payne of Ohio, Eppa Hunton of Virginia,

---

[4] 23:351–52.
[5] 23:379–80. Dec. 28, 1876.
[6] Cong. Rec., 44–2, 6.

[7] Ibid., 11–16.
[8] Ibid., 91–92.
[9] Ibid., 197–98.

Abram S. Hewitt, and William Springer of Illinois, Democrats; also McCrary, George F. Hoar of Massachusetts, and George Willard of Michigan.

The Senate voted on the eighteenth to respond.[10] The President pro tem. appointed Edmunds, Morton, Frelinghuysen, and Logan, Republicans; also Thurman, Bayard, and Matt W. Ransom of North Carolina.[11] Logan telegraphed that he could not return in time to serve. (The session of the Illinois legislature was at hand, and Logan was seeking reelection.) Conkling was appointed in his stead.[12]

Chairman Payne, as we know, set on foot the compilation of *Counting Electoral Votes*, which is invaluable in assessing the performance of the several members of the Commission.[13]

After the holiday recess each committee went to work. Payne sought agreement on the proposition that the President of the Senate had no function in counting the votes. Hoar and McCrary opposed: it was unwise to rule out what might be the only solution if the two Houses reached no agreement. Presently a proposal by McCrary matured into an informal acceptance of a tribunal consisting of the five senior Associate Justices, Clifford, Swayne, Miller, Davis, and Field. That was two Democrats (Clifford and Field), two Republicans (Swayne and Miller), and Davis, who was supposed to be independent.

Meanwhile the Senate committee had worked on a proposal by Edmunds which became a tribunal of five members from each House and the four senior Associate Justices: then one of the Congressional members would be eliminated by lot.

Beginning on January 12 the two committees met together, and came near to agreement on a tribunal that would contain five members from each House; then from the six senior Associate Justices one would be excluded by lot.

That idea leaked out and was reported in the press on Sunday, December 14. It was not well received. An editorial in the *New York Times* suggested that ''a simpler way to settle the matter would be for Mr. Hayes and Mr. Tilden to be blindfolded on the portico of the Capitol, and 'draw cuts' for the Presidency.''

When the joint committee resumed on Monday it was recognized that resort to chance was impractical. Then attention was turned to what seemed to be the probable action of various Justices, and particularly to that of Justice Davis. Edmunds was scornful: Davis was an ''independent'' like Chase and Horace Greeley—ready to accept a Democratic nomination for the Presidency. Springer of Illinois professed to be intimate with the Justice: at home he was not thought of as a Democrat, but

---

[10] Ibid., 258.
[11] Ibid., 343.
[12] Ibid., 388.

[13] House Misc. Doc. No. 13, 44–2; supra, p. 10.

was known to be absolutely honest and fair. Hewitt had taken pains to investigate, and his information was that Davis was neutral. Then on January 17 Payne announced that Davis was competing against the Democratic candidate for Senator in Illinois.

Morton expressed his continuing doubt about the power to submit the question to a tribunal outside of Congress; but if the power did exist, he would call in the entire Court: that would avoid the appearance of being "fixed," and all parties would be better satisfied by its decision. (That had been his position when his bills to regulate the counting of the votes were being debated.)

Hewitt had had little to say in the discussion: he was known to be close to Tilden and he wished, he said, to avoid an inference that he was expressing the candidate's views. Without consultation with anyone he suggested that the five Justices might be arrived at by taking the two senior Justices (Clifford and Swayne); let each then select another; then let the four select the fifth.

After an adjournment to consider, Edmunds announced that the Senate committee rejected Hewitt's proposal and made a counter-proposal: take the Justices from the First, Third, Eighth, and Ninth Circuits (Clifford, Strong, Miller, and Field), and let them choose the fifth. Thereupon the House committee retired; on returning Payne reported that the proposal was accepted. Edmunds and Payne with the aid of others prepared a draft bill. On Thursday morning, January 18, a report drafted by Edmunds and Thurman to accompany the bill was accepted, and signed by all except Morton.[14]

On that same day Edmunds introduced the bill, S. 1153, in the Senate, and explained it at length. The decision of the Commission by a majority would be read at a Joint Session and would govern unless objection be made by at least five Senators and five Representatives, and the two Houses separately concurred in ordering otherwise.

Morton followed on Monday, arguing that the bill was unconstitutional and unnecessary. He saw in this the "product of 'the Mississippi plan' whose shadow had entered the Chamber"; members were "acting under the apprehension of violence."[15] Frelinghuysen and Conkling,

---

[14] Milton H. Northrup, clerk of the House Committee on Banking and Currency, was employed as clerk of the special committee of the House. A quarter of a century later he published in the *Century Magazine* "A Grave Crisis in American History. The Inner History of the Origin and Formation of the Electoral Commission of 1877," 62: 923–34 (Oct. 1901). From his notes he traced the evolution of the plan for the Commission. The summary account above is derived from Northrup's article.

[15] In anticipation of the election of 1875 in Mississippi, measures of intimidation, physical and economic, were so effective that a Democratic victory was secured while the day was said to have passed peacefully. Hence "the Mississippi Plan." The debate continued on Tuesday, and on Wednesday through the night to 7 A.M.

Thurman and Bayard, defended the measure against Sherman of Ohio and Sargent of California.

Dawes of Massachusetts objected that the Commission would be allowed an unbounded jurisdiction by the provision that it might "take into view such petitions, depositions, and other papers, if any, as shall, by the Constitution and now existing laws, be competent and pertinent in such consideration." That would permit it to invade "the prerogatives of the States to settle the title of their own electors."[16] Christiancy of Michigan, who until recently had been chief justice of that State's supreme court, made a most judicious defense of the bill. What Dawes viewed as a matter of jurisdiction was "only a question of the admissibility of evidence . . .; nothing more, nothing less."[17] Blaine, newly come to the Senate, denied the power to make this delegation to a commission; apparently he thought that only the President of the Senate could count the electoral votes.[18]

Merrimon, whose opinion had been that "we have no power to delegate to . . . any tribunal whatsoever" a controversy over electoral votes,[19] now said "I feel constrained to yield doubts in favor of this bill. It may have the effect of preserving the life of the Republic."[20]

When at last the vote was taken the response was yea from 47 Senators (26 Democrats and 21 Republicans); voting nay were 16 Republicans and 1 Democrat, Eaton of Connecticut.[21] To reach a vote the legislative day of Wednesday the twenty-fourth had run on to 7 A.M. on Thursday.

Five hours later the House met, at noon on Thursday, January 25. At once Chairman Payne asked unanimous consent to take up the bill; he wished to call for a vote at 2 P.M. on Friday. Garfield and others asked for more time, and it was settled that the debate would continue that evening; that the House would meet at 10 on Friday, when speeches would be limited to ten minutes; and that Payne would call for a vote at 3 P.M.; Members were free to extend their remarks in the *Record*. Payne then reported the bill out of the select committee.[22]

McCrary led off, followed by Hunton and Hoar in supporting arguments that fully covered the ground. Others were heard, chiefly in support.

In the evening Garfield made the leading argument against the bill. It "assumes the right of Congress to go down into the [electoral] colleges and inquire into all the acts and facts connected with their work."

---

[16] Cong. Rec., 44–2, 877, 888.
[17] Ibid., 886–88.
[18] Ibid., 898.
[19] Supra, p. 31.

[20] Cong. Rec., 44–2, 905.
[21] Ibid., 913.
[22] Ibid., 930–31.

Gentlemen on the other side of the House have expressed their indignation that one or two States . . . have established returning boards to examine and purge the returns of the ballot-boxes of their States; and I must say for myself that I would not tolerate such a board unless intimidation, outrage, and murder made it necessary to preserve the right of voters. All the evils that have been charged against all the returning boards of the Southern States, this bill invites and welcomes to the Capitol of the nation. It makes Congress a vast, irresponsible returning board, with all the vices of and none of the excuses for the returning boards of the States.[23]

He recognized honest differences over the constitutional provision that the President of the Senate would open the certificates "and the votes shall then be counted." Admitting the difficulty, he would accept the exposition of the venerable Chancellor Kent that in the absence of legislation on the subject it would be the duty of the President of the Senate to count the votes and declare the result. The delegation of the power of the two Houses was, in his view, unconstitutional. The Commission would have the same power as either House to take into view such papers, "if any," as were pertinent: on this he commented ruefully that "this House certainly has shown its power to send for persons and papers beyond any other of its great powers. [Laughter.]"

At 11 P.M. the House recessed to 10 A.M. on the morrow.

At that time Charles E. Hooker of Mississippi, who as a Confederate colonel had lost an arm at Vicksburg, deprecated any "allusion to the subject of war. I never have doubted that this question would be solved . . . without regard to anything like force."[24] Julian Hartridge of Georgia, former Confederate soldier and Congressman, closed his speech in favor of the bill with the remark that "There is the arch of the Constitution, supported by the three pillars, upon which respectively are inscribed the words 'wisdom,' 'justice,' and 'moderation.' " Those words should be "the talismans to control our action."[25] Representative Benjamin H. Hill of Georgia, formerly a Confederate Senator, soon to enter the United States Senate, gave "hearty and warm approval" to the bill. He said that the voice of the South cried "Peace! Peace! Civil war redresses no wrong, preserves no right; if you doubt, look here and be convinced."[26]

Amidst these harbingers of peace Roger Q. Mills of Texas sounded a call to resistance. "What is needed, sir, is not a more accurate method of ascertaining who is the elected President. . . . But what is wanting . . . is a disposition to obey the popular will. . . . " Recently the House had appointed a committee on its powers and privileges, which had re-

---

23 Ibid., 970.
24 Ibid., 973–75.

25 Ibid., 975–76.
26 Ibid., 1008–89.

ported "That in the counting of the electoral vote no vote can be counted against the judgment and determination of the House of Representatives."[27] Mills demanded, "Why have Members retreated from it now? Have they taken counsel from their fears? . . . If popular government is to be overthrown, and a minority is to dictate to the majority and enforce its orders by the military power of the Government, I will not legalize the robbery nor do any act to screen its deformity from the eyes of the people."

When a Member objected that Mills had exceeded his time, numerous others, friends and opponents of the bill, asked that he have an hour.

Ignoring the claims of others who had asked to speak, Mills wandered farther from the subject. Presently he related how "a recusant son of the South, [President Johnson], demanded of [General Grant] that he consent that Robert E. Lee might be brought to the scaffold and stand upon its treacherous triggers to make treason odious," but Grant had written his name in the hearts of the Southern people by saying No. "Look upon the pictures, then and now. *Then* he stood before the country like Saul amidst the hosts of Israel . . . higher than all the people."

> *Now* he lies there,
> And none so poor to do him reverence.

The speech[28] breathed hostility and bitterness at a nervous moment when many Southerners spoke of reconciliation and submission, and of eagerness for an orderly decision.

L. Q. C. Lamar of Mississippi followed. He had "listened with great pleasure to the able argument just submitted by the gentleman from Texas, mixed however with regret that I am forced to contest the views and to combat the course" there indicated. He went on to sustain the bill. "Its enactment into law will be a great triumph of patriotism, nationality, harmony, and zeal for the public good over faction, selfishness, and struggle for party ascendancy." "Indeed [the bill] is so in harmony with the genius of the Constitution, so promotive of the scheme of the framers, that had this commission of reference been part of the original Constitution itself, there would have been no language too extravagant to describe its far-sighted wisdom."

Lamar welcomed the participation by Justices of the Supreme Court: the people of the South did not forget that the Court had protected them from harsh and oppressive legislation. "Its decision in the Slaughterhouse[29] and other cases justified us in believing that there was one refuge

---

[27] H.R. Rep. 100, 44–2, of Jan. 12, 1877.

[28] Cong. Rec., 44–2, 978–82.
[29] 16 Wall. 36 (1873); VI, ch. 21.

for those who claimed that protection." He closed with an appeal for "the old good feelings and the old good humor."[30]

Less than three hours remained before the time when the chairman had hoped to call for a vote; many spoke briefly and elaborated in the *Congressional Record*. Among these was Henry Watterson, editor of the *Louisville Courier-Journal*, who was filling a term of seven months. His essay closed with "The Proposed Compromise," for which he would vote. "I am the readier to do this since I regard Tilden's case as a good one; but I shall vote for the bill with the full consciousness that the action of the commission may bitterly disappoint me and those who feel and think with me. If it does, I shall have discharged my duty in that manner which was best calculated to preserve constitutional forms and keep the peace of the country at the time when the Republic was menaced and the people were not prepared for war."[31]

At 4 P.M. Payne moved the previous question, to which there was no dissent. He was then entitled to one hour, almost all of which he yielded to seven speakers: four who supported the bill, three who opposed.[32]

In eight final minutes Payne gave thanks that "this hour of deliverance" had arrived. The bill repudiated the claim that the President of the Senate was authorized to count the votes; the great majority of the people would regard an attempt to decide the contest by that means as "a bold and unjustifiable usurpation." To those Democrats who held that the Constitution was sufficient in itself and that the power to count lay in the Houses, he replied that the two were co-equal and opposed: how could they be brought to agree before March 4? The bill offered the only available solution.

A hush fell on the House as the vote was taken. At the end the Speaker directed that his name be called, then answered *yea*. The count was announced: yeas from 191; nays from 86; 14 did not vote.[33] The *New York Times* on January 27 gave this analysis: voting for the bill were 159 Democrats and 32 Republicans.[34] The minority included 68 Republicans and 18 Democrats: of these 18, five came from Kentucky, four from Alabama, and three from Ohio.

On Monday, January 29, the bill became law with President Grant's signature.[35]

---

[30] Cong. Rec., 44–2, 997–99.

[31] Ibid., 1005–08.

[32] One of the opponents, William Lawrence of Ohio, a Republican, extended his remarks to fill eight pages in the *Record*: the President of the Senate was alone empowered to count the votes; Hayes was entitled to all of those in question; but the bill put his right in jeopardy. Ibid., 104–48.

[33] Ibid., 1050.

[34] In an adjacent column on the first page the Associated Press reported the vote as 158 to 33.

[35] 19 Stat. 227.

The Act provided that "each House shall, by viva voce vote, appoint five of its members" to be Commissioners. It was understood that each House would name three from its majority party and two from the minority. That was carried out by means of the party caucus. The Democrats of the Senate had no difficulty in choosing Thurman and Bayard. The Republicans of the House voted for Garfield and Hoar. The Senate Republicans held two meetings in reaching their selection. Sherman, who had led the opposition to the bill, stated at once that his group wanted Morton; the friends of the bill looked to Edmunds; and Frelinghuysen was chosen as being acceptable to both groups. The House Democratic caucus ran through five ballots. Payne and Hunton received a majority on the second ballot, and Abbott of Massachusetts on the fifth.[36]

Then came the viva voce elections. Senator Cragin of New Hampshire made known the Republican caucus selections by suggesting that Edmunds, Morton, and Frelinghuysen be chosen; and Senator Stevenson of Kentucky, chairman of the Democratic caucus, added the names of Thurman and Bayard, hoping that the election of these five would be unanimous. The roll was called, and each Senator rose and voted for the same five, save that each Senator named refrained from voting for himself. Thus each received 68 votes.[37]

In the House, Lamar nominated the five chosen in the respective caucuses. The roll was called and each Representative announced the five for whom he voted. Some Democrats in their caucus had indicated an unwillingness to vote for Garfield, presumably because of his opposition to the bill for which the Democrats had massed such strength. The result of the election was that Hoar received 264 votes; Payne, Hunton, and Abbott, 263; and Garfield, 240. Ten others received five, three, two, or one vote each.[38]

The expectation in the agreement on the Electoral Commission Bill had been that Justice Davis would be the fifth judicial member. His conduct on and away from the Court had over the years established the belief that he was indeed independent in politics. On January 24 and 25, however, as the bill was being passed by the Houses, the anticipated course of events had been thrown askew. William T. Pelton, Tilden's imprudent nephew, had contrived to cause pressure to be brought on Democrats in the Illinois legislature to elect Davis as the State's next Senator. Pelton's fatuous purpose had been to create in the Justice's mind a feeling that as a member of the Commission he should respond by voting for Tilden. Tilden had had no awareness of this unfortunate meddling. Nor had the Democrats in Congress, to whose interest it seemed unfriendly.

---

[36] These details were reported in the newspapers on January 30 and 31.

[37] Cong. Rec., 44–2, 1107–09. Jan. 30.

[38] Ibid., 1113–14. Jan. 30.

On January 26, representative Martin I. Townsend, a witty New York Republican, seized the occasion to lampoon the hapless Democrats. He told the House,

> Our democratic friends wanted a fair count. They are the fairest set of men that God ever made . . . . [Laughter]. And they wanted not only a fair but an impartial count. But in order that the umpire might be perfectly fair and impartial, in order that every bias should be removed from the mind of the umpire, an order was forwarded from Gramercy Park [Tilden's residence] to the democrats of Illinois that they should elect Judge Davis United States Senator. Not that there is any wrong in it; not the least in the world. It is done simply for the purpose of making Judge Davis unbiased. [Laughter]. . . .[39]

It was a moment of banter, before the parties became caught up in bitterness and misrepresentation.

---

[39] Ibid., 1024–26, at 1025. A full account of Pelton's intervention is given in Willard L. King's *Lincoln's Manager, David Davis* (Cambridge, Mass.: Harvard University Press, 1960), 290–93 and footnotes.

PART TWO

Proceedings
of the Electoral Commission

"I am afraid that [Senator Morton] is over-sanguine in supposing that that day of political millennium has arrived in
which he and his party friends, and I and mine, shall be
able to look at facts imbued with all the color of party
feeling, yet decide them as though we were entirely indifferent to the result of our decison."

Senator Thomas F. Bayard, April 19, 1876

GARFIELD'S DIARY for Wednesday, January 31, 1877, gives his
account of the organization of the Commission:

At eleven a.m. went to the Supreme Court room and met the
Commission. . . . The President, Mr. Justice Clifford was sworn by
the Clerk of the Sup. Ct and then administered the oath to the other
fourteen members. Each kissing the bible, and subscribing the oath
prescribed in the law. The members took seats at the table in the centre
of the Sup. Ct. room, in the following order:

Frelinghuysen   Morton   Edmunds   Payne   Hunton   Abbot

Thurman

Bayard

$\longrightarrow$ N

Hoar

Garfield

Thus the Justices were seated with their backs to the Bench.

Bradley   Field   Clifford   Miller   Strong

A committee of six was appointed to draft rules, and the Committee adjourned until 4 p.m. I learned from one of the Judges that
there had been a long struggle to decide the fifth Justice. . . .

He returned at 4 P.M.,

when the Commission met again, and sat nearly two hours adopting
rules. I think they allow too much time for debate. David D. Field is

56

anxious to be made a manager. He followed me to the door of the Ct. Room urging me to vote for allowing each House to appoint managers. A clause was reported in one of the rules by the Committee to allow members of either House to act as counsel. This was voted down–a blow to the hopes of D.D.F.

(David Dudley Field had taken his seat on January 11 to fill a vacancy until the end of the session on March 3. For a busy lawyer in New York City this seemed an odd thing to do. The explanation was that Tilden, his neighbor, desired that he do it in order to promote Tilden's immediate interests.)

But a place was provided for him by Thurman's amendment to let objectors to returns speak before the Commission. When it grew dark candles were brought, there being no gas fixtures in the Supreme Ct room. . . .

The President [Clifford] had been requested, in consultation with Edmunds and Payne, to nominate officers. James M. McKenney, who was second to the Clerk of the Supreme Court, was named as Secretary of the Commission. One of his duties was to keep the Journal.

"On the way home," Garfield added in his diary, "Strong J. told me that all the Judges *except one* were very sorry to be called to the Commission. . . ."[1]

David Dudley Field was anxious to play a leading part, and one Justice was not sorry to be a member: one cannot doubt that the willing one was brother Stephen.

Also on Wednesday the House received the report of its committee to investigate the election in Florida, that the electoral votes cast for Tilden were the legal votes. A mass of exhibits were laid before the House.[2] There would be a minority report as soon as it could be prepared. (On February 14 the majority report was adopted by vote of 142 to 82.[3]

As provided in Section 1 of the Electoral Commission Act, the two Houses met at 1 P.M. on the first Thursday in February to count the electoral votes.[4] The President of the Senate opened and handed to the tellers the certificate from Alabama, and one of the tellers announced ten votes for Tilden and for Hendricks. The like procedure was followed for Arkansas, California, Colorado, Connecticut, and Delaware.

---

[1] The diary is among the Garfield Papers in the Library of Congress; the papers are available on microfilm.

[2] Cong. Rec., 44–2, 1157–72.

[3] Ibid., 1562–66.

[4] Page 9, Proceedings of the Electoral Commission and of the Two Houses of Congress in Joint Meeting relative to the Count of Electoral Votes cast December 6, 1876, for the Presidential Term commencing March 4, 1877 (Washington, D.C.: Government Printing Office, 1877); a volume of 1,087 pages.

Then the President handed the tellers a certificate from Florida, and a teller read *in extenso* the certificate giving four votes to Hayes and to Wheeler. A second certificate handed to the tellers, giving four votes to Tilden and to Hendricks, was read. A third certificate, "received by messenger, January 31," was then read, it too giving four votes to Tilden and to Hendricks. The President of the Senate inquired, "Are there objections to the certificates from Florida?"

An objection by Senator Jones of Florida and other Senators and David Dudley Field and other Representatives to the first certificate was read. Then objections to the second and to the third certificates were made by Republican Senators and Representatives. The Presiding Officer announced that all the certificates and accompanying papers, as well as the objections, would be transmitted to the Electoral Commission.

By the Commission's Rule IV,

> The objectors to any certificate or vote may select two of their number to support their objections in oral argument and to advocate the validity of any certificate or vote the validity of which they maintain; and in like manner the objectors to any other certificate may select two of their number for like purpose; but, under this rule, not more than four persons shall speak, and neither side shall occupy more than two hours.[5]

After the objections had been presented, counsel would argue the merits.

The State's election law of August 6, 1868, as amended by an act of February 27, 1872, provided:

> On the sixth day after election or sooner if the returns have been received, it shall be the duty of the county judge and the clerk of the circuit court to meet at the office of said clerk, and take to their assistance a justice of the peace of the county, (and in case of the absence . . . or . . . disability of the county judge or clerk, the sheriff shall act in his place,) and shall publicly proceed to canvass the vote given for the several officers . . . as shown by the return on file in the office of said clerk or judge, and shall then make and sign duplicate certificates containing . . . the whole number of votes given for each officer. . . .

One certificate would be sent to the secretary of state and the other to the Governor.

When the returns from the several counties had been received

> the Secretary of State, Attorney General, and the Comptroller of Public Accounts, or any two of them, together with any other member of

---

[5] Ibid., 8.

the cabinet who may be designated by them shall meet at the office of the Secretary of State . . . and form a Board of State Canvassers, and proceed to canvass the returns of said election, and determine and declare who shall have been elected . . . as shown by such returns. . . .

Then came a most important provision:

If any such returns shall be shown or shall appear to be so irregular, false, or fraudulent, that the board shall be unable to determine the true vote for such officer . . . , they shall so certify, and shall not include such return in their determination and declaration. . . .

The secretary of state would preserve all such returns and papers received.

The . . . board shall . . . sign a certificate, containing . . . the whole number of votes given for each office . . . and therein declare the result. . . .

Representative David Dudley Field would support Objection No. 1, brought by Democratic Senators and Representatives.[6] He began by asserting that at the election on November 7 there "was a majority in favor of the [Tilden] electors. . . . Nevertheless, a certificate comes here signed by the then governor certifying that the Hayes electors had a majority of the votes. By what sort of juggling that resulted I now take it upon me to explain."

He would speak of one county (Baker, in the northeastern portion of the State). *Ex uno disce omnes*: by this one the other counties may be judged. He related that when the county judge and then the sheriff refused to join the county clerk in canvassing the vote of the county's four precincts, the clerk summoned a justice of the peace; and on November 10 they made the true count, which was reported to the State board of canvassers. However, also on November 10, the county judge issued a notice to the clerk and a justice of the peace to join him on the thirteenth to make the canvass. On the thirteenth the clerk and the justice of the peace attended as called, but the judge was not there. The clerk summoned another justice of the peace and on November 13 the two recanvassed the vote and sent that return to the State board. On the evening of the thirteenth the judge with the sheriff and a third justice of the peace, just commissioned by Governor Stearns, entered the clerk's office, took the returns from a drawer, and made another canvass by throwing out two precincts, and sent that return to the State board.

---

[6] Ibid., 24–26, 35–45.

[To clarify we extract from the majority (Democratic) report to the Florida legislature. The earliest of the three returns was executed on November 10 by Clerk Coxe (a Democrat) and a justice of the peace. The report to the legislature explained that "the county judge contemplated committing a most base and wicked fraud in the canvass and he did not believe the clerk . . . would become a party to it." This earliest return showed 238 votes for Democratic electors and 143 for the Republicans.

[The second return by Coxe and a different justice of the peace showed the same result.

[The third return, by county judge, sheriff in place of clerk, and a third justice, reported 130 Democratic votes and 89 Republican.

[In respect of composition, only the certificate signed by the three officers satisfied the statute.

[The majority report impeached the certificate by quoting testimony of the sheriff.]

Field read a portion:

Q. Why did you throw away Johnsville precinct? A. We believed that there was some intimidation there; that there was one party prevented from voting.

Q. How did you know that one man was intimidated at Johnsville precinct? A. Well, we heard it rumored around at the time.

Q. You next threw out Darbeyville precinct? A. Yes, sir.

Q. For what reason did you do so? A. We believed that there was some illegal votes cast there.

Q. Did you have any evidence before you? A. No, sir.

Field continued in addressing the Commission:

Now let me go from this county canvass to the State canvass.

. . . They [the canvassers] took the third canvass from Baker County and amended it, as appears in the *Congressional Record* of February 1, page 65, and added "amended by canvassing all the precinct returns," and that amendment in the full canvass is the true one for Baker County; that is, they got at a true result in respect of that county by taking the false certificate and amending it so as to take in all the returns.

[That brought the return for Baker County to 238 Democratic votes and 143 Republican.]

But what did they then do? Stearns was a candidate for the office of governor. He was then governor and he was a candidate for the succession. His opponent was Mr. Drew. The canvassers were Stearns's appointees, to go out of office with him or to remain in office if he was counted in. They took the returns from the other counties and threw out enough to give the State to the Hayes electors and to Stearns as governor.

The matter to which Field referred is to be found in the permanent edition of the *Congressional Record* for the 44th Congress, Second Session, for January 31 at pages 1157 to 1166, with exhibits at 1166 to 1172. This is the report of the majority of the House committee sent to "investigate the recent election in the State of Florida." [The minority report appears at pages 1172–81.]

Much that was said in argument for the Tilden electors was concerned with matters presented in the majority report with exhibits.

"These are all facts," Field continued, "which we offer to make good by evidence as the Commission may prescribe, by a cloud of witnesses and by a host of documents." How far the objectors would be called upon to justify these allegations would depend on what the Commission held to be the proper scope of its inquiry.

"This monstrous fraud being thus far accomplished, the people of the State took it upon themselves to see if they could not right the wrong. . . ."

Field told the Commission that the Supreme Court of Florida, only three weeks past, in *State ex rel. Drew v. McLin et al.*[7] by mandamus had directed the canvassing board to restore the votes of one county and of precincts of certain other counties it had eliminated, and that in obedience to that judgment the board certified a majority for Drew for Governor. Field added, "The same rectification, applied to the electoral votes, would of course give a majority to the Tilden electors. . . ."

In fact Drew had informed the court that the board "went behind the face of the election returns from divers counties . . . and did, upon [affidavits and other pretended evidence] discard the vote of the county of Manitee "and did exclude returns from precincts in Jackson, Hamilton, and Monroe counties, and that had these returns been counted, he would have been elected Governor.

What the court held was that the canvassing board was limited by the letter of the statute to excluding only where it appeared that a return was "so irregular, false or fraudulent that the board shall be unable to determine the true vote." "True vote," the court held, meant an *actual vote,* not necessarily a *legal vote.* The answer of the respondents showed that they had not so limited their exclusions; they had thrown out so many votes here, and added so many there. . . . It was held that in so doing they had assumed "judicial power" in violation of the State constitution's division of powers.

---

[7] 16 Fla. 1.

The recanvass of votes for Governor as ordered by the court had resulted in the election of Drew.

(The matter of the canvass for electoral votes was not before the court, and it did not follow that a recanvass of those votes "would of course give a majority to the Tilden electors.")

Besides Drew's case, on December 6—the day when the Hayes electors cast their votes—an information in quo warranto had been brought in the circuit court for Leon County by the four who claimed to have been elected to vote for Tilden.[8] Presently that brought a judgment that the respondents had been "mere usurpers."

"So much for the action of the judicial department of Florida," Field continued. Then the legislature by a statute of January 17, 1877, enacted that the secretary of state, the attorney general, and the comptroller of public accounts should forthwith make a recanvass of the votes. The result was a determination in favor of the Tilden electors. Thereupon the legislature by an act of January 26 declared that the Tilden electors, by name, were the electors chosen at the election of November 7, 1876.

Could it be, Field asked, that the certificate of Governor Stearns forwarded to Washington "countervails all this evidence, and that no matter what amount of testimony we may offer" that signature could not be invalidated? It was erroneous to say "you cannot go behind the certificate." The true question was, "Can the certificate go before the truth and conceal it?" By the Constitution, "the person having the greatest number of votes" shall be President. "I argue that here before this Electoral Commission, invested with all the functions of the two Houses, . . . you can inquire into the truth, no matter what may have been certified to the contrary."

After more on that theme Field concluded,

> Here is the certificate; one feels reluctant to touch it. Hold it up to the light. It is black with crime. Pass it round; let every eye see it; and then tell me whether it is fit to bestow power and create dignity against the will of the people. . . .

Representative John Randolph Tucker of Virginia supported Field's argument:[9]

> We object to these votes [by Hayes electors] being counted, because we say that these men were not elected according to the law of Florida. . . . ; secondly, we hold that, even if they had been elected according to the forms of the law of Florida, their election was tainted with fraud

---

[8] State *ex rel.* Call *et al.* (Tilden Electors) v. Humphreys *et al.* (Hayes Electors).

[9] Proc., 45–52.

and is void; and the whole question presented to this tribunal, the question presented to the two Houses of Congress, and which they have substituted this tribunal in their stead to decide, is simply this: Is there any power in the Constitution under which we live by which a fraudulent and illegal title to the office of President can be prevented? Must a man that everybody knows to be a usurper be pronounced . . . to have a valid title to the office when all the world knows he has not? . . .

Near the expiration of his time Tucker spoke of the objection filed by Senator Jones of Florida to the counting of the vote of Frederick C. Humphreys, one of the Hayes electors, on the additional ground that he was ineligible because of holding the federal office of shipping commissioner.[10] Tucker said that this man "was appointed in 1872 . . . ; continued to hold the office on the day that he voted, . . . and continues to hold it now, so far as I know. . . ."

Justice Clifford then called for an objector on the other side, and Representative John W. Kasson of Iowa stepped forward.[11] He and his colleague, McCrary of Iowa, had only that moment had access to the printed certificates and papers involved; in consideration of the magnitude of the questions presented they asked for a delay until the morrow.

Justice Miller spoke out: "Mr. Kasson, much as I would like to oblige you, for myself I must say that looking at the emergency and the necessity of getting along and the number of persons to be heard in all these cases, if we set this example the Commission probably would never get through. I must for myself vote against any delay unless it be to three o'clock, so as to allow an opportunity to take lunch in the mean time."

The Commission agreed to recess from 12:52 until 3:00.

These were Miller's friends; McCrary was a close friend, a fellow townsman who had prepared for the bar in Miller's office. Here and throughout the proceedings, Miller was always pressing to get on with the hearing.

When the session resumed Kasson began, "What is the case before the Commission? First a certificate, as required by the Constitution and laws of the United States and in conformity with the statutes of the State of Florida, certifying the electoral vote" of the State of Florida. That was the one first opened in the Joint Session of the Houses on February 1, giving the votes to Hayes.

The second certificate, also opened before the Joint Session, was prefaced by a statement by the attorney general of Florida that it appeared

---

[10] By Art. II, Sec. 1, cl. 2, "no . . . Person holding an Office of Trust or Profit under the United States, shall be appointed an Elector."

[11] Proc., 52–64.

that at the election on November 7, 1876, Call, Yonge, Bullock, and Hilton had been elected electors of the President. With that document came a sworn statement by Call, Yonge, Bullock, and Hilton that they as duly elected electors cast their votes for Tilden. Then they certified that they had notified the Governor of their election, but that he refused to deliver to them a certificate of their appointment.

"There is a third certificate still more extraordinary, still more wanting in all the legal elements of electoral verification . . . which is thoroughly *ex post facto*, certified by" the subsequently elected Governor Drew, reciting the subsequent proceedings in the circuit court, and those in the superior State court, "the latter expressly excluding the electoral question"; [2] also a certified copy of the statute of January 17, 1877, calling for a recanvass of the returns of the election of electors, and [3] a certificate executed on January 19, 1877, declaring that the recanvass showed the election of Call, Yonge, Hilton, and Bullock. Then [4] there was a certificate, executed on January 26, 1877, by Call, Yonge, Hilton, and Bullock that they had met on December 6, 1876, and cast their votes for Tilden. And [5] Governor Drew on January 26 certified that "in pursuance of . . . an Act to declare and establish the appointment by the State of Florida of electors of President and Vice-President of the United States," approved January 26, 1877, he certified that Call, Yonge, Hilton, and Bullock had been chosen, appointed, and declared electors.

(Certificate No. 3 had been delivered to the Presiding Officer of the Senate by messenger on January 31, and opened by him before the Joint Session of the Houses on February 1.)

The latter two, said Kasson, did not conform to federal law or to the law of Florida on December 6 "when the functions of the electors were ended." If Certificate No. 1 was accepted, there would be no need to consider the others.

The objection to Certificate No. 1 was that there was fraud behind it, behind the electoral college, on the part of local and State canvassing officers, "away behind all action of the presidential electors themselves." If the objector had been right in this, then, the proponents of Certificate No. 1 would say,

> if you go into . . . Baker County to verify his assertions, we should inevitably ask that you go into Jackson County, where, under other political domination, they rejected 271 votes actually cast for the Hayes electors [and . . .] into Alachua County and find at one precinct a railroad train of non-resident passengers getting off . . . and voting the ticket which was supported by the objector [Mr. Field]. . . . We should invoke your attention to Waldo precinct of the same county to find that they had vitiated that poll also by what is called stuffing the ballot-box. And so on with other counties. . . .
> If we go for fraud, let us go to the bottom of it. . . .

He thought, however, that the Constitution and laws would not permit the Commission "to go to the extent that would be required if it attempted to probe these mutual allegations of fraudulent voting and . . . canvassing to the bottom. . . ."

If there was fraud or conspiracy in a canvass of electoral votes, could it be overturned? Kasson replied, "Yes, if legal provision is made therefor." Where? "I answer, within the jurisdiction where the laws provide for the appellate or original determination of rights." But if the State had not made such provision, that was no reason for claiming a federal remedy that the Constitution did not allow. There was need for a final determination, but that lay within the jurisdiction of the State, before the point where federal jurisdiction attached.[12]

"The Constitution," Kasson told the Commission, "says that we have very little to do with this matter of elections by States. . . . It gave us no authority to overrule State action; and the alleged right to change a duly certified result contains within itself a claim of right, and without appeal, to deny to the States that exclusive right which the Constitution took such extraordinary pains to confirm to them." If you go behind the State's certificate, "unless simply to determine the verity of the several authentications and their conformity to law, . . . you launch yourselves into a tumultuous sea of allegations of fraud, irregularity, and bad motive. . . . There is no limit unless we draw the constitutional line narrowly."

Thurman asked, Suppose Florida chose four Members of Congress to be electors, would we be bound to count them? Kasson needed to reflect on that question; he was aware that an objection of ineligibility was involved in the Florida case.

Kasson admonished the Commissioners in words that may sound strange, coming from a Republican opposing a demand on behalf of a State for energetic action by federal authority:

> We must clear our minds from what has grown within the later years to be most dangerous to the reserved rights of the States and to the rights of the people, namely, the assertion of unlimited universal power of each House, or of both Houses, to assume jurisdiction over all things or questions having a national aspect or relation. . . .

In closing Kasson asked the Commission to give attention to the recent decision of the Supreme Court of Florida in *State ex rel. Drew v. McLin et al.*,[13] where the court "says that this canvassing-board cannot do anything except the ministerial act of determining upon the face of the

---

[12] Accord: Senator Merrimon's speech on March 23, 1876, and his S. 1049 in the Second Session of the 44th Congress.

[13] 16 Fla. 1.

returns irregularity, fraud, &c.; and by a strange inconsistency of argument, the gentlemen on the other side, coming to Washington in the case of Florida, ask this Commission to take the other ground, which has been overruled in Florida, and say that we, who have not the powers conferred by statute upon the Florida board, have immensely larger powers, which have not been hinted at in the Constitution and laws of the United States, and do have the right to exercise judicial functions." He commended to the Commission that decision on which Field had relied so heavily.

McCrary opened by recalling that the Commission was charged to "decide whether any, and what, votes from a State are the votes provided for by the Constitution."[14] Objectors to Certificate No. 1 had spoken as though the Commission sat as a court to try title to the office of Presidential elector. That was "utterly impossible." If one case could be made against one elector requiring the Commission to go down and decide how many votes were legally cast for this candidate or that, the same might be done against another, and this business might be interminable.

The Constitution provided that the certificates from the States would be opened "and the votes shall then be counted": that denoted "the narrowest possible ministerial duty"; to count was simply to enumerate, one by one.

The quo warranto proceeding had been brought in the circuit court on December 6 and a judgment had been reached almost two months later; an appeal was pending. It was claimed on the other side that the judgment related back to the time of filing, vitiating all that had been done in the meantime. But that was not the law: he cited many decisions. He was confident that the Commission would treat the matter as having no effect upon its own duties.

McCrary drew attention to Sections 135 to 140 of the Revised Statutes, originating in the Act of Congress of March 1, 1792: it was the duty of the executive of the State to give three certified lists of the electors to each one of them on or before the first Wednesday in December, when they were to meet and cast their votes. The electors would make and sign three certificates of the persons voted for, and annex to each certificate one of the lists furnished by the executive. The electors would seal up the certificates so made by them, and certify upon each that the list of all the votes for President and the list of all the votes for Vice President[15] were contained therein. One certificate was to be sent by messenger and delivered to the President of the Senate before the first Wednesday in January; one was to be forwarded to him by the post office; and the third

---

[14] Proc., 64–72.
[15] Separately listed under the statute of March 26, 1804, enacted in response to the Twelfth Amendment, which required separate votes for the Vice President.

was to be delivered to the Judge of the District wherein the electors assembled.

The Constitution prescribes that the day when the electoral colleges vote "shall be the same throughout the United States," and Congress had fixed upon the first Wednesday in December. McCrary continued:

> Now, if it be true that after the college in any State has . . . discharged its duties, it remains to any court in the State to review its decision after its action has been transmitted to the seat of Government, then I say the Constitution in one of its most vital provisions has been . . . violated, for in that case, after the time fixed by law, after the result of the election in the whole Union has been ascertained, after it has been discovered that by changing the vote of a single State the result of the election in the whole nation may be changed, parties may institute their proceedings, may bring the action of quo warranto, may proceed to try the case, and may determine that the electors who have discharged this duty on the day fixed were not the legal electors. . . .

And if an inferior court in one State might entertain such a petition to aid one party, a judge in another State might render judgment in favor of the other party. And so instead of the certitude the Constitution provided for the counting of the electoral votes there would be an investigation of the decisions of these courts.

In the matter of the objection to the vote of Humphreys, sometime shipping commissioner, McCrary was advised that at the time of the election he no longer held that office. There were no papers accompanying the votes relating to an alleged ineligibility. "I apprehend that it is not competent . . . for any member of either House to make any objection he pleases and refer to any papers he pleases."

Kasson returned "to answer after a little reflection" the question put to him by Thurman: Was the Commission bound to count the vote of an elector who fell within a class the Constitution had barred from appointment? Kasson answered "according to my best judgment, submitting it very deferentially to the able counsel who are likely perhaps to consider the same question, for I understand it is presented by an objection, though not in any proper form appearing upon any of the certificates. I answer the question in accordance with the spirit of the division of powers of the different branches of Government. Congress, under its power to give effect by legislation to constitutional provisions, might probably provide" for a judicial adjudication of such disqualification, "but without such legislation, it is not, in my judgment, a question to be considered in counting. . . ."[16]

---

[16] Proc., 72.

At that point, as Edmunds observed, "the objectors have exhausted their functions, and the rest of the case belongs to counsel."[17]

In accord with that view the President (Justice Clifford) "asked counsel whether they proposed to offer evidence before proceeding with the argument?"

Merrick replied,

> Mr. O'Conor requests me to answer . . . that we expect to offer evidence, which is now here, before proceeding with the argument. We have been under the impression that the evidence was already before the Commission, without any necessity for a further offer on our part.

Justice Miller spoke out:

> I wish to say, as one of the Commissioners, that I do not understand that any evidence has yet been admitted in this case; and I suggest to the counsel who propose to offer evidence to-morrow morning, that they make a brief synopsis or a brief statement of what it is they propose to offer altogether, instead of offering it in detail and having objections raised to every particular piece of testimony. This is a mere suggestion from myself.

The President:

> Now we will hear the reply of the counsel on the other side.

Mr. Evarts:

> We have no evidence to offer, unless there should be a determination to admit evidence inquiring into facts, and evidence should be produced against us which we should then need to meet.

The President:

> Should the Commission decide to receive evidence, you expect to have the privilege of offering it afterward?

Mr. Evarts:

> We do. To apply it to this particular fact of Humphreys, whenever it is made to appear by evidence which is admitted by this Commission that Mr. Humphreys at any time held an office, we shall need to give evidence, perhaps, that he resigned it before the election.

---

[17] Proc., 73–74.

Part Two: *Proceedings of the Electoral Commission*

The President:

Of course no such question would arise if the Commission should decide that it was not admissible.

Mr. Evarts:

Undoubtedly; and we suppose we may say on this point that if there is to be an inquiry which adduces evidence, that evidence is to be proved according to the rules which make its production evidence— by the system of the common law.

The President:

I did not put the inquiry by direction of the Commission. It was merely, as we are to have private consultation, that we might know what was expected on one side or the other.

Commissioner Thurman:

I suppose it is the inclination of counsel to aid the Commission and facilitate its labors as much as possible. There are a number of facts, I suppose, about which there is no controversy; I mean as to the existence of the facts themselves. Whether proof of them is admissible in this proceeding is a question of law, and wholly different from the question of whether the facts exist or not. Now, if counsel would agree, as far as they can, in respect of those facts of which there can be no controversy, leaving the question of their admissibility as a question of law to the decision of the tribunal, it would very much tend to save our time, much more than to have proof of the facts offered piecemeal and objections offered *pro* and *con.* . . .

At 5:03 the Commission adjourned.

When the Commission met at 10:30 on Saturday, February 3, the President observed that the stage of objections was closed and that proceedings thereafter would be governed by Rule III: in arguments on the merits of any question each side would be allowed two hours to be used by not more than two counsel; on interlocutory questions one counsel on each side would be heard for not more than fifteen minutes; the Commission might see fit to allow more time. Printed arguments would be received.[18]

Attention should now be given to the matter of introducing evidence.

Shortly Jere. Black, who ranked after Charles O'Conor among counsel opposing Certificate No. 1, gave his view.[19] It had been "absolutely

---

[18] Proc., 74–82.

[19] Ibid., 82–84.

necessary that the conscience of the two Houses should be informed concerning the truth of the case which they were to decide, and accordingly . . . they sent their committees and had evidence taken. These committees collected the documents, put the whole thing into a proper form, and then came back and offered it to the two Houses, by whom it was received and made a part of the record of this case." When the two Houses made the Commission the keepers of their conscience, "they required you to tell them what they ought to do . . . to make the decision . . . upon the evidence that was before them. . . . The President of the Senate . . . handed this evidence, all of it, over in bulk to be used here by this Commission. . . ." Black could not think of anything more wrong than that before this evidence was introduced it must "be submitted to the scrutiny of counsel who will apply to it those snapperadoes of *nisi prius* practice," as though this was a case on the price of a sheep "instead of concerning the rights of a whole nation." The Commission would sift the mass of evidence "to separate the chaff from the wheat upon the final hearing of the case."

When Black's fifteen minutes had expired, Justice Miller spoke:

> I move that counsel on each side be allowed two hours to discuss the question . . . whether any other testimony will be considered . . . than that which was laid before the two Houses by the presiding officer of the Senate.

Thurman would include whether "we are to take into consideration the testimony which has been taken by either of the Houses, and also the question what further testimony may be offered here."

Miller agreed to the inclusion, and as thus modified the motion was adopted.[20]

Two hours were allowed for each side, and presently it was agreed that three counsel might participate.

Merrick opened for the objectors to Certificate No. 1.[21] He said that he was "indifferently prepared to enter upon the discussion."

He read the pertinent provision of the statute of January 29. When plural returns had been received from a State and objections were made,

> all such certificates, votes, and papers so objected to, and all papers accompanying the same, together with said objections, shall be forthwith submitted to the said Commission, . . .

which would proceed to consider them, "with the same powers, if any, now possessed for that purpose by the two Houses acting separately or

---

[20] Ibid., 84–88. | [21] Ibid., 89–96.

together, and, by a majority of votes, decide whether any and what votes from such State are the votes provided for by the Constitution . . . , and how many and what persons were duly appointed elector,'' and the Commission may

> take into view such petitions, depositions, and other papers, if any, as shall, by the Constitution and now existing law, be competent and pertinent to such consideration. . . .

Merrick pointed to the reports Congressional committees had made on Florida, Louisiana, South Carolina, and Oregon, and submitted that "this evidence . . . is now before the Commission and properly in the cause."

> And I may remark that when the House committee took this testimony [in Florida] there was full opportunity given to all parties interested . . . to summon whatever witnesses they might desire. . . . The examination-in-chief was taken subject to the established rules of evidence, and cross-examination was permitted with the broadest latitude those rules allow. . . .

If it now were required to repeat such inquiry, probably it would yield nothing more than was reported by the committee.[22]

Merrick quoted the constitutional provision: "and the votes shall then be counted." The electoral *votes* was the critical part. "We . . . submit that any legitimate evidence going to determine what are the true votes is proper and competent evidence before this tribunal."

Black followed, and we quote a fair sample:[23]

> Now, remember the argument that Mr. Merrick made . . . ; let it sink into your hearts, and do not forget it, because it is God's truth. . . . "The *votes* shall then be counted;" the *votes*, mind you; not the frauds nor the forgeries. . . . I affirm, everybody affirms, and I hope to God that nobody here, even on the other side, will attempt to deny, that the Congress . . . has the verifying power, the power that enables it to inquire whether this is a forgery or not; and . . . you have a right to inquire whether it is . . . invalidated by the base fraud in which this thing was concocted. The work of the counterfeiter is as well entitled to be received for truth as this spawn of a criminal conspiracy got up

---

[22] There was a minority report by the two Republican members of that committee wherein one read that they were "debarred from all access to the documentary evidence" collected, and "were compelled throughout the entire investigation to grope our way in the dark." Nevertheless they had collected a considerable amount of material tending to support their conclusion that the Hayes electors had been elected.

[23] Proc., 96–101.

to cheat the State and the Union, overturning . . . the great principle that lies at the foundation of all our security.

Merrick filed a brief prepared by an associate, Ashbel Green of New Jersey; it was a clear, full, and able discussion which his colleagues unanimously approved. This was entitled, "Brief as to the conclusive character of lists of the Executive. . . ." Its purpose was to show that the certificates given by Governor Stearns, Republican, to the Republican electors, were not conclusive. Evidently counsel on his side believed that their opponents would base their case on that contention.[24]

The Constitution, by Article II, Section I, clause 3, and then the Twelfth Amendment, required simply that the electors "sign and certify [their votes] and transmit sealed to the seat of the Government of the United States, directed to the President of the Senate. . . ." The Act of Congress on March 1, 1792—which entered into Section 136 of the Revised Statutes—declared that the executive of each State would cause three lists of the names of the electors to be made and certified and to be delivered to the electors on or before the day on which they were required to meet. Green wrote that this was "a very suitable precautionary enactment." It was only directory ". . . as a recommendation, and operative only through the presumable respect of the State authorities for the wishes of Congress." It did not "declare that the lists . . . shall be conclusive evidence, or the only evidence. . . ."

Although the brief did not mention it, Florida's general election law of November 20, 1872, provided in its Section 32 that

> When any person shall be elected to the office of elector of President and Vice President, or Representative in Congress, the governor shall make out, sign, and cause to be sealed with the seal of the State, and transmit to such person a certificate of his election.

Green's brief was of high quality, but he was mistaken in supposing that his opponents were relying on the ground at which he aimed.

Stanley Matthews opened for the Hayes electors, and took the earliest opportunity to *deny* that his side held that the Governor's certificate of the list of electors was conclusive.[25]

By the spirit of the Constitution, Matthews argued, by the interpretation of the generation that adopted it, electors were *selected,* and they "not only have the *power* in the sense of *might,* but . . . *power* in the sense of *right,* to vote on the day named, for the persons who, in their judgment, ought to be . . . the chief executive officers of the nation."

---

[24] Ibid., 729–34.   [25] Ibid., 101–08.

Part Two: *Proceedings of the Electoral Commission*

Each State had the right to prescribe the mode of their appointment. This had come to be by popular election.

That election consisted of a number of acts: the voting in the local unit, whose result was carried to the county seat and there compiled; that result was reported to the third and highest returning officer or canvassing board,

> who exercise the powers conferred upon them by law and make that which . . . is *the completion and consummation of this appointment.* The board sitting upon these returns make their final return of the fact, as it appears to them, . . . under their responsibility as public officers. . . .
>
> Up to that point the State alone acts in the appointment. . . . Congress, under the Constitution . . . , may designate the day on which the appointment shall be made, and it shall designate the day on which the electors . . . shall deposit their ballots for President and Vice President. In that interval . . . I am willing to admit, any and everything that may be claimed on the other side as to the existence of State authority to inquire into and affect that record. But when that day has passed when in pursuance of the authority of law conferred by that appointment under the statutes of the State, on the day named by Congress, the body which has, according to the forms of law, been invested with the apparent title to act as the constituents of that great electoral body, and when they are required by the Constitution and law to accomplish the act for which . . . alone they have been brought into being, then that transaction, so far as State authority is concerned, passed beyond the limit of its control. It has become a Federal act. It then becomes one of those things which pass into the jurisdiction . . . of Federal power. It is the deposit of the vote of the elector in the ballot-box of the United States, and the nation takes charge of its ballot-box.

The electoral votes so given were to be sealed and transmitted to the President of the Senate, to be kept by him unopened until the day named when he opened the certificates before the two Houses, and *the votes shall then be counted.*

It had been a matter of debate *who* should count the votes. That was immaterial now; the question was, *What is it that is to be done?* Counting in its primary meaning was merely enumeration; but as said on the other side, it was an important question, What is to be counted? The Commission undoubtedly had a certain discretion and judgment, as to determine whether a certificate was genuine or a forgery, or whether if proved by a seal the seal was genuine. But that must be distinguished from a judicial power to try the title to an office. In exercising the jurisdiction in quo warranto a court with the machinery of trial by jury goes *to the very truth and right of the matter.* ''Is it proposed here to do that?''

"I think it is plain that this Commission is not engaged in the exercise of that jurisdiction." Matthews did not doubt that the power to try the title to the office of President or Vice President might be vested in the federal courts; but until then it remained dormant.

He denied that a State could through its courts exercise jurisdiction over the office and function of an elector after he had cast his vote. Otherwise "it would be in the power of a party and faction at any time, when beaten at the polls by the popular vote, to resort to . . . extraordinary writs . . . and defeat their adversaries by the interminable delays of litigation." Although the State might by such machinery and mode of proof as it chose verify its appointment of electors, that must be carried out prior to the time when, by the Constitution, those who had the indicia and the color of office had cast their votes.

> It is said, "Fraud vitiates everything." No, it does not. It makes things voidable, but it does not vitiate everything. If my friend, [Mr. Black,] by the arts and stratagems of other people, (which I know his guileless soul does not possess,) should hoodwink me by fraudulent misrepresentation into voting for his candidate—if that be a possible supposition—I cannot retract my ballot, nor can the scrutiny set aside the result, because fraud upon private persons is sometimes insignificant when compared with public interests. Frauds by trustees or persons in fiduciary capacities do not make void their fraudulent transactions. . . .

Black had recalled an incident in 1839 when the Whig Governor of New Jersey rejected the returns from certain local units and gave to the candidates of his own party certificates of election under the seal of the State. But the House made its own inquiry and in 1840 declared Democratic claimants entitled to the seats. Matthews explained that the supposed analogy "fails utterly, because by the express terms of the Federal Constitution the House of Representatives was the judge of the elections, returns and qualifications of its own members." There was no comparable authority for a federal inquiry into the election of Presidential electors.

With admirable precision Matthews had discussed the issue of the evidence admissible before the Commission.

The Commission had consented that *three* counsel be heard on each side of that question. Edwin W. Stoughton would follow Matthews, and Evarts would conclude.

Stoughton went to the jurisdiction of the Commission.[26] The statute authorized it to exercise the same powers, *if any*, that Congress or either House possessed. This was not a jurisdiction to descend to "voting-polls and places whence it cannot emerge in many days."

---

[26] Ibid., 109–13.

Judicial notice might be taken of the statutes of Florida. That of 1872 was quoted, creating an ultimate returning board having capacity to certify the number of votes cast and who were elected. Congress had no authority to go behind that determination. The Commission was authorized to take into view such depositions and papers, *if any,* as shall, by the Constitution and law, be "competent and pertinent" for its consideration. That meant only such proof as the common law had sanctified "to be employed to affect the rights of men." It did not mean the inquiries by Congressional committees which might permit "the breath of calumny to be blown in a way which, thank God, courts of justice take care to prevent."

Undoubtedly the Commission might go behind the certificate of the Governor, as for instance on questions of forgery or mistake, but not behind "the certification of the lawful returning board." Even if the board had made a mistake, its conclusion was not to be undone by any subsequent judicial action or by ex post facto legislation.

The Commission then adjourned until 11 o'clock on Monday, February 5.

(Here let it be interjected for future reference, Justice Bradley recorded in his diary for Sunday, February 4, that "Judge Field called." Field was intensely purposeful.)

When the Commission resumed on Monday, Evarts summed up for the Hayes electors on the question of the scope of the inquiry.[27] "I have said that this Commission cannot receive evidence in addition to the certificates, of the nature of that which is offered [by the other side]; that is, evidence that goes behind the State's record of its election, which has been certified by the governor as resulting in the appointment of these electors." On the matter of receiving testimony to show the ineligibility of Humphreys, "our proposition is that, at that stage . . . of the election, the two Houses cannot entertain any subject of extraneous proof. The process of counting must go on. If a disqualified elector has passed the observation of any sentinels or safeguards that may have been provided by the State law . . . it must stand unchallengeable and unimpeachable in the count."

On "the general doctrine," subject to the constitutional provisions, federal concern began with the deposit of the sealed vote of the electors chosen by the State.

O'Conor, closing for the objectors[28] to Certificate No. 1, said, "We maintain, as representing what are called the Tilden electors, that this tribunal has full authority to investigate by all just and legitimate means of proof the very fact, and thereby to ascertain what was the electoral

---

[27] Ibid., 113–24.

[28] Ibid., 124–36.

vote of Florida.'' The implied power to do this arose ''from the absolute necessity of the case.'' That view had been resisted on the ground of the ''overwhelming inconvenience'' and the ''intolerably protracted litigation'' that would be involved. ''We say that there is no limit to the power of investigation for the purpose of reaching the ends of justice, except such as a due regard for the public convenience and the interests of public justice and society at large may impose. . . .'' But it would not be necessary ''to go further than to make a correction of the unlawful extrajudicial acts of the canvassing-board.''

> So then, in this case of rivalry between these two sets of electors, it appears to me that we present the best legal title. That we have the moral right is the common sentiment of all mankind. It will be the judgment of posterity. There lives not a man, so far as I know, upon the face of this earth, who . . . could look an honest man in the face and assert that the Hayes electors were truly elected. The whole question, therefore, is whether in what has taken place there has been such an observance of form as is totally fatal to justice, and beyond the reach of any curative process. . . .

This claim of moral superiority brought a prompt riposte from Evarts. He put into the record, not as evidence ''but for your honors' information,'' figures from the minority report of the House investigation committee, such as the November 28 report by the secretary of state to the canvassing board, showing the gross vote: the Hayes electors had a majority of 43.[29]

The majority report of the committee set out the returns of the county canvassers of the election on November 7,[30] which being totaled showed

For Tilden electors	24,439
For Hayes electors	24,349
Tilden majority	90

After showing this narrow majority the House committee, in a narrative of, say, 18,000 words, recited details of their journeying into nine counties. Besides recording the prevalence of irregularity and fraud, they undertook to make corrections in the count. At once they added 23 votes to the 90, making a Tilden majority of 113. Then they revised the count for Baker and eight other counties according to ''different theories suggested.'' The first theory caused the figure to be raised to 543. Then further additions and subtractions on another theory resulted in ''a clear majority'' of the Tilden electors of 1,600.[31]

---

[29] Cong. Rec., 44–2, 1159.
[30] Ibid., 1159.

[31] Ibid., 1159–65.

The minority had claimed for the Hayes electors a majority of over 925.

What the majority reported after visiting nine counties leaves one with the belief that Florida's elections were conducted with great looseness, and that figures of votes cast were very soft.

Evarts was not placing confidence in the figures in the minority report. To sustain Certificate No. 1 there was no need to do so. It certified that Humphreys, Pearce, Holden, and Long, being duly appointed electors, had assembled at the seat of government on the sixth day of December, 1876, and there cast ballots for Hayes for President and for Wheeler for Vice President, and annexed thereto the Governor's certificate of their appointment. When they had complied with what the Constitution and the statute of 1792 required as to signing, sealing, and transmitting, they had fulfilled their function.

O'Conor and his associates bore the burden of supporting Objection No. 1. He argued that when the Constitution provided that the President of the Senate shall "open *all* the certificates" it meant "all the packets that may come to him"; and from that flowed a power in the Houses to investigate, "if necessary, a selection of the actual votes from the mass of papers produced and physically present before the Houses." It was competent for the Houses "to do whatever may be needful to the accomplishment of justice." And the Commission had for this purpose all the powers possessed by the House.

His opponents, O'Conor told the Commission, had argued that such an investigation would be so inconvenient "that it is better to let injustice triumph and permit a usurper to enter the executive office by the most unholy of avenues, that which is paved with falsehood, fraud, and corruption. They say it is better to submit to all that and to any other more enormous evil, if a more enormous one can be imagined, than to submit to the shocking and monstrous inconvenience that is thus to result from any attempt to inquire into the validity of the election!"

But then O'Conor descended somewhat tamely from that lofty plane to assure the Commission that he really did not want an investigation that went down to the actual vote cast; he would be satisfied with such a revision of the action of the canvassing board as would sustain the Tilden electors.

Ashbel Green filed his Brief No. 2,[32] whose object was to persuade that Certificate No. 3, received by the President pro tem. on January 31— the day immediately preceding the Joint Session to count the electoral votes—should be deemed to satisfy the pertinent requirements of the Constitution and of the Act of 1792 to enforce them. "There is no possible utility of having these papers in the hands of their depositaries before

---

[32] Proc., 745–60.

they can be opened and used, except to make certain that they shall be there when they are needed for the use of the count.'' And the Florida statute of January 26, 1877, to declare and establish the appointment of electors was ''evidence of a higher nature, of greater authority'' than the certificate executed in accord with the Constitution and federal statute. ''Of the competency of the legislative power . . . to pass a curative statute of this nature, and of the complete efficacy of that statute to remedy such an informality, there can be no doubt. . . . It is allowing an act to be done *nunc pro tunc* in furtherance of right and justice. . . .''

The effort lacked nothing in the boldness of its assertions.

ARGUMENT CLOSES AND THE COMMISSION DELIBERATES

ON MONDAY, FEBRUARY 5, the Commission met in public session at 11 o'clock, when Evarts and O'Conor made their concluding arguments on the pending question, Whether the Commission would hear any evidence other than what was submitted to the two Houses by the President of the Senate, and if so, What evidence could properly be considered?

As Garfield recorded in his diary, he escorted his mother and his wife to witness the proceedings. His comment was that ''[Evarts'] speech was very clear and scholarly and in parts able but his sentences were too long and involved and I think he lacked his usual fervor and force.'' O'Conor ''was suffering from feebleness and he did not come up to my expectations though he exhibited great clearness of mind and conciseness of statement.''

''After a recess of a quarter of an hour the Commission went into secret session for deliberation. After a little conversation in which Judge Bradley expressed a desire to take the evening and tomorrow morning for study of the case in which opinion he was endorsed by Edmunds and Thurman we adjourned to meet at 12 o'clock tomorrow when the Commission must wrestle with the merits of the case.''

[To be specific he should have written, ''to wrestle with the question of admissibility of evidence.'' But as he well knew, if the ruling was against admission of other evidence, that would probably be substantially decisive of the case.]

As the Journal for Monday, February 5 records, on motion by Thurman it was

> *Ordered*, That the public session of the Commission be adjourned until Wednesday (the 7th instant,) at 11 o'clock a.m.

Then the Commission adjourned to meet for deliberation at noon on Tuesday, February 6.

Part Two: *Proceedings of the Electoral Commission*

The Journal is properly taciturn on the doings in the secret session. We have, however, Garfield's diary, which will be supplemented at points from the notes Justice Bradley took for his own use. "Worked at my desk until 12 o'clock [presumably he referred to his desk in the House of Representatives], when I went to the Commission. Bradley and Frelinghuysen were a little late, but at 20 minutes past 12 all the members were present. After an impressive pause in which each member seemed disinclined to begin, Edmunds delivered his opinion of the case in quite a conversational tone, speaking on the question of what evidence if any we should consider. He spoke until 1.10, and was followed by Morton who spoke until 1.35. Thurman spoke for 45 minutes reading a part of his remarks from manuscript."

Bradley's note on Thurman's remarks was:

> The *action* of the *Canvassing* Board is part of the *manner* directed by the legislature of the State.
> If the Board exceeded its jurisdiction it did not act "in the manner" prescribed.
> The Board went *beyond its jurisdiction, an usurpation of power.* This *vitiated their action.*

Garfield's diary goes on: "Frelinghuysen gave his opinion and occupied about 20 minutes. Bayard spoke commencing 2.45 until 3. Then a recess for half an hour. Bayard resumed and closed at 4.42. Hoar read until 5.08. Mr Hunton spoke 50 minutes ended at 5.55. Desultory discussion between Thurman and Edmunds until 6.30."

Bradley recorded that Bayard "Examines the resolution and powers of the Commission—All the evidence which Congress may use, we may use." And Hoar made the point that "The Canvassing Board is made by law the final arbiter."

Among Bradley's notes on Hunton's argument are these:

> The objectors have offered to prove that the Hayes electors were not elected but that the Tilden were—
> Shall we let them prove it?
> Congress more than once have set aside the certificate of a Governor and gone contrary to it.
> In 1873 the votes of Louisiana were rejected notwithstanding the certificate of the Governor—
> The certificate of the Returning Board is not the appointment—but only evidence of the appointment. The *State makes* the appointment—When the last ballot was cast the appointment was made.
> *De facto* elector cannot exist when there is a *de jure* elector—

Then "Morton explains about election of 1873—"

It seems likely that the "desultory discussion between Thurman and Edmunds" had concerned the inference to be drawn from debate on January 7, 1873, on a resolution offered by Senator Sherman to inquire whether the recent election of electors in Louisiana and Arkansas had been in accord with the Constitution and laws. In the view of Democrats that was a precedent for "going behind" the action of the electors, while Republicans held that it had no such meaning.[33]

Garfield's diary continued: "I spoke 25 minutes and closed at 6.55. Abbott opened at 7 and spoke until 7.35. All the Senators and members [of the House] having spoken except Mr Payne. The proceedings were very impressive and the debate very able. . . . I have never spent a day in closer and severer intellectual work with more sharp incitement from the presence of able and trained minds. . . ."

Adjournment on Tuesday, February 6, came at 7:45, to meet on the morrow at 10 A.M.[34]

Later, on February 27, as the work of the Commission was all but complete, Justice Strong moved

> That the members of the Commission be at liberty to reduce to writing the remarks made by them during the consultations of the Commission, and cause them to be published in the printed proceedings on or before the 15th day of March next.

That was carried over the dissent of Abbott, Field, Hunton, and Payne.[35]

---

[33] Both Louisiana and Arkansas had been in political disorder when the election of November 1872 was held; as to each it was to be anticipated that the counting of the State's electoral vote might be drawn in question. In the Senate on January 6, 1873, Sherman offered a resolution to direct the Committee on Privileges and Elections to inquire and report whether the recent elections had been conducted in accord with the Constitution and laws of the United States. The resolution, however, was so broadly drawn as to include a call for inquiry as to contests over the election of electors, and what measures were required to provide for the determination of such contests and to guard against and determine like contests in the future. In debate next day Thurman said at once that "I shall vote for this resolution, because there is an urgent necessity for action. . . ." The drafting seemed, however, to have implications that he could not accept. "I know of no power in Congress to pass any law [on the election of electors] except one fixing the time when the electors shall be chosen. . . ." Then followed a statement that would be quoted approvingly by Senator Frelinghuysen in his opinion in the Electoral Commission. Proc., 844–53 at 847.

Sherman replied that he had intended to avoid any constitutional debate; he sought only an urgent general inquiry. After comments by Frelinghuysen, Trumbull, Edmunds, Stewart, and Conkling showed that the constitutional question was held in abeyance, the resolution to refer the matter to the committee was passed without division. Cong. Globe, 42–3, 364–68.

In the outcome the votes for those States were not counted.

[34] Proc., 138.
[35] Ibid., 703–04.

Part Two: *Proceedings of the Electoral Commission*

It is thanks to this action that we may know what members chose to report they had said under the injunction of secrecy. Much had been made in disappointed comment in the press of the fact that the Commission had done its work *in secret*; yet in the end it was four Democratic members who opposed publication. Representative Payne withheld his opinion from publication.

What the Congressional members had said on Tuesday, February 6, as they reported for publication, will be summarized. After that will come the matter of highest interest, the opinions of the five Justices, most important of all being that of Justice Bradley.

One reads in the Appendix of Opinions in the volume of *Proceedings* that Edmunds, ''who was the first speaker in the deliberations on the Florida case, was taken ill early in March and . . . was unable to write out his remarks by the time limited by the Commission's resolution.''[36] Certainly he recognized his responsibility as spokesman for the Republican members drawn from the Congress.

Much the same may be said of his friend and counterpart, Thurman, as spokesman and most responsible among the Democrats. He broke down before the proceedings were completed. On February 23, while the Oregon case was pending, the Commission was informed by Mrs. Thurman that

> Mr. Thurman has been in bed all morning and now suffering such intense pain that it will be impossible for him to meet the Commission to-day.

As arranged, the Commission adjourned that afternoon to his home and there with his participation completed the voting on the case from Oregon.[37]

On Monday, February 26, Thurman gave notice that he would be unable to continue. On that day the Senate chose Francis Kernan of New York as replacement,[38] and he sat in the case from South Carolina.

Thurman's opinion on Florida held that the decision of the board could be impeached for want of jurisdiction to do what it did. It had thrown out the votes of counties and precincts, which the Supreme Court of Florida had held was beyond the board's power. Furthermore in quo warranto proceedings the circuit court had held that it was the Tilden electors who were duly appointed. ''It is said that if we go behind the decision of the canvassing-board we must go to the bottom, and may thus be led to investigate the doings of hundreds of thousands of election officers in the United States. . . .'' Thurman replied, ''It is not sound

---

[36] Ibid., 817.
[37] Ibid., 637–42.

[38] Ibid., 654–55.

logic to say, that because we cannot investigate everything we shall investigate nothing; that because we cannot correct all errors and frauds we shall correct none. The law never requires impossibilities, but it does require what is possible."[39]

Morton said that the Constitution made the States absolutely independent in their appointment of electors. The election of those named in Certificate No. 1 was declared in due form, and it seemed absurd that a new Governor, a new legislature, and a new canvassing board could change what had been lawfully done.[40]

Frelinghuysen consolidated in one opinion his views on the four contests.[41] The State was sovereign in its right finally to determine who had been chosen as electors:

> The impracticability of the two Houses when met to count the votes . . . going behind the final decision of the States, and attempting to find out which set of electors in very truth have received the most votes, is a conclusive argument against the existence of any such power. . . .

He *agreed* with what *Thurman* had said four years earlier on January 7, 1873:

> Now if there is to be a contest of the right of persons to hold the office of elector, it seems to me to have been the contemplation of the framers of the Constitution that that was a matter to be provided for by the States themselves; that each State must determine for itself the election of electors, and determine in such mode as it shall provide any question that may arise between different persons claiming to be elected to that office. No jurisdiction over the subject seems to have been given to Congress. . . .[42]

Frelinghuysen also *agreed* with what *Bayard* had affirmed two years earlier on February 25, 1875, when Morton's S. 1251 to provide for counting the electoral votes was under consideration:

> There is no pretext that for any cause whatever Congress has any power . . . to refuse to receive and count the result of the action of the voters in the States in that election as certified by the electors they have chosen. . . .[43]

---

[39] Ibid., 833–36.
[40] Ibid., 817–25.
[41] Ibid., 844–53.

[42] Cong. Globe, 42–3, 364; *Counting*, 336.
[43] Cong. Rec., 43–2, App. 159, 160; *Counting*, 473.

Bayard, who now followed in the Commission's discussion, made no reference to what he had said two years earlier. He stressed the range to which the inquiry should extend:

> It is plain to me that from the very nature of this proceeding all the testimony, all the information known to parliamentary law and usage which was and is in the possession of either or both Houses of Congress, must necessarily be considered as being to-day before this Commission and subject to its examination; also that if other and further testimony is needed by us in relation to any fact to satisfy our minds prior to reaching a decision, it is our duty and power to take it, having always in view that it shall be competent and pertinent, and regulating our action so that the law under which we proceed will not be defeated by prolonged delays.

So the time allowed for taking testimony, hearing counsel and objectors would be measured by a due sense of the great end in view, that a decision be reached by the third of March.[44]

George F. Hoar of Massachusetts was by family association and conscience a Free Soiler, then a Republican. After service in the legislature he came to the House in 1869. His opinion in Florida dealt strictly with the law of the case.[45] Quoting the State's statute on the appointment of electors, he said "It seems to me that this determination of the canvassing board is in the nature of a judgment. It must be performed before the electors receive their authority or cast their votes. It is the conclusive evidence of their authority." . . .

"I do not think that any evidence can be received to overcome the effect of this determination of the State authority as to who were lawfully appointed, made before the electors cast their vote on the 6th of December. Further, I do not think that the evidence offered or suggested by the counsel or objectors tends to overcome it."

The power expressly given to each House to "judge of the elections, returns, and qualifications" of its own Members barred any implication of a like power over the appointment of electors. Moreover, such a power would be "utterly impracticable for Congress to exercise between the time certificates are brought officially to its knowledge and the time when it must be determined who has been chosen President." Indeed O'Conor had "conceded this difficulty, to which his only answer is the suggestion that such an inquiry, like the right to the writ of *quo warranto*, must be limited by discretion; in other words, that the two Houses may go as far into the inquiry, who were duly chosen electors in any State, as they in their discretion think fit, as time will permit."

---

[44] Proc., 855–70.

[45] Ibid., 955–59.

"The statement of this position seems to be its refutation." It was a question of *jurisdiction*—who had the power to determine who had been duly chosen to be electors. "It is gravely answered that it is in Congress when the State to be investigated is near the seat of Government, or the inquiry relates to a few election-precincts only, but is to be left to the State in other cases; that Congress may exert a power of inquiry into an election in Delaware which is impossible in California, or inquire into one election district in New York, but cannot into twenty or a hundred. This claim would never have arisen in any man's mind before the days of railroads and telegraphs. Such investigations, possible only in the most limited degree now, would have been wholly impossible as to most of the States when the Constitution was adopted."

Surely Hoar would not have fabricated such paltering answers by his opponents, yet no Democrat admitted having made them.

O'Conor had sought to offer evidence "that the board of State canvassers, acting on certain erroneous views in making their canvass, rejected certain returns." That seemed immaterial, said Hoar: first, because the question was to be judged by the board and not by Congress; "second, because the evidence would not affect the count of the vote unless it were further shown that the actual result of the election was declared otherwise than truly, to show which must open to both sides the whole question as to the votes actually cast for electors in Florida, a question which the two Houses of Congress cannot investigate or determine."

Hoar had spoken only twenty minutes.

Eppa Hunton of Virginia, the only Southerner on the Commission, spoke next.[46] After distinguished military service he had resumed the practice of law, engaged in conservative politics, and in 1873 had come to the House. His opinion on the Florida case was elaborate, with much citation of authority. "We must determine which of these returns is the true return. . . . To do this demands examination, scrutiny, and consideration of all the facts on which the several sets of electors proceeded to cast their votes. . . ."

He dwelt on the elements upon which Certificate No. 3 was based: the quo warranto judgment in favor of the Tilden electors in the circuit court; the decision of the supreme court in Drew's suit against Stearns; the statute of January 17 directing the new board of canvassers to make a new canvass; the resulting certificate that Tilden electors had been elected on November 7; the legislature's enactment that these were the true electors, and the Governor's certificate of January 26 to that effect.

> . . . Thus the State of Florida has, through all of its three several departments, declared that according to her laws the Tilden electors

---

[46] Ibid., 901–12.

were duly chosen. . . . She is suffering under a grievous State wrong, and through all her departments has tried to correct it, and is now stretching out her hands to us for relief. I cannot believe that this Commission will refuse to hear this testimony, and (if it comes up to the offer of proof) to correct this foul wrong.

In his argument Hunton had said "The two Houses possess this power" to determine what persons were *duly* appointed electors, citing the action on Louisiana in 1873.[47] Bradley's notes show that Morton interrupted at that point, and that he and Edmunds gave their interpretation of the incident, taking five minutes to do so. Hunton made his reply. When he closed it was an hour and a quarter after he began.

Garfield followed, beginning at 6:20 and speaking until nearly 7 P.M.[48] At the outset he repelled the assumption that those who opposed the proffer of evidence were seeking to protect fraud while virtue and right were on the side of the Democrats.[49] David Dudley Field as objector had asked the Commission to hear evidence that the canvassers of Baker County had thrown out the votes of Darbyville and Johnsonville precincts. O'Conor had looked to a much wider field; he proffered evidence to show erroneous rejection of returns from several counties. "From the reports of the committees of the Senate and House . . . I observe that testimony has been taken in reference to polls in seventeen different counties of the State. A portion of that testimony I have no doubt is contained in the large packages brought before us, but not yet opened. Much of the testimony referred to in the Senate report, relates to the proceedings at polling-places, to alleged frauds on the part of voters, and to errors on the part of officers who conducted the election."

"This summary of the evidence proffered is sufficient," Garfield continued "to show that we cannot take one step beyond the final determination which the State itself had made without going to the bottom of the poll; in brief, this Commission must assume to be the canvassing and returning board of Florida. A bare statement of the proposition shows that its accomplishment by us is not merely inconvenient; it is utterly impossible. . . .

". . . We are far into the sixth day of our proceedings. This is the first of four cases to be submitted; and we are now debating, not the merits of the case, but a preliminary question of procedure. It is not too much to say that the admission of the evidence proffered will wholly defeat the object of the bill."

The testimony taken for legislative purposes, Garfield added, did not meet the standard for evidence in a judicial trial.

---

[47] Supra, p. 80, n. 33.
[48] Proc., 959–66.

[49] Using the same official reports that Evarts had cited the previous day. Supra, pp. 76–77.

85

Josiah G. Abbott of Massachusetts, a graduate of Harvard College, was a dedicated Democrat, a delegate to his party's national conventions, often an unsuccessful candidate for office in a climate politically uncongenial. Briefly he had been Judge of the Superior Court. He was seated in the House on July 28, 1876, as victor in an election contest,[50] and departed at the end of that Congress.

Abbott spoke with exasperation at the Republicans' claim, which was "abhorrent to the sense of justice and right of every fair-minded man in the land. Nothing but the strongest, clearest, and most incontrovertible reasons can ever compel the public conscience and judgment to assent to it."[51]

> Each and every State has the greatest interest not only in its own vote for President but in the vote of each of the other States. No greater wrong could be done to the people of all the other States than to have a President imposed upon them, not by the honest, real vote of a single State, but by a fraudulent and wicked misrepresentation of that vote. . . .
>
> . . . It is claimed . . . that the doctrine of State rights bars the way to any inquiry into the question whether the persons from any State claiming to cast its vote are true electors, and compels Congress to confine itself merely to counting. . . . I yield to no one in my fidelity to the doctrine of State rights, but I am not willing to carry it to the extent of doing in its name the greatest wrongs to States, instead of upholding their rights. There never was a clearer case of stealing "the livery of Heaven to serve the devil in," than in thus attempting to wrest the doctrine of State rights to excuse and justify this great wrong to States. . . .

The Commission was asked to sustain the Hayes electors "because two irresponsible ministerial officers . . . have so declared," although the State courts, the legislature, and the Governor had declared to the contrary.

> If this attempt to authorize these two irresponsible officers . . . to appoint presidential electors . . . is by the judgment of this Com-

---

[50] See Abbott v. Frost, infra, p. 174. Abbott had lost two sons in the Union Army. Henry L., at nineteen a lieutenant in the 20th Massachusetts, was killed three years later while commanding the regiment. He was pleased to refer to the 20th as "the copperhead regiment." This was the "Little Abbott" whom Holmes revered in his war-time letters and always thereafter. These expressions abound in *Touched with Fire: Civil War Letters and Diary of Oliver Wendell Holmes, Jr.*, edited by Mark De Wolfe Howe (Cambridge, Mass.: Harvard University Press, 1947), and Howe's *Justice Oliver Wendell Holmes*, Volume I: *The Shaping Years, 1841–1870* (Cambridge, Mass.: Belknap Press of Harvard University Press, 1957).

[51] Proc., 932–39.

mission to be crowned with success, [it] would proclaim to the world that, to obtain and enjoy the office of President of the United States, . . . a candidate and party, as lacking in principle as they are rich in money, can, by buying a few weak, wicked, and irresponsible State canvassers, gain possession and hold that high office. . . . In fine, such a judgment would proclaim that this government is no longer one of the people, under the Constitution and law, but that it is a Government of returning-boards and their creatures.

When the Commission met on Wednesday, February 7, Justice Clifford recalled that on the fifth it had been ordered that there would be a public session at 11 A.M. on Wednesday. Now, since the deliberations had not ended, it was ordered that at 11 o'clock the doors would be considered as opened, and that the Commission would at once adjourn for deliberation.

Garfield recorded in his diary that "Mr Payne made a speech of 35 minutes having in it more partisan bitterness than any yet made. He had the bad taste to speak sneeringly of colored men in Florida. . . ." (The speech was not reported in the *Proceedings*.)

The time had come when the judicial members must speak: did Florida's votes go to make Tilden President—or were they to be counted for Hayes? How each Justice performed upon that memorable scene is the great concern that has brought us to this point.

JUSTICE FIELD'S OPINION

JUSTICE FIELD said that the main question, to which all other inquiries were subordinate, was "how many and what persons were *duly appointed* electors" in the State of Florida.[52]

By the Constitution the manner of appointment was left entirely to the State legislature. "Any substantial departure from the manner prescribed must necessarily vitiate the whole proceeding. . . . If . . . the legislature should prescribe that the appointment should be made by a majority of the votes cast at [a prescribed] election, and the canvassers, or other officers of election, should declare as elected those who had received only a plurality or a minority of the votes, or the votes of only a portion of the State, the declaration would be . . . invalid as not conforming to the legislative direction; and the appointment of the parties thus declared elected could only be treated as a nullity."

The legislature of Florida directed that electors were to be chosen by a majority of the qualified voters. "When their votes were cast on the

---

[52] Ibid., 974–88.

7th of November, the electors were appointed, and all that remained was to ascertain and declare the result. . . . What subsequently was required . . . was an authentic declaration of the result.'' Field related the steps by which the returns were sent up to the canvassing board, whose duty was to ''declare who were elected *as shown by such returns.*' The duty of the canvassers under the law of the State was ministerial. . . . Such was the construction given to the statute by the supreme court of the State. . . .'' in *Drew v. Stearns.*

''The construction given to a statute of a State by its supreme court is, as we all know, considered as part of the statute itself, as much so as if embodied in the very text.'' The Florida court had held that the canvassing board had acted in excess of its authority. In that erroneous way the board had concluded that the Hayes electors were chosen—which result ''was without any validity whatever.''

Field had asked the gentlemen supporting the Hayes electors, Suppose the canvassing board made an error in addition; suppose they acted in pursuance of bribery or conspiracy; suppose they acted under force with pistols at their heads: did they hold that the Houses of Congress could not remedy the falsity of their certificate? To each question, allegedly, gentlemen had answered that there was no remedy.

This doctrine, which seems to me to be as unsound in law as it is shocking in morals, is supported upon the notion that if we are permitted to look behind the certificate of the governor, and of the canvassing board . . . we shall open the door to an investigation which may not be brought to a close before the 4th of March. . . . I admit . . . that no proceedings can be permitted which will postpone the counting [so as to prevent the timely election of a President]. But this limitation of time . . . is a reason for immediate action to correct [mistake] and expose [fraud]. Whatever is done to overthrow the *prima facie* evidence presented by the certificate by the governor must be commenced, carried forward, and completed, so that the result of the proceeding can be considered by the two Houses of Congress when the certificates are opened in their presence and the votes counted. The countervailing evidence must be presented in some authoritative form, like the judgment of a competent tribunal, or the legislative declaration of a State, or the finding of an appropriate committee approved by the House appointing it; and then it will constitute a basis for the action of the Houses without delaying their proceedings. . . . I admit that the proceeding cannot be had, *except by permission of the two Houses*, by reason of the delay it would occasion. . . . [B]ut if the fact of forgery or falsity has already been found by competent authority, and the finding is laid before the two Houses, . . . it would be their manifest duty to act upon the finding, in order that the nation might not be defrauded in its choice of a Chief Magistrate.

Here there was "the highest possible evidence of the action of the State of Florida"—in the adjudication of a court of competent jurisdiction (*State ex rel. Call et al. v. Humphreys et al.* in the circuit court, which while appealed had full force in the meantime); in the declaration of the legislature; and in the certificate of Governor Drew based upon a recanvass. Moreover the House of Representatives had sent a committee to Florida to investigate, whose report "declared that the evidence was perfectly conclusive that the State of Florida had cast her vote for the Tilden electors"; and the House had adopted a resolution to that effect by a vote of 142 to 82.

Concluding, "I desire that this Commission should succeed and give by its judgment peace to the country. But such a result can only be attained by disposing of the questions submitted to us on the merits. It cannot be attained by a resort to technical subtleties and ingenious devices to avoid looking at the evidence. . . ."

Comment: "Any substantial departure from the manner prescribed [by *state legislation* on the appointment of electors] must necessarily vitiate the whole proceeding." But a complete departure from what the *Constitution* prescribed for the election of a President could be overlooked when as an alternative the State presented "the highest possible evidence" of its action, not so late as to prevent a declaration of the result in time to induct a President on March 4.

That seems highly unpersuasive.

JUSTICE STRONG'S OPINION

JUSTICE STRONG'S OPINION[53] dwelt on the proposition that the Commission had no authority to revise the determination of the board of canvassers.

"What we are asked to do . . . is to recanvass a State election for State agents or officers, or, rather, to try a contested election for presidential electors, such a contested election as is provided for in most of the States by established tribunals created for the purpose of determining election contests. . . ."

"Has this Commission power to try a case of contested election in a State?" Neither Congress nor either House—whose powers in this behalf have been conferred on this Commission—has been given such a power by any provision of the Constitution; nor can it be implied. "The scheme of the Constitution was to make the appointment of electors exclusively a State affair, free from interference of the legislative department of the Government," save that Congress may determine the time for

---

[53] Ibid., 994–1001.

choosing electors, and the day on which they shall give their votes, which day shall be the same throughout the Union.

"If, then, Congress has not the power to enter into the consideration of the evidence offered, it would be idle to admit it."

But we are asked, Is there no way of avoiding the possibility of having electoral votes cast on the faith of false returns of elections? Can no inquiry be made into the correctness of such returns? To such questions I reply, there is ample power in the State. She may provide in any way to purify her elections, and may devise means to correct an erroneous canvass, or rectify false returns, or throw out illegal votes. She may do this in the most summary way. She may accomplish it completely before the day for casting the electoral vote arrives. But I find no power in Congress, either express or implied, to do this work which the State may do.

Strong sketched the provisions of Florida law whereby the result of the popular vote "shall be *determined* and *declared* by a State board of canvassers constituted as directed." After that the Governor is required to give a certificate to the persons chosen as electors. In this case it is not suggested that Governor Stearns' certificate did not truly represent the determination of the State board. "It was neither untrue nor fraudulent." "I admit that the governor's certificate is not unimpeachable. It may be shown to be untrue by proof that it does not correspond with the determination of the canvassing-board. It may be proved to be a forgery." But nothing of that sort had been alleged. "The determination, I have said, may be the subject of revision by process of State law, but until annulled it was the pronounced action of the State."

Now, then, the persons who voted for Hayes on the 6th of December had all the insignia of title when they voted. . . . No other persons had even a *prima facie* right. The Tilden electors had no decision in their favor of any board or tribunal authorized by law to ascertain and declare the results of the election. They had no certificate from anybody empowered to certify that they were electors. They were not even electors *de facto*.

In my judgment, it follows inevitably that what was done in Florida after the 6th of December is immaterial. Neither the action of the legislature, nor a *post hac* decision of a court, can affect an act rightfully done, when it is done and completed before the legislature and the court attempted to annul the authority for it. . . . There must be a finality in ascertaining the results of an election, and when the election is a mode of appointment of persons to cast a vote for a State on an appointed day, the finality must be on or before that day, else nothing can be settled.

90

Strong cited a number of cases on that point.

> My conclusions, then, are that neither Congress nor this Commission has authority under the Constitution to recanvass the vote of Florida for State electors; that the first determination of the State canvassing-board was conclusive until it was reversed by State authority; that while it remained unreversed it conferred upon the persons declared by it to have been chosen electors rightful authority to cast the vote of the State; and that the act which those electors were appointed to do having been done, it was not in the power even of the State afterward to undo the act and call in question the authority by which it was done.

Accordingly the evidence proffered was impertinent to any question the Commission could decide, and ought not to be admitted.

JUSTICE MILLER'S OPINION

IN THE FLORIDA case, as Miller saw it, "the only question . . . properly before the Commission is . . . whether any other evidence can be received and considered . . . than that which was submitted by the President of the Senate to the two Houses . . . , being the different certificates and the papers accompanying the same." It was urged that "a large pile of papers, a half-bushel perhaps in quantity, of the contents of which both this Commission and the two Houses are profoundly ignorant," should be received because they were in a very general way referred to in objections to Certificate No. 1. These papers were not identified in any way. "They may be *ex parte* affidavits taken in the morasses of Florida, in the slums of New York, or the private office of retained counsel in this city." It seemed very clear to him that the statute did not charge the Commission to consider such papers.[54]

> It is said by way of impeachment of this certificate [No. 1] that the board of canvassers exceeded its jurisdiction by rejecting returns which were neither irregular, false, nor fraudulent; and that this can now be shown by proof before this Commission. But what is the *jurisdiction* of this board? It is not merely to count up and compare the returns, but upon all the facts submitted to them to determine, that is, to decide, who is elected. This is its duty, and its jurisdiction is commensurate with its duty. If it mistakes the law, or does not properly weigh the facts, these do not affect the jurisdiction, or invalidate the judgment which it renders.
>
> Jurisdiction is the power to examine and decide, to hear and determine, the subject matter submitted to the tribunal by which the

---

[54] Ibid., 1006–15.

jurisdiction is to be exercised. When jurisdiction is given over the whole subject, as in this case, to decide who are elected, it cannot be limited to that which is directory in the mode of proceeding. It may not follow that mode, yet its decision be valid. Its decision may be erroneous, but it is nevertheless the decision of the only tribunal having jurisdiction, and it must be conclusive. I say it must be conclusive, because there is no other tribunal which is by law authorized to review this decision or to correct its errors if any exist. . . .

Then reliance had been placed on decisions by two courts in Florida. The holding in *State ex rel. Drew v. McLin* seemed "so much at variance with the language and spirit of the statute" on the powers of the canvassing board "as to have little weight with me." It had also been claimed that the decision of a local circuit court sustaining the Tilden electors in a suit against Hayes electors had the effect of overturning the decision of the State canvassing board. "Can the right to cast one of the electoral votes of a State for President be thus tried in a court of law? It is not asserted that any such right is found in any act of Congress or in any statute of Florida." An elector exhausted his function when he had cast his vote: there was no need for a proceeding by quo warranto; an injunction would be much more appropriate, if any judicial remedy existed at all, for by that writ the single act which the elector performs might be prohibited. The soundness of judicial restraint of an elector by quo warranto might be tested by its consequences: in New York there were thirty-two courts of original jurisdiction, and by that reasoning a judge in any one of them could prevent the thirty-five electoral votes of that State from being counted. "It is safe to say that no such power exists in any man or in any tribunal, unless placed there by the expressed will of the law-making power."

On the objection to Humphreys' vote, Miller saw two reasons why evidence to show that he held a federal office when chosen was inadmissible. First, the vote being in fact accomplished could not be annulled by any subsequent proceeding. Second, there were many provisions in the Constitution that were not self-executing, and the one here in question was one that had never been called into action by appropriate legislation.

Miller turned to considerations which in his view were conclusive of the question before the Commission. It was manifestly the duty of the State to decide upon the means by which the appointment of Presidential electors was authenticated and certified. In Florida they were chosen by popular suffrage in a mode well defined by a statute of 1872. Certain officers were to constitute the board of State canvassers; the returns were sent to them, and when they had performed their duties as there set out, the board would "make and sign a certificate . . . and therein declare the result. . . ." By another statute the Governor was required to make out, sign, and cause to be sealed with the seal of the State, and transmit to each person elected a certificate of his election.

"These two provisions prescribe the manner in which the result of an election for electors shall be '*determined and declared*' and how that result shall be duly authenticated. When the canvassing-board herein mentioned has canvassed the returns of the election, has determined who is elected, and has declared that fact by signing the certificate, which is to be deposited with the secretary of state, the person named in that certificate is from that moment a duly appointed elector.''

"In all governments where rights are secured by law, it has been found necessary where those rights, whether public or private, depend upon the existence of certain facts, to appoint an officer, a commission, a tribunal, by whatever name it may be called, to ascertain these facts and declare the rights which they give. . . . And except where there is a provision in the law for an appeal from such decision, or a review of it in some recognized legal mode, it *must* be conclusive. As regards courts of justice, this principle is everywhere recognized and is acted on every day. There is no reason why it should not be equally applicable to all other tribunals acting within the scope of their authority, and it is so. As illustrations I will cite a few instances from the highest judicial authority in this country with whose decisions I am familiar. . . . ''

He told of the long line of decisions, from *Knox County v. Aspinwall*[55] in 1859 to *Town of Coloma v. Eaves*[56] in 1876, holding that where legislative authority had been given to a municipality to subscribe to railroad stock and to issue bonds in payment, and where it was to be gathered from the enactment that the officers of the municipality were authorized to decide whether a condition precedent had been complied with, their recital that it had been, made in the bonds held by a bona fide purchaser, were conclusive of the fact. (Miller had been distressed with the result of giving such authority, where too often corruption, misrepresentation, or improvidence had caused enormous indebtedness to be saddled upon municipalities; but there was no question that this was the law of the Court.)

"Again, in the administration of the system of public lands of the United States, questions of conflicting rights are perpetually arising which by the acts of Congress are to be decided by the officers of the Land Department of the Government. Many applications have been made to the courts to control the action of these officers by writs of mandamus to compel them to do something, or of injunction to restrain them; but the Supreme Court has uniformly held that in the performance of their functions, which required the exercise of judgment or discretion, they were beyond the control of the courts, because to them, and to them alone,

---

[55] 21 How. 539.   [56] 92 U.S. 484. VI, 1047, 1058–60.

had the law confided the exercise of that judgment, and, except as by appeal from one officer of that department to another, no right of reviewing that judgment had been provided.''

"That the same principle applies to affairs of more public character is shown by the cases of Luther v. Borden[57] and the Commonwealth of Virginia v. West Virginia.''[58] In the former the issue in an action of trespass depended upon which was the true government of the State of Rhode Island, that known as the Dorr government, which was alleged to have the support of a majority of the popular vote, or the ancient charter government which was resisting overthrow by the Dorr movement. The Court declined to make any inquiry into the facts on which the respective parties relied; it held that the Constitution had confided to the political department of the Government the right to determine that question; the Court was bound by the action of the President, who by proclamation had required the supporters of the Dorr government to disperse and had recognized the ancient government as the true one.

In the latter case a statute of Virginia had authorized the Governor to call an election in Berkeley and Jefferson counties on the question whether the voters chose to become a part of West Virginia; the Governor was to determine the result and, if carried, to certify the same to the Governor of West Virginia, whereupon those counties became a part of the new State. All this was done. Some years later, however, the Commonwealth of Virginia brought suit in the Supreme Court to recover those counties, alleging that no fair vote was taken, that the majority had been the other way, and that the Governor had been imposed upon by false and fraudulent returns. The case was heard on demurrer, and the Court held:

> We are of the opinion that the action of the governor is conclusive of the vote as between the States of Virginia and West Virginia. He was in legal effect the State of Virginia in this matter. In addition to his position as executive head of the State, the legislature had delegated to him all its own power in the premises. It vested him with large control as to the time of taking the vote, and it made his *opinion* of the result the condition of final action.

"This language," Miller concluded, "is eminently applicable to the case before us. The legislature of Florida has vested in her board of canvassers the authority to determine who are elected electors. It has conferred no power on any tribunal to revise that decision. The board in this respect represents the State. Its judgment is her judgment and its official certificate is her authorized expression of what she has done in the matter, and it is conclusive.''

---

[57] 7 How. 1 (1849). VI, 395. | [58] 11 Wall. 39 (1871). VI, 619–27.

Briefly he added his concurrence with Justice Strong's opinion. Miller indulged in a personal comment:

Much has been said of the danger of the device of returning-boards, and it may be that they have exercised their power in a manner not always worthy of commendation. But I take the liberty of saying that such a power lodged in one or in both Houses of Congress would be a far more permanent menace to the liberty of the people, to the legitimate result of the popular vote, than any device for counting these votes which has as yet been adopted by the States.

(There will be occasion to notice the manner in which the House of Representatives exercised its power to judge of the elections, returns, and qualifications of its own Members.[59])

JUSTICE BRADLEY'S OPINION

GARFIELD'S DIARY ENTRY for Wednesday, February 7, after remarks on the opinions of Payne and Justices Field, Strong, and Miller, came to Justice Bradley. This was the high point in the entire course of the Electoral Commission, and no outsider was present. Garfield's account is especially significant, particularly because it contradicts what has been the accepted account.

Garfield wrote: "Judge Bradley arose at 2.13 to read his opinion. All were intent, because B. held the casting vote. It was a curious study to watch the faces as he read. All were making a manifest effort to appear unconcerned. It was ten minutes before it became evident that he was against the authority to hear extrinsic evidence. His opinion was clear and strong. Near the close he surprised us all by holding that we could hear testimony as to the eligibility of Humphreys."

(In the *Proceedings* the Remarks of Mr. Commissioner Bradley are prefaced with this statement: "The following opinions and remarks have been somewhat abbreviated, and repetition of similar arguments in the different cases has been omitted."

(The Florida opinion runs to 6 pages; that for Louisiana, 8; for Oregon, 4; and for South Carolina, 2½.)

Because of attacks upon this Florida opinion by those embittered over the outcome, because those reproaches have been perpetuated in historical accounts, and because commentators have shown little acquaintance with the text, it is in order to set it out at length. *It is the most important document in the history of the Electoral Commission.*[60]

---

[59] Abbott v. Frost, infra, p. 174. [60] Proc., 1019–25.

There will be interruptions for comment, particularly to recall utterances in the Senate in the years immediately prior to the election of 1876—notably the opinions of Democratic Senators, precisely in accord with the reasoning in Bradley's opinion.

Comments will be indented, in reduced italic type, yielding prime importance to the opinion.

The report begins, "I assume that the powers of the Commission are precisely those, and no other, which the two Houses of Congress possess in the matter submitted to our consideration; and that the extent of those powers is one of the questions submitted. This is my interpretation of the act under which we are organized.

"The first question, therefore, is, whether, and how far, the two Houses, in the exercise of the special jurisdiction conferred on them in the matter of counting the electoral votes, have power to inquire into the validity of the votes transmitted to the President of the Senate. Their power to make any inquiry at all is disputed by, or on behalf of, the President of the Senate himself. But I think the practice of the Government, as well as the true construction of the Constitution, has settled that the powers of the President of the Senate are merely ministerial, conferred upon him as a matter of convenience, as being the presiding officer of one of the two bodies which are to meet for the counting of the votes and determining the election. He is not invested with any authority for making any investigation outside of the joint meeting of the two Houses. He cannot send for persons or papers. He is utterly without the means or the power to do anything more than to inspect the documents sent to him; and he cannot inspect them until he opens them in the presence of the two Houses. It would seem to be clear, therefore, that, if any examination at all is to be gone into, or any judgment is to be exercised in relation to the votes received, it must be performed and exercised by the two Houses."

This sustains the view upon which the Electoral Commission Act was based, that it does not belong to the President of the Senate to count the electoral votes. When in 1875 and again in 1876 Morton's bill to regulate the counting of the electoral vote was debated, Hamilton, Whyte, and Stevenson, Democrats, had insisted that the Constitution did fasten that function upon the President of the Senate.

Then in January 1877 Morton and Garfield had taken that position in opposing the Electoral Commission Bill. On January 5 Governor Hayes wrote: "I believe the V.P. alone has the constitutional power to count the votes and declare the result."

To Thurman it had seemed almost beyond comprehension that anyone looking at the Constitution could suppose that the power was so conferred. Now in restrained language Justice Bradley agrees with this conclusion.

Part Two: *Proceedings of the Electoral Commission*

"Then arises the question, How far can the two Houses go in questioning the votes received, without trenching upon the power reserved to the States themselves?

"The extreme reticence of the Constitution on the subject leaves wide room for inference. Each State has a just right to have the entire and exclusive control of its own vote for the Chief Magistrate and head of the republic, without any interference on the part of any other State, acting either separately or in congress with others. If there is any State right of which it is and should be more jealous than of any other, it is this. And such seems to have been the spirit manifested by the framers of the Constitution. This is evidenced by the terms in which the mode of choosing the President and Vice President is expressed: 'Each State shall appoint, in such manner as the legislature thereof may direct, a number of electors equal to the whole number of Senators and Representatives to which the State may be entitled in the Congress; but no Senator or Representative, or person holding an office of trust or profit under the United States, shall be appointed an elector. The electors shall meet in their respective States and vote by ballot,' &c. Almost every clause here cited is fraught with the sentiment to which I have alluded. The appointment and mode of appointment belong exclusively to the State. Congress has nothing to do with it, and no control over it, except that, in a subsequent clause, Congress is empowered to determine the time of choosing the electors, and the day on which they shall give their votes, which is required to be the same day throughout the United States. In all other respects the jurisdiction and power of the State is controlling and exclusive until the functions of the electors have been performed. So completely is congressional and Federal influence excluded, that not a member of Congress nor an officer of the General Government is allowed to be an elector. Of course, this exclusive power and control of the State is ended and determined when the day fixed by Congress for voting has arrived, and the electors have deposited their votes and made out the lists and certificates required by the Constitution. Up to that time the whole proceeding (except the time of election) is conducted under State law and State authority. All machinery, whether of police, examining boards, or judicial tribunals, deemed requisite and necessary for securing and preserving the true voice of the State in the appointment of electors, is prescribed and provided for by the State itself and not by Congress. All rules and regulations for the employment of this machinery are also within the exclusive province of the State. Over all this field of jurisdiction the State must be deemed to have ordained, enacted, and provided all that it considers necessary and proper to be done."

The above construction of the Constitution could not seriously be questioned. Thurman had said: "each State must determine for itself

97

*the election of electors, and determine in such mode as it shall provide
any question that may arise between different persons claiming to be
elected to that office. No jurisdiction over the subject seems to have
been given to Congress. . . ."*[61]

Senator Merrimon of North Carolina: *"I do not believe that Congress or any national authority has any right to contest the election of
President and Vice President. . . . The manner of the election of President is one of those provisions of the Constitution which . . . provide
for and uphold, the autonomy of the States. . . . The whole matter [of
the appointment of electors] is within the jurisdiction of the States, each
for itself."*[62]

Lyman Trumbull, a Republican Senator when he spoke in 1873,
now counsel for the Tilden electors in Louisiana, had thought that *"the
intention was to leave the appointment of electors exclusively to the
States, and that the only jurisdiction which the Federal Government
had was to designate the time when these electors should be appointed;
but the manner of their appointment and everything else connected with
their selection is to be left to the State, and that the jurisdiction . . .
of Congress . . . extends no further than to inquire whether these are
the electors appointed by that State."*[63]

"This being so, can Congress or the two Houses institute a scrutiny
into the action of the State authorities and sit in judgment on what they
have done? Are not the findings and recorded determinations of the State
board or constituted authorities binding and conclusive since the State
can only act through its constituted authorities?"

Senator Bayard: *"nowhere is power given to either House of
Congress to pass upon the election, either the manner or the fact, of
electors for President and Vice President; and if the Congress . . . ,
shall assume, under the guise or pretext of telling or counting a vote,
to decide the fact of the election of electors . . . , then they will have
taken upon themselves an authority for which I, for one, can find no
warrant in this charter of limited powers. . . ."*[64]

Senator Charles W. Jones of Florida, a Democrat, professed,
ten months before the case of Florida came before the Electoral Commission, that the selection of electors *"was left exclusively to the States,
and every question arising out of their election or appointment was left
of necessity with the same authority. The laws of the State provide the
manner in which these persons shall be chosen, and they may provide
also who shall determine in cases of contest and difficulty the person
who has been duly elected. Whatever may be the decision of the State
authorities, or by whom made, is binding on the United States."*[65]

---

[61] *Counting*, 336.
[62] Supra, p. 20.
[63] *Counting*, 340.

[64] Supra, p. 15.
[65] Supra, p. 28.

"But it is asked, must the two Houses of Congress submit to outrageous frauds and permit them to prevail without any effort to circumvent them? Certainly not, if it is within their jurisdiction to inquire into such frauds. But there is the very question to be solved. Where is such jurisdiction to be found? If it does not exist, how are the two Houses constitutionally to know that frauds have been committed? It is the business and the jurisdiction of the State to prevent frauds from being perpetrated in the appointment of its electors, and not the business or jurisdiction of the Congress. The State is a sovereign power within its own jurisdiction, and Congress can no more control or review the exercise of that jurisdiction than it can that of a foreign government. That which exclusively belongs to one tribunal or government cannot be passed upon by another. The determination of each is conclusive within its own sphere."

Prior to November 1876, disinterested opinions were unanimously in accord with Bradley's conclusion in 1877.

Senator Merrimon's statement was unqualified: "If it should be suggested when the electoral vote is cast and is sent to Congress that great frauds have been perpetrated by one party or the other; that votes have been bought by the score and by the thousand, and that force and intimidation have been used, that would be impertinent and vain; for it would be a matter clearly without the jurisdiction of Congress. It is a matter to be investigated, considered, and disposed of entirely by the State. . . ." The context has been quoted more fully above.[66]

Frelinghuysen had said, "The States possess the right of determining who shall be elected and who has been elected an elector, as entirely as the United States Government possesses the right to decide who shall represent the country in England or be an embassador at Geneva."[67]

Morton regretted that although States had passed laws for contesting the election of Governor and other State officers, "no State has provided any method of contesting the election of electors" although "this election may be distinguished by fraud, . . . by violence, by tumult. . . ." Thus "whatever electors are certified to by the State authorities have the right to cast the vote, and there is no power in Congress . . . to prevent them from doing it, although it may be known to the whole world that they were not honestly elected. . . ."[68]

A fortnight later Morton substantially repeated the statement.[69]

On both of these occasions Bayard and Thurman were participating in the discussion. They did not dissent from Morton's statement; they did not then affirm that "fraud vitiates everything." Morton's view on this point point was their own as well.

---

[66] *Counting,* 637.
[67] Ibid., 338.

[68] Ibid., 424.
[69] Ibid., 498.

"It seems to me to be clear, therefore, that Congress cannot institute a scrutiny into the appointment of electors by a State. It would be taking it out of the hands of the State, to which it properly belongs. This never could have been contemplated by the people of the States when they agreed to the Constitution. It would be going one step farther back than that instrument allows. While the two Houses of Congress are authorized to canvass the electoral votes, no authority is given to them to canvass the election of the electors themselves. To revise the canvass of that election, as made by the State authorities, on the suggestion of fraud, or for any other cause, would be tantamount to a recanvass."

On January 7, 1873, when the Senate was considering a proposal to inquire whether the election of electors in Arkansas and Louisiana had been in accord with the Constitution, Thurman said: "I know of no power in Congress to pass any law on this subject [of a State's conduct of its election of electors] except a law fixing the time when the electors shall be chosen. . . . The provision is not as it is in regard to the election of Senators and Representatives. . . ."[70]

"The case of elections of Senators and Representatives is different. The Constitution expressly declares that 'each House shall be the judge of the elections, returns, and qualifications of its own members.' No such power is given, and none ever would have been given if proposed, over the election or appointment of the presidential electors. Again, while the Constitution declares that 'the times, places, and manner of holding elections of Senators and Representatives shall be prescribed in each State by the legislature thereof,' it adds, 'but the Congress may at any time by law make or alter such regulations, except as to the places of choosing Senators.' No such power is given to Congress to regulate the election or appointment of presidential electors. Their appointment, and all regulations for making it, and the manner of making it, are left exclusively with the States.

"This want of jurisdiction over the subject makes it clear to my mind that the two Houses of Congress cannot institute any scrutiny into the appointment of presidential electors, as they may and do in reference to the election of their own members. The utmost they can do is to ascertain whether the State has made an appointment according to the form prescribed by its laws.

"This view receives corroboration from the form of a bill introduced into Congress in 1800 for prescribing the mode of deciding disputed elections of President and Vice-President, and which was passed by the Senate. It proposed a grand committee to inquire into the constitutional

---

[70] Supra, p. 80, n. 33.

qualifications of the persons voted for as President and Vice-President, and of the electors appointed by the States, and various other matters with regard to their appointment and transactions; but it contained a proviso, in which both Houses seem to have concurred, that no petition or exception should be granted or allowed which should have for its object to draw into question the number of votes on which any elector had been elected.

"This bill was the proposition of the federal party of that day, which, as is well known, entertained strong views with regard to the power of the Federal Government as related to the State governments. It was defeated by the opposition of the republican side, as being too great an interference with the independence of the States in reference to the election of President and Vice-President. And taken even as the federal view of the subject, it only shows what matters were regarded as subject to examination under the regulation of law, and not that the two Houses of Congress, when assembled to count the votes, could do the same without the aid of legislation. The bill was rather an admission that legislation was necessary in order to provide the proper machinery for making extrinsic inquiries."[71]

Note that Bradley, in addressing the Federalists' bill of 1800, puts aside the question of the power of Congress to confer, by legislation, broader powers of inquiry into disputed elections; the 1877 Act gave the Commission such authority as the two Houses possessed under existing law.

"It is unnecessary to enlarge upon the danger of Congress assuming powers in this behalf that do not clearly belong to it. The appetite for power in that body, if indulged in without great prudence, would have a strong tendency to interfere with that freedom and independence which it was intended the States should enjoy in the choice of the national Chief Magistrate, and to give Congress a control over the subject which it was intended it should not have.

---

[71] This incident was recorded at 16–29 in the House Document *Counting Electoral Votes* cited heretofore. A bill by Federalist Senator James Ross of Pennsylvania would provide for a Grand Committee of six Senators, six Representatives, and the Chief Justice, to be constituted before each Presidential election, to examine and finally to decide all disputes relating to the election. By a proviso in Section 8, no objection would be considered that would draw in question "the number of votes on which any elector in any of the States shall have been appointed." The bill failed in the House of Representatives. John Marshall in the House had seen in the bill a partisan attempt to seize the Presidency and, by an amendment he supported, that feature had been blunted. Albert J. Beveridge records this in *The Life of John Marshall*, 4 vols. (Boston and New York: Houghton Mifflin Co., 1916–19), II, 452–58.

"As the power of Congress, therefore, does not extend to the making of a general scrutiny into the appointment of electors, inasmuch as it would thereby invade the right of the States, so neither can it draw in question, nor sit in judgment upon, the determination and conclusion of the regularly constituted authorities or tribunals appointed by the laws of the States for ascertaining and certifying such appointment.

"And here the inquiry naturally arises, as to the manner in which the electors appointed by a State are to be accredited. What are the proper credentials by which it is to be made known who have been appointed? Obviously, if no provision of law existed on the subject, the proper mode would be for the governor of the State, as its political head and chief, through whom its acts are made known and by whom its external intercourse is conducted, to issue such credentials. But we are not without law on the subject. The Constitution, it is true, is silent; but Congress by the act of 1792 directed that 'it shall be the duty of the executive of each State to cause three lists of the names of the electors of such State to be made and certified and to be delivered to the electors on or before the day on which they are required to meet;' and one of these certificates is directed to be annexed to each of the certificates of the votes given by the electors. And if it should be contended that this enactment of Congress is not binding upon the State executive, the laws of Florida, in the case before us, impose upon the governor of that State the same duty. I think, therefore, that it cannot be denied that the certificate of the governor is the proper and regular credential of the appointment and official character of the electors. Certainly it is at least *prima facie* evidence of a very high character."

The paragraphs that follow consider the limited extent to which the Governor's certificate may be the subject of inquiry. It does not have "the full sanctity which . . . belongs to the proceedings and recorded acts of the board of canvassers." The board's determination is "the act of the State" and "the most authentic evidence of the appointment" of electors.

"But the Houses of Congress may undoubtedly inquire whether the supposed certificate of the executive is genuine; and I think they may also inquire whether it is plainly false, or whether it contains a clear mistake of fact, inasmuch as it is not itself the appointment, nor the ascertainment thereof, but only a certificate of the fact of appointment. While it must be held as a document of high nature, not to be lightly questioned, it seems to me that a State ought not to be deprived of its vote by a clear mistake of fact inadvertently contained in the governor's certificate, or (if such a case may be supposed) by a willfully false statement. It has not the full sanctity which belongs to a court of record, or which, in my judgment, belongs to the proceedings and recorded acts of the final board of canvassers.

"In this case, it is not claimed that the certificate of the governor contains any mistake of fact, or that it is willfully false and fraudulent. It truly represents the result of the State canvass, and if erroneous at all, it is erroneous because the proceedings of the canvassing-board were erroneous or based on erroneous principles and findings.

"It seems to me that the two Houses of Congress, in proceeding with the count, are bound to recognize the determination of the State board of canvassers as the act of the State, and as the most authentic evidence of the appointment made by the State; and that while they may go behind the governor's certificate, if necessary, they can only do so for the purpose of ascertaining whether he has truly certified the results to which the board arrived. They cannot sit as a court of appeals on the action of that board."

"The law of Florida declares as follows": Here was set out the pertinent part of the statute creating the board of State canvassers, which would "proceed to canvass the returns of said election and *determine and declare who shall have been elected to any such office or as such member, as shown by such returns.*" [Emphasis supplied.]

"The governor's certificate is *prima facie* evidence that the State canvassers performed their duty. Indeed, it is conceded by the objectors that they made a canvass and certified or declared the same. It is not the failure of the board to act, or to certify and declare the result of their action, but an illegal canvass, of which they complain. To review that canvass, in my judgment, the Houses of Congress have no jurisdiction or power."

> *So far the opinion had been paved by propositions formerly accepted on both sides of the Senate, professed most insistently by adherents to State-Rights Democratic doctrine.*

"The question then arises, whether the subsequent action of the courts or legislature of Florida can change the result arrived at and declared by the board of State canvassers, and consummated by the vote of the electors and the complete execution of their functions?

"If the action of the State board of canvassers were a mere statement of a fact, like the certificate of the governor, and did not involve the exercise of decision and judgment, perhaps it might be controverted by evidence of an equally high character. . . ."

> *Was the quo warranto judgment of the circuit court of so high a character as to overcome the action of the board of State canvassers? (Justice Field had seen "the highest possible evidence of the action of*

the State" in that judgment which, though appealed, "had the full force in the meantime.") Bradley had given the idea the most serious consideration, and here explains why it must be rejected:

"Looking at the subject in this point of view, I was at one time inclined to think that the proceedings on *quo warranto* in the circuit court of Florida, if still in force and effect, might be sufficient to contradict the finding and determination of the board of canvassers—supposing that the court had jurisdiction of the case. But the action of the board involved more than a mere statement of fact. It was a determination, a decision quasi-judicial. The powers of the board as defined by the statute which created it are expressed in the following terms: 'They shall proceed to canvass the returns of said election and determine and declare who shall have been elected to any office;' and 'if any such returns shall be shown, or shall appear to be, so irregular, false, or fraudulent that the board shall be unable to determine the true vote for any such officer or member, they shall so certify, and shall not include such return in their determination and declaration.' This clearly requires quasi-judicial action. To controvert the finding of the board, therefore, would not be to correct a mere statement of fact, but to reverse the decision and determination of a tribunal. The judgment on the *quo warranto* was an attempted reversal of this decision and the rendering of another decision. If the court had had jurisdiction of the subject-matter, and had rendered its decision before the votes of the electors were cast, its judgment, instead of that of the returning-board, would have been the final declaration of the result of the election. But its decision being rendered after the votes were given, it cannot have the operation to change or affect the vote, whatever effect it might have in a future judicial proceeding in relation to the presidential election. The judicial acts of officers *de facto*, until they are ousted by judicial process or otherwise, are valid and binding.

"But it is a grave question whether any courts can thus interfere with the course of the election for President and Vice-President. The remarks of Mr. Justice Miller on this subject are of great force and weight."

Justice Bradley then recognized, as had Justice Strong, what a State might do to effect a review of the action of the canvassing authority, prior to the time appointed by Congress for the casting of the electors' votes:

"The State may, undoubtedly, provide by law for reviewing the action of the board of canvassers at any time before the electors have executed their functions. It may provide any safeguard it pleases to prevent or counteract fraud, mistake, or illegality on the part of the canvassers. The legislature may pass a law requiring the attendance of the supreme court or any other tribunal to supervise the action of the board, and to reverse it, if wrong. But no such provision being made, the final action of the board must be accepted as the action of the State. No tampering with the result can be admitted after the day fixed by Congress for casting the electoral votes, and after it has become manifest where the pinch of the contest for the Presidency lies, and how it may be manipulated.''

Then came a rejection of the measures taken after December 6
to supersede the action of the certificated electors on that day:

"I am entirely clear that the judicial proceedings is this case were destitute of validity to affect the votes given by the electors. Declared by the board of canvassers to have been elected, they were entitled, by virtue of that declaration, to act as such against all the world until ousted of their office. They proceeded to perform the entire functions of that office. They deposited their votes in a regular manner, and on the proper and only day designated for that purpose, and their act could not be annulled by the subsequent proceedings on the quo warranto, however valid these might be for other purposes. When their votes were given, they were the legally constituted electors for the State of Florida.

"The supreme court of Florida said in the Drew case, it is true, that the board of canvassers exceeded their jurisdiction, and that their acts were absolutely void. In this assertion I do not concur; and it was not necessary to the judgment, which merely set aside the finding of the board and directed a new canvass. Under the Florida statute, the board had power to cast out returns. They did so. The court thought they ought to have cast out on a different principle from that which they adopted. This was at most error, not want or excess of jurisdiction. They certainly acted within the scope of their power, though they may have acted erroneously. This is the most that can be said in any event; and of this the Houses of Congress cannot sit in judgment as a court of appeal.

"The question is asked, whether for no cause whatever the declaration and certificate of the board of canvassers can be disregarded? as if they should certify an election when no election had been held, and other extreme cases of that sort. I do not say that a clear and evident mistake of fact, inadvertently made, and admitted to have been made by the canvassers themselves, or that such a gross fraud and violation of duty as that supposed, might not be corrected, or that it might not affect the validity of the vote. On that subject, as it is not necessary in this case, I express no opinion. Such extreme cases, when they occur, generally suggest some special rule for themselves without unsettling those general rules and principles which are the only safe guides in ordinary cases. The difficulty is that the two Houses are not made the judges of the election and return of the presidential electors.

"I think no importance is to be attached to the acts performed by the board of canvassers after the 6th day of December, nor to the acts of the Florida legislature in reference to the canvass. In my judgment, they are all unconstitutional and void. To allow a State legislature in any way to change the appointment of electors after they have been elected and given their votes, would be extremely dangerous. It would, in effect, make the legislature for the time being the electors, and would subvert the design of the Constitution in requiring all the electoral votes to be given on the same day.

"My conclusion is that the validity of the first certificate cannot be controverted by evidence of the proceedings had in the courts of Florida by *quo warranto*, and that said evidence should not be received."

Then came the statement which, as Garfield recorded, "surprised us all."

"It is further objected that Humphreys, one of the Hayes electors, held an office of trust and profit under the Government of the United States at the time of the general election, and at the time of giving his vote. I think the evidence of this fact should be admitted. Such an office is a constitutional disqualification. I do not think it requires legislation to make it binding. What may be the effect of the evidence now produced, I am not prepared to say. I should like to hear further argument on the subject before deciding the question."

Thus at the close Justice Bradley held out to the supporters of Tilden the bright possibility that the vote of one Hayes elector might be rejected.

JUSTICE CLIFFORD'S OPINION

As PRESIDENT OF THE COMMISSION, Justice Clifford spoke last.[72] His opinion was more than twice as long as that of Justice Bradley; "a dull speech, but strongly Democratic," wrote Garfield. Aside from reference to the oath to "give true judgment agreeably to the Constitution and the laws," he said very little about the Constitution. Of the laws of the United States, that creating the Commission was cited, and there was one reference to the "rules of decision" provision in the Judiciary Act of 1789.[73] Nothing was made of the consideration that the question arose

---

[72] Proc., 1042–58. [73] Sec. 34, 1 Stat. 73.

in the context of the federal relations between State and Nation: it seemed as if the Commission was charged to decide a controversy on the flat plane of municipal law.

To summarize the reasoning: Certificate No. 1 if unexplained showed that Hayes electors were chosen, while Nos. 2 and 3 made a like showing for Tilden electors. "All just and intelligent persons must admit" that this calls for an inquiry into the facts; but "an amazing proposition was advanced that the inquiry cannot extend beyond the examination of the papers presented by the President of the Senate to the two Houses." This view is defended by "the most extravagant suppositions that ingenious minds can devise or imagine," based upon supposed inconvenience.

The Commission is not expected to scrutinize the votes cast at the general election: the controversy concerns only the conduct of the board of State canvassers.

Both sets of electors voted on December 6: Certificate No. 1 was signed by Governor Stearns, but objectors allege that it is untrue and corruptly procured, and it has been declared void by the new Governor, the legislature, and the judiciary. The attorney general, a dissenting member of the board, signed Certificate No. 2. His conduct appears frank and open.

The salient events were traced: the quo warranto proceedings; the new canvass by a new board created by the new legislature; the statute of January 26 declaring that the Tilden electors had been duly elected; and Certificate No. 3 signed by the new Governor.

"Viewed in any light, it must be admitted that it is 'confirmation strong as proofs of Holy Writ' that Certificate No. 2, signed by the attorney general, is true, and that it gave the true and honest result of the election."

It comes as a surprise to find Clifford borrowing from Shakespeare; ordinarily his quoting was confined to workaday materials. He could not have been aware of the context: the malign Iago, intending to arouse in Othello a false suspicion that leads him to kill Desdemona, says

> Trifles light as air
> Are to the jealous confirmations strong
> As proofs of Holy Writ.[74]

As it turned out in the case of the Electoral Commission, rumors light as air were to the disappointed Democrats "confirmations strong as proofs of Holy Writ," and have remained so for a hundred years.

Clifford continued: Counsel supporting Certificate No. 1 make the startling contention that under the Florida statute of 1872 the decision of

---

[74] *Othello*, III, iii, 322–24.

the board of State canvassers is conclusive; but that statute directs the board to determine and declare who was elected *"as shown by such returns,"* and in doing this they are to throw out returns "so irregular, false, or fraudulent" that they are unable to *determine the true vote.* "Candid men everywhere will agree" that the board had no right to exclude any return except such as was so irregular, etc., that they were unable to ascertain the true vote. *Objectors* to Certificate No. 1 seek to prove that the board threw out returns that were not so irregular, etc., in order to change the result of the election; but the argument is made that neither Congress nor the Commission has jurisdiction to try such an issue.

The Act of Congress creating the Commission directs it to determine what were the true electoral votes, and authorizes it to take into view all petitions and other papers admissible by the Constitution and existing laws and pertinent to the matter under consideration. "Every person of ordinary intelligence" would know that that cannot be done without considering the authentic documents from the office of the secretary of state and the judgment of the State courts showing that it was the certificate of the attorney general that expressed the true result of the election.

To refuse to consider this evidence amounts to a decision in favor of Certificate No. 1.

In a contest between the rival candidates for Governor the supreme court of the State on December 25 held that the State board had no authority to exclude votes except when the canvassers were unable to ascertain for whom the votes were cast. This decision of the State court must be regarded as the rule of decision (citing Section 34 of the Judiciary Act).

But the proposition is advanced that the determination who were the duly elected electors must be made *before* the electors meet and vote. This is monstrous and makes a mockery of justice. Inasmuch as the decision of the State court furnishes the rule of decision it must be held that Certificate No. 1 is void for irregularity and fraud.

Clifford closed by invoking the authority of the English courts:

> Proper opportunity to investigate such charges ought to be permitted at some time, and if it is not possible to accomplish that object before the day appointed for the meeting of the electors, justice and necessity demand that it shall be allowed subsequent to that time, for it would be too great a triumph for injustice to hold that it must be postponed forever because the outrage was committed so near to the time designated for the performance of the duty that it was impossible to institute and close the scrutiny before the accessories to the guilt have actually enjoyed the stolen privilege which belonged to the complaining party. (Queen *vs.* Vestrymen of Pancras, 11 Ad. & Ell., 25.)
>
> Three points were decided by the exchequer chamber in Rochester *vs.* the Queen, (1 Ell., Bl., & Ell., 1031,) which support the proposition

Rutherford B. Hayes
(Library of Congress)

Samuel J. Tilden
(Library of Congress)

Abram S. Hewitt
(Brady-Handy photo. Library of Congress)

Justice Nathan Clifford
(Library of Congress)

Justice Samuel F. Miller
(Library of Congress)

Justice Stephen J. Field
(Library of Congress)

Justice William Strong
(Library of Congress)

Justice Joseph P. Bradley
(Library of Congress)

Senator George F. Edmunds
(Library of Congress)

Senator Allen G. Thurman
(Library of Congress)

Senator Frederick T. Frelinghuysen
(Library of Congress)

Senator Thomas F. Bayard
(Brady-Handy photo. Library of Congress)

Senator Oliver P. Morton
(Library of Congress)

Representative Henry B. Payne
(Library of Congress)

Representative George F. Hoar
(Library of Congress)

Representative Josiah G. Abbott
(Brady-Handy photo. Library of Congress)

Representative James A. Garfield
(Library of Congress)

Representative Eppa Hunton
(Library of Congress)

William M. Evarts
Republican Counsel
(Library of Congress)

Charles O'Conor
Democratic Counsel
(Library of Congress)

Edwin W. Stoughton
Republican Counsel
(Library of Congress)

Jeremiah S. Black
Democratic Counsel
(Brady-Handy photo. Library of Congress)

Stanley Matthews
Republican Counsel
(Library of Congress)

Richard T. Merrick
Democratic Counsel
(Library of Congress)

Matthew H. Carpenter
Republican Counsel
(Library of Congress)

George Hoadley
Democratic Counsel
(Library of Congress)

John A. Kasson
Republican Objector in Florida Case
(Brady-Handy photo. Library of Congress)

David Dudley Field
Democratic Objector in Florida Case
(L. C. Handy Studios)

George W. McCrary
Republican Objector in Florida Case
(Library of Congress)

Henry Cooper
Democratic Objector in Florida Case
(Library of Congress)

Aaron A. Sargent
Republican Objector in Oregon Case
(Library of Congress)

Joseph E. McDonald
Democratic Objector in Louisiana Case
(Library of Congress)

that it was not too late to make the investigation: (1) That the court ought to compel the performance of a public duty by a public officer although the time prescribed by statute for the performance of the same has passed. (2) That if the public officer to whom belongs the performance of such a duty has in the mean time quitted his office and has been succeeded by another, it is the duty of the successor to obey the commands of the court. (3) That all statutes are to be construed with reference to the known, acknowledged, recognized, and established power of the proper court to superintend and control inferior jurisdictions and authorities of every kind.

To explain in context: In the first case cited the facts were that a meeting to elect vestrymen and auditors of the Parish of St. Pancras was held on May 6, 1839; both churchwardens and ratepayers [taxpayers] were to participate in the voting. The churchwardens presided and did the counting, in a room that was crowded, and declared the result (which was favorable to "partizans of the parish"). Some disappointed ratepayers, contending that the counting had been unfair, brought mandamus to hold a new election. Sir Frederick Pollock [grandfather of Justice Holmes' correspondent of the same name] argued that if the chairman determined the vote bona fide, even if erroneously, it could not be impeached; if mala fide, he was punishable but the election was not defeated. The Queen's Bench, however, in November ordered a new election, even though the time fixed by law was long passed. It was a "well known practice of this Court to set aside vicious proceedings held at the regular period, and direct others in their place afterwards."

In Justice Clifford's second case, the Mayor and assessors of Rochester were directed by law to revise the list of burgesses [citizens having full municipal rights] between the first and the fifteenth of October every year. In January 1857 mandamus had been sought, alleging that for insufficient reason no list had been made in the previous year. The return by the Mayor was that he did not hold that office in 1856, but would comply if lawfully he could. An assessor returned that he was advised that he could not lawfully comply. The Court of Exchequer Chamber held that the Mayor in office was the proper person to perform this public duty, and that he ought to perform it. Furthermore, "common sense requires that, if the burgess list . . . be not properly revised at the proper time, it should be done afterwards." Mandamus, "to amend all errors which tend to the oppression of the subject or other misgovernment ought to be used when the law has provided no specific remedy, and justice and good government require that there ought to be one for the execution of the common law or the provisions of a statute."

For the reasons given, Clifford concluded, the proffered evidence ought to be admitted.

(To set up English decisions on filling such offices as vestryman and burgess in order to justify departures from the Constitution's prescriptions on the election of a President tended to belittle the strength of the case for the Tilden electors.

(In their respective opinions on the Florida case, Justice Bradley had covered 6 pages in the *Proceedings*; Strong, 7; Miller, 9; Field, 13. And Clifford consumed 17 pages while keeping the discussion on a parochial level.)

After that, as Garfield recorded, "Thurman made a short speech, showing his dissatisfaction with the result. Edmunds closed with a short opinion on the validity of the acts of *de facto* officers. At three a vote was taken."

It was decided by vote of 8 to 7 that no evidence would be received or considered that had not been submitted to the two Houses by the President of the Senate—except for the matter of the eligibility of Humphreys. So far Bradley joined with the other Republican members.

Then Abbott proposed an order to receive evidence in Humphreys' case. In accordance with the concluding statement that had "surprised us all," Bradley voted with the Democrats to receive such evidence.

There was reason for hearing testimony on that point, *unless* it seemed perfectly clear that, absent legislation by Congress to enforce the disability, this was not a matter to be considered in counting the State's vote. If it appeared that Humphreys had effectively resigned prior to the November election it would seem that there was no basis for objection. There might, however, be a question whether a resignation had been effective. If Humphreys had resigned between the election and his voting as elector, that would present a different problem. If he had held federal office at the time he voted, that would be still another situation.

Notice was sent to counsel of the result of the votes: they should be prepared to go forward at 11 A.M. on the morrow. Then at 3:45 the Commission adjourned.[75]

A special dispatch carried the news to the *Chicago Tribune*:

[As three o'clock] approached little bands of anxious people began to gather in the corridor leading from the Supreme Court room to the Senate Chamber.[76] Among them were Senators and Representatives, journalists, and not a few of the politicians of both parties of national reputation now in Washington watching the progress of events. During the half-hour of waiting many rumors were afloat as to the decision of the Commission, and furnished for the time being topics of discussion among those assembled. None of these rumors had a sub-

---

[75] Proc., 138–39.

[76] The plan of the main floor of the Capitol is shown in VI at 64.

stantial foundation, for no one came from the Supreme Court room to give an intimation of what was going on within the closed doors. Soon after half-past 3 there was a movement in the crowd, and Senator Edmunds was seen to come from the court-room with several law-books under his arm. He threaded his way through the obstructed corridors and passed into the Senate without stopping to speak to any one. The satisfied look which overspread his face gave the Republicans some hope. He was followed a few minutes later by Senator Morton, who walked with some difficulty. . . . A personal friend joined him . . . and, walking by his side to the door of the Senate Chamber, got the first news of the Commission's decision. Then, as if telegraphed, the word went around, eight to seven against testimony. A moment later several other members . . . appeared, and the result was known more in detail throughout the crowd. . . .

After all, everything depends upon the 5th Judge. The action of the Electoral Commission to-day shows that Judge Bradley holds the balance of power upon all questions affecting the final result. . . .[77]

In the Tilden Papers in the New York Public Library is a letter from John P. Stockton, written from the office of Robert Gilchrist at Jersey City on February 8:

My Dear Govr
    Please look over the enclosed brief, and if you think it worth while send it to where it can do some good. Mr. Gilchrist and myself have a more intimate knowledge of Judge Bradley's habit of thought than any one else, and the enclosed is the result of an hour's talk with him this morning.

Stockton (1826–1900) had served in the Senate from March 15, 1865, until unseated on March 27, 1866, by reason of a challenge by members of the New Jersey legislature on the ground that his election had been by only a plurality of the Joint Session. He served again for a full term from March 4, 1869. He was the State's attorney general from 1877 to 1892.

Gilchrist (1825–88) had served in the Union Army and had been a Republican up to the close of the war, changing thereafter his party affiliation. He had been the State's attorney general from 1873 to 1877.

Each was an able lawyer, and well acquainted with Bradley's professional work.

Writing on February 8, they likely recognized that Bradley's open mind on the problem of constitutional ineligibility of an elector, as shown by his action on the seventh, offered a useful line for Democratic persuasion. It was indeed a point to which Bradley gave continued thought.

---

[77] *Chicago Tribune*, Feb. 8, p. 1, under the headline "TALLY ONE!"

Stockton and Gilchrist were counsel of standing and understanding: it is not to be supposed that they called upon the Justice with any thought of applying "pressure," but only to inquire whether a line of argument might be useful.

On the next day Stockton called on Tilden.

CONCLUSION OF THE FLORIDA CASE

ON THURSDAY, FEBRUARY 8, witnesses were heard. It appeared that Humphreys had been appointed shipping commissioner by the Circuit Court for the Northern District of Florida. On September 24, 1876, he had sent his resignation to Circuit Judge Woods, who was then in Ohio. On October 2 Woods had replied that "your resignation is accepted. The vacancy can only be filled by the circuit court, and until I can go to Pensacola to open the court for that purpose, the duties of the office will have to be discharged by the collector." The collector on October 5 acknowledged to Humphreys his assumption of the duties.

George Hoadly of Cincinnati, counsel for objectors to Certificate No. 1, argued that the resignation could only be accepted by the court in session; that in the meantime Humphreys continued in a federal office.

Ashbel Green continued on the same side. He argued that simply on the evidence before the Commission it should hold that the Tilden electors had been elected. This was on the line of his Brief No. 2, already described.

Samuel Shellabarger, an able lawyer with long service as a Congressman from Ohio, then practicing at Washington, replied for the Hayes electors. "If when the electoral vote of a State has once been cast by men endowed with every muniment of title to the office of elector which the laws of the State enabled them to hold at the time when they must do their first and last official act, the power of the State to manipulate that vote, its jurisdiction over it had gone away from the State to the nation."

Evarts closed for the defenders of Certificate No. 1. Rebutting Hoadly's argument, he cited the provisions of law punishing officers of the military and naval services who, having tendered a resignation, quit without leave with intent to remain permanently absent. But as to civil officers he quoted Justice McLean on the circuit in *United States v. Wright*:[78] "There can be no doubt that a civil officer has a right to resign his office at pleasure, and it is not in the power of the executive to compel him to remain in office. It is only necessary that the resignation be received to take effect. . . ."

---

[78] Fed. Case No. 16,775 (1839).

Evarts concluded on the main theme of the case, that the Constitution made the election of a President final upon the observance of the prescribed steps, and that the result could not be undone by ''new officers, new interests, new legislators.''

Merrick closed for the other side in an hour filled with critical questioning by Republicans and helpful suggestions from their opponents.

Then the Democrats joined by Bradley carried a motion to adjourn until 10 o'clock on the morrow.

Friday, February 9, was a trying day behind closed doors.[79] It was time to reach a final decision on Florida.

In the afternoon Thurman offered a resolution,

> That F. C. Humphreys was not a United States shipping commissioner on the 7th of November, 1876.

After some discussion that was withdrawn.[80]

Clifford was of opinion that Humphreys had *not* made ''a complete legal resignation of the office before November 7''; however,

> inasmuch as the evidence shows that both the judge and the incumbent regarded the resignation as complete, and it appears that the incumbent never did perform any subsequent official act, I am of the opinion that, in an equitable view, the person named ought to be regarded as having been eligible as an elector on the day when the election was held.[81]

Bradley's view was that ''It being shown that Humphreys resigned his office before the election, the question of ineligibility became unimportant.'' He added, however, an opinion to which he had now come:

> that the constitutional prohibition, that no member of Congress or officer of the Government should be appointed an elector, is only a form of declaring a disqualification for the electoral office, and does not have the effect of annulling the vote given by one who, though disqualified, is regularly elected, and acts as an elector; likening it to the case of other officers *de facto*.[82]

---

[79] Proc., 194–98.

[80] The *New York Evening Post* of Saturday, February 10, was able to report the Commission's Journal for the ninth, the injunction of secrecy having been removed. The *Post* went on to give this account of what had been heard about the discussion:

This resolution was criticised by several Republican members on the ground that it might carry an implication that, if Humphreys had been such commissioner on the seventh of November his vote would have been invalid, and the resolution was not urged, there seeming to be practically a unanimity of opinion that Humphreys's resignation was legally effectual, having been tendered and accepted before the election.

[81] Proc., 1058–59.

[82] Ibid., at 1025.

Presently Garfield offered a resolution, that Humphreys and the three others, Hayes electors, were duly appointed. This was carried by eight votes. Edmunds, Bradley, and Miller were appointed to draft a report to that effect. At 6:05 the Commission adjourned for an hour.

On resuming, Edmunds presented a report in several paragraphs, addressed to the President of the Senate presiding at the Joint Session of the two Houses. It stated that the Commission had decided that the votes of Humphreys, Pearce, Holden, and Long, named in the certificate of Governor Stearns, as appeared in Certificate No. 1, were the votes provided for in the Constitution.

The ground for this decision was that it was not competent to go into evidence *aliunde*[83] the papers opened by the President of the Senate before the two Houses to prove that other persons than those regularly certified by the Governor in accord with the determination and declaration of the State board of canvassers had been appointed electors.

As to the eligibility of Humphreys, the Commission was of the opinion that, without reference to the question of the effect of the vote of an ineligible elector, the evidence did not show that he had the office of shipping commissioner on the day when the electors were appointed.

In consequence of the foregoing, the certificates of electoral votes, Nos. 2 and 3, were rejected.

This report was adopted by vote of 8 to 7, and signed by Miller, Strong, Bradley, Edmunds, Morton, Frelinghuysen, Garfield, and Hoar.[84]

A letter transmitting the report to the President pro tem. of the Senate was prepared for the signature of Nathan Clifford, as President of the Commission; also one to the Speaker, advising him that the report was being sent to the President of the Senate.

On motion of Abbott the injunction of secrecy on the action had that day was removed.

At 8:05 P.M. the Commission adjourned.[85]

PROCEEDINGS IN THE TWO HOUSES

AT A JOINT SESSION on Saturday, February 10, the decision of the Commission was read before the two Houses. The Presiding Officer asked, Are there objections? Representative David Dudley Field presented an objection signed by six Senators and twelve Representatives (Abram S. Hewitt among them). Eight grounds were specified: that the Commission had decided in favor of Hayes electors whereas Tilden electors had been elected in accord with the Constitution; that it excluded material

---

[83] "From another place" [than].
[84] Proc., 195–97.

[85] Proc., 197–98.

evidence in half a dozen matters; and that it refused to recognize the right of the courts of Florida to review the judgment of the canvassing board.[86]

The Senate withdrew and returned to its chamber. Promptly it sustained the decision by vote of 44 to 24.[87]

The House was in no mood for prompt action. By vote of 162 to 107 it put the matter over to Monday the twelfth at 10 A.M.[88] When that hour arrived there was no quorum in the chamber.

After protracted exercises in parliamentary law (not counted in the two hours allowed by the statute for debate on the report of the Commission), David Dudley Field yielded to John Randolph Tucker of Virginia, who said among other things that "upon a question of this kind the whole organism of the State must speak its voice." "The vote cast by electors . . . is not effectual until opened and counted. The act of voting on December 6, 1876, by them was inchoate. It now claims to be made consummate. In the interval the inchoate act is declared to be usurpation. . . . Shall we make the inchoate usurpation consummate by our judgment?"[89]

Tucker, formerly and subsequently a professor of law, was affirming something not to be found in any law-book: that the vote of an elector was imperfect, tentative, subject to recall, up to the moment of counting.

Republicans also were heard, and the remarks of Mark H. Dunnell of Minnesota are worthy of mention. A native of Maine and educated there for the bar, he had moved to Minnesota in 1865 to be secretary of the territory. He had been in Congress since 1871, and was one of two minority members on the investigating committee sent to Florida:

> We of the minority, in our simplicity supposed that . . . there would be placed before us as a committee, the affidavits, the evidence, and the testimony upon which the returning board of Florida had acted; for we were called upon and directed to report to Congress the action of the returning board. . . . But the majority of the committee said no. . . . And, from the beginning to the end, not one particle of evidence that went before the canvassing board did we have.
>
> There was left over at Tallahassee from the raid made by democratic politicians from the city of New York a certain . . . politician. . . . [He] was caught up and made the secretary of this investigating committee. He had papers; he had affidavits; he had telegrams; but they were only to be read . . . by the democratic portion of this committee; they were never once seen . . . by the minority.

---

[86] Ibid., 199–201; Cong. Rec., 44–2, 1481.

[87] Proc., 201–02, where the vote is given as 44 to 25; Cong. Rec., 44–2, 1473–77.

[88] Proc., 202; Cong. Rec., 44–2, 1481–87.

[89] Cong. Rec. 44–2, 1493–96, at 1494.

MR. THOMPSON [of Massachusetts, chairman of the Florida committee]. Will the gentleman–

MR. DUNNELL. No, sir; I was voted down in Florida by the majority of the committee, and I propose now to have my ten minutes. . . . No one was more surprised than I, to read and hear the report of that committee. . . .[90]

One of the objections to the Commission's decision was that it had excluded evidence taken by committees concerning frauds and irregularities. Justice Field's opinion held that this report, being adopted by the House, should "if not accepted as final, at least be considered by us." But partisan feeling, on both sides, was so strong in these investigations that one should view them with profound misgiving.

When the time for debate had run a vote was taken on a motion by Representative Field to reject the decision of the Commission: this received 168 votes of yea and 103 of nay.[91]

Then in a Joint Session, the Houses not having agreed to reverse the decision, it stood and Florida's votes were counted for Hayes and Wheeler. The Presiding Officer proceeded with the opening of the certificates.

SUBSEQUENT CASES

IN THE CONTEST FROM LOUISIANA,[92] Certificate No. 1 from the "Kellogg board" gave eight votes to Hayes. Objections to this were (1) that the board was not constituted according to law, in that it had only four members of one political party when there should have been five members drawn from different parties; (2) that the board acted fraudulently in counting the votes; and (3) that two of the electors were ineligible by reason of holding a federal office at the time of their election.

All of these contentions were rejected by vote of the eight Commissioners who were members of the Republican party. On the first objection it was held that the board was legally constituted by virtue of legislation previously held valid by the State's supreme court. On the second it was held (as in the case from Florida) that it was not competent to consider evidence *aliunde* the papers opened in the presence of the two Houses. Third, it would be of no avail to receive evidence that persons chosen elector had held federal office at the time of their appointment.

Bradley was the only Justice who filed an opinion in this case.[93] His view on the issue of ineligibility will be considered in a moment.

---

[90] Ibid., 1499–1500.
[91] Cong. Rec., 44–2, 1502; Proc., 203.
[92] Proc., 265–423.
[93] Ibid., 1026–34.

Part Two: *Proceedings of the Electoral Commission*

The decision of the majority was certified on February 16. The Senate accepted it by vote of 41 to 28; the House rejected, 173 to 99. On February 20 it was announced that the decision stood.

Certificate No. 1 from Oregon[94] showed that the secretary of state had in the presence of the Governor canvassed the result of the election, and found that Odell, Watts, and Cartwright had received the highest number of votes, and that they had voted for Hayes. Certificate No. 2, made by the Governor, stated that Odell, Cartwright, and Cronin, "having received the highest number of votes cast . . . for persons eligible, under the Constitution of the United States," had cast two votes for Hayes and one for Tilden.

By the laws of Oregon, the votes for electors were to be canvassed by the secretary of state in the presence of the Governor; the former would make lists of the persons elected and affix the seal of the State, which would be signed by the Governor and the secretary of state. There was no question but that the majority of popular votes had been cast for Republican electors. Watts, being a postmaster, had resigned after his election. Oregon law provided that in case of vacancy by death, neglect to attend, or otherwise, the remaining electors should immediately choose a replacement. Odell and Cartwright chose Watts, who joined them and cast his vote. The Governor, however, refused to sign a certificate for those three persons.

On February 23 the Commission by vote of 8 to 7 held that the certificate of the secretary of state recorded the effective determination; that the refusal of the Governor to sign did not defeat the appointment; and that the latter's certificate to Cronin was without authority and void.

The Senate accepted by vote of 41 to 24; the House rejected by vote of 158 to 112. Thus Oregon's three votes were counted for Hayes.

The case from South Carolina was lodged with the Commission on Monday, February 26; on the morrow it was heard and determined.[95] Certificate No. 1, signed by Governor D. H. Chamberlain and the secretary of state, covered the votes of seven electors for Hayes. There was a Certificate No. 2 by persons claiming to have cast electoral votes for Tilden, whose suit to establish that they were the true electors was pending in the State court. No member of the Commission supported their claim.

The contention of objectors to Certificate No. 1 was (1) that the election was void because the legislature had never acted under a provision of the constitution of 1868 that it was the duty of the legislature "to provide from time to time for the registration of all electors"; (2) that on November 7, 1876, the presence of federal marshals and detachments of the United States Army had prevented the full exercise of the right of

---

[94] Ibid., 463–641.

[95] Ibid., 666–703.

suffrage; that in fact on that day South Carolina did not have a republican form of government.

Of counsel, Stanley Matthews and Samuel Shellabarger appeared on the Republican side and Montgomery Blair and Jere. Black opposed. Black made the closing speech, in this tone:[96]

> I had not and have not now any intention to argue this case. I never heard the objections . . . until they were read in your presence this morning. . . .
>
> I am so fallen from the proud estate of a free citizen, you have so abjected me, that I am fit for nothing on earth but to represent the poor, defrauded, broken-down democracy. And because I suffer more, they think me more good for nothing than the rest, and . . . send me out on this forlorn hope. . . .
>
> If . . . the law you have made for this occasion shall be the law for all occasions, we can never expect such a thing as an honest election again. . . . You need only to know what kind of scoundrels constitute the returning-boards, and how much it will take to buy them.
>
> But I think even that will end some day. At present you have us down and under your feet. . . . But . . . wait a little while. The waters of truth will rise gradually. . . . Wait: retribution will come in due time. Justice travels with a leaden heel but strikes with an iron hand. . . .

Bradley noted, ''Black—Made an insolent speech.'' Garfield wrote in his diary, ''a bitter and insulting speech of 3/4 of an hour.''

Still on February 27, when the chamber had been cleared for deliberation, Bayard delivered an opinion in which he said ''The Constitution provides that the electors shall be appointed *by the State*''; but on election day South Carolina was ''controlled by the unlawful presence of the agents and officials of the Government of the United States.'' The Tilden electors had sought relief in the State courts from the false returns by the board of State canvassers, but before a decision could be had the board of canvassers adjourned.

While Bayard was calling on the Commission to take notice of these contentions, Senator Frelinghuysen laid before him the *Congressional Record* opened at a marked passage where on February 25, 1875, Bayard had been dwelling on the theme that ''nowhere is power given to either House of Congress to pass upon the election, either the manner or the fact, of electors for President or Vice President; and if the Congress . . . shall assume, under the guise or pretext of telling or counting the vote, to decide the fact of the election of electors . . . , they will have taken upon themselves an authority for which I . . . can find no warrant in this charter of limited powers.''

---

[96] Black's speech on February 27, ibid., 695–99.

Bayard read the marked passage, and said "I must freely admit that within the two years which have elapsed I have had a better opportunity for the study . . . of this subject. . . . I trust the time will never come when I shall cling obstinately to an error. . . ." "In 1875 . . . I was considering a case where '*the State*' had chosen her electors in fact," where here "two South Carolinas appear," one of which must be false.[97]

Thus at the close of the Commission's deliberations Bayard was brought to recognize openly what he and his associates had so recently abjured—the ground on which Senators of both parties had agreed in 1875 and early 1876, from which the majority of the Commission was refusing to be budged.

In one respect Bayard was perfectly consistent: on April 18, 1876, he had said that Morton was "over-sanguine in supposing that he and his party, and I and mine, shall be able to look at facts imbued with all the color of party feeling, yet decide them as though we were entirely indifferent to the result of our decision."

Bradley was the only Justice to file an opinion on South Carolina; doubtless he felt it incumbent on him to state his reasoning.

The failure to pass a law on registration was a neglect of a legislative duty, but it ought not to prejudice the people or the State.

The only objection of any weight alleged that disturbance of the election and interference of federal troops had made it impossible to know what was the will of the State. But the two Houses meeting to count votes had no authority to make such an inquiry. The objections and the evidence offered to support them were insufficient, and the electoral votes should be counted.

The Commission was unanimous in rejecting Certificate No. 2. Then by vote of 8 to 7 it was decided that South Carolina's eight electoral votes had been given to Hayes.

The Senate accepted the decision by vote of 39 to 22. The House refused to concur in the decision by 190 votes to 72.

On Friday, March 2 the Commission met at 11 A.M., the judicial members and five others being present. A report on allowances to be paid to officers and employees was accepted. The time for filing opinions was extended to the end of March. It was ordered that 450 copies of the record of proceedings with the arguments of the Commissioners be distributed equally to the members.

Thereupon at 11:30 the Commission adjourned sine die.[98]

---

[97] This is in the Appendix of Opinions, at 897–901, where at 898–99 Frelinghuysen had placed before Bayard the marked passage of what the latter had said on February 25, 1875.

Frelinghuysen filed a comprehensive opinion at 844–53. At 847 he quoted Bayard's remarks on February 25, 1875, as above.

[98] Proc., 728.

March 4 fell on Sunday, and to insure continuity the oath of office was administered to President Hayes by the Chief Justice at the White House on that day. Sunday was, as Bradley wrote in his diary, "A day of anxiety."

The inaugural ceremony on Monday proceeded without disturbance. Justice Davis sat with his brethren for the last time; Clifford and Field were absent.

Justice Miller wrote to his brother-in-law, William Pitt Ballinger of Galveston, Texas:

> I am just returned from the inauguration ceremonies and the cannon are peacefully playing the last part in that drama. It is to me a great relief. . . .
>
> The last ten days have demonstrated how well founded were my fears. If it was with the utmost difficulty the House of Representatives could be induced to proceed with counting the vote after the decision of a tribunal which the majority in that house had created, and which had been favored and supported by every democrat in the Senate but one, how far would its count have proceeded without such a tribunal? It is now too clear for disputation, that the Senate and House would have separated without completing the count. That each body would have declared a different man President and no human wisdom can now tell what evils would have followed.
>
> The peaceful inauguration of Hayes as President is due largely, very largely, to the discretion, forbearance, good sense and patriotism of the southern leaders of the democratic party. . . .
>
> Their conduct in the matter has made an impression on republicans that must have good results. I have never known such a revulsion in public feeling and I feel very sure that the period of harsh feeling and misconception and foolish prejudice is rapidly passing away. . . .[99]

JUSTICE BRADLEY PURSUES INELIGIBILITY TO A CONCLUSION

THE PROBLEM of constitutional ineligibility as it arose in Florida, in Louisiana, and Oregon, was novel, obscure, and, it might prove, decisive. Bradley was not prepared to dismiss it out of hand, as did Justice Miller, as inadmissible in the absence of enforcing legislation. (On mature reflection, however, Bradley came to that view.) In the Commission he felt his way from case to case. In his file of "Notes taken & made in the Electoral Commission" he left the following:

---

[99] Part of this letter appears in Charles Fairman, *Mr. Justice Miller and the Supreme Court, 1862–1890,* (Cambridge, Mass.: Harvard University Press, 1939) at 291.

Four different views may be taken of the effect of constitutional ineligibility on an elector.

1. That his election, or appointment, is void:

2. That his election is only voidable, but if he act as elector without a removal of the disqualification his vote will be void.

3. That his election is voidable, but if he act his vote will be good—as the official act of an elector *de facto*.

4. That his election is neither void, nor voidable until some provision has been made by law for ascertaining and providing the ineligibility.

I have had great difficulty in coming to a satisfactory conclusion as to which of these views is the proper and sound one. My first impression was that the appointment was void; but I did not feel clear on the subject. Hence in the Florida case, I voted that the evidence of Humphrey's ineligibility, which was charged to have continued until after he had cast his vote, should be taken; reserving the effect of the proof for further consideration. At the close of the argument of that case, I had come to the conclusion that, whatever might have been done in reference to his election before he cast his vote, if not set aside until then, his vote was valid.

I thought then, however, and I think now, that a proceeding might be prescribed by the state legislature for ascertaining and giving effect to the fact of ineligibility. In the Florida case, however, the fact turned out to be that Humphreys had resigned before the election.

When the Louisiana case came before us, the charge of Constitutional ineligibility had relation only to the time of the election, and not to the time of the electoral vote. It became necessary, therefore, to examine the subject further. In looking at the history of the Convention which framed the Constitution, and the fact that the electors were originally intended to be uncommitted to candidates for the Presidency, and to act on their own wisdom and discretion, I became satisfied that the great object of the ineligibility of members of Congress and officers of Government as electors was, that they should be free from the bias and partiality which such an official connection with the general government would be likely to create; and that if they were qualified when they cast their votes, and no proceeding had been taken to oust them before they were qualified, it was sufficient,—like the case of members of Congress ineligible when elected on account of age, &c. but, the disqualification being removed, entitled to their seats.

In the Oregon Case the evidence shows that Watts was an officer at the time of the election and resigned, and was reappointed by the others. In my view of the case there was a vacancy to be filled, whether the election of Watts was void, or only voidable. On the first supposition there was a vacancy from the start; on the second, it arose when he resigned. Hence the remaining electors were authorized in either view, to fill the vacancy.

[In red ink, apparently written after some delay:]

I have not had, or expressed, an opinion on the subject from the first, that would have changed the result in either case. And, on a review of the whole matter now, I am more and more inclined to the last view, that until a law is passed providing a mode of ascertaining the fact of ineligibility, the issue cannot be raised when the two Houses are met to count the vote. They have no machinery for entering upon such a trial. Before their meeting they have no jurisdiction on the subject. They have no authority, it seems to me, to use for this purpose, their ordinary power as legislative bodies, by which they take evidence all over the country by committees—without regard to its character or to the right of cross-examination.

PART THREE

"Immense Gratuitous and Unfounded Abuse"

JUSTICE BRADLEY IN 1878

> Although every member of the Commission took the same oath "impartially [to] examine and consider . . . and a true judgment give . . . ," it was assumed from the outset that this imposed a unique duty upon the fifth justice, Bradley.

OUTSTANDING among newspapers devoted to Tilden was the *New York Sun,* which daily provided "all the news for 2 cents" to a circulation of 140,000. On February 1, 1877—the day the Commission met to begin work—the *Sun* expressed resentment that "the almost absolute decision of the Presidential question is left to Judge Joseph P. Bradley of Newark, a politician to whom the party never looked in vain . . . ."

On the eleventh, when the Florida case had been decided, the *Sun* declared that there was "no process or method by which fraud can be converted into honest reality. [But] Judge Bradley seems to-day to have the ability, as well as the intention, to attempt such a miracle. . . ."

Charles A. Dana, editor of the *Sun,* and many other ardent supporters of Tilden were quick to suppose that those who stood in their disfavor had a bad character and evil intention, an assumption which in truth might be quite unfounded. Bradley was not "a politician" ready to do dirty jobs for his party. He had been an unsuccessful candidate for Congress in 1862 in a Democratic stronghold. Then he had been a candidate for Presidential elector in 1868, on which occasion he had defended "the measures of the great Union party," including particularly "the National legal tender." Now in 1877 he did not obey the call to the Commission with any "intent" to make Hayes President. Along with Waite and Strong, he was the least "political" among the members of the Court.

A far more discerning appraisal appeared in the *Chicago Tribune* of February 14, agreeing upon its own information with an estimate recently appearing in Murat Halstead's *Cincinnati Commercial*:

The fear that the Republicans have is that Bradley is an intensely legal man, even more legal than Republican, and that he will not hesitate to give the Presidency to Tilden if the technical points should be in his favor. . . . These persons fear that Bradley is more lawyer than Republican, and the Democrats fear that he is more Republican than lawyer.

The Nashville *Daily American* (Democratic) repeated this estimate with approval; a fortnight earlier it had described Bradley as "a fair judicial officer from whom a strictly legal opinion is to be expected on a point of law and a fair determination upon a matter of fact"; it was through his action in the *Grant Parish Case* that "innocents almost the victims of a foul judicial and political conspiracy [were] saved from punishment."[1]

On March 3 the *Sun*, its columns heavily blackened as a sign of national humiliation, denounced "the infamous eight," particularly the three Justices who "from the first act . . . were more partisan than the politicians, and less careful in hiding their bias. . . . It is not surprising that these Judges . . . who treated their solemn obligations as dicer's oaths, should have taken the precaution . . . to exclude reporters from their secret sessions, and thus to deny a betrayed people the poor privilege of seeing the record of their treachery and perjury."[2]

The *Sun* and the Democratic leadership were in close affiliation. Abram S. Hewitt, national chairman, employed A. M. Gibson, Washington correspondent of the *Sun*, to help him in writing the arguments that poured out of the party headquarters;[3] then Tilden engaged him to write *A Political Crime: The History of the Great Fraud.*[4]

In mid-February 1877 Attorney General Alphonso Taft wrote to Governor Hayes:

> The discussion before the Commission is progressing favorably. We passed Florida without damage and I think we shall pass Louisiana in the same way . . . . But what I want to write about now is, that one of my secret service men who seems to be intimate with Gov. Tilden

---

[1] Bradley's opinion in the Grant Parish Case, United States v. Cruikshank, Fed. Case No. 14,897 (1874), held that none of the counts in the indictment could be sustained. See VII, 261—69. That opinion was sustained in United States v. Cruikshank, 92 U.S. 542 (1876).

[2] No person faithful to the purpose of the Commission would have desired that its deliberations be open to reporters. Reporters for the *Sun*, for instance, would have denounced opinions op-posed by their paper. In the end, when a vote on printing the opinions of the Commissioners was taken, there were four votes in the negative, from Justice Field and Congressmen Abbott, Hunton, and Payne—all Democrats.

[3] Allan Nevins, *Abram S. Hewitt, with Some Account of Peter Cooper* (New York: Harper & Brothers, 1935), 309.

[4] New York: William S. Gottsberger, 1885.

reports that he was present at a meeting for consultation between Tilden & Dana & Bartlett of the New York Sun, and heard them agree upon this general plan. To abuse Judge Bradley & the Commission tremendously, and to go for a new election. They consider that the commission wd decide against them. But they thought that the decisions could be postponed to the 4th March. They have great confidence that they can force a new election. I do not apprehend much danger however . . . .[5]

Such a report is to be treated with great caution. It was true, however, that Bradley was singled out for persistent abuse. On the twelfth the *Sun* reported that "Joe Bradley, who is now engaged in making Hayes President, was formerly conspicuous as the attorney of the Camden and Amboy Railroad, for which he rendered valuable service in maintaining the New Jersey Legislature."

On that day the *Sun*'s leading editorial, "The Democrats in the House," declared that in creating the Electoral Commission the Democrats unwittingly had acted unconstitutionally; instead, they should have adopted a resolution declaring that Hayes was not elected and that the President of the Senate ought not to declare to the contrary.

This would leave the title to the office open to be contested before the Courts. The only trouble about this is that we have not, any longer, a Supreme Court of the United States. *The fury of an honest and indignant public opinion, however, rising, as it assuredly will, like a whirlwind and a storm, may safely be trusted to drive the present nominal judges from their places upon the bench, substituting a judiciary for that political body.*[6]

At its Commencement on June 27, 1877, Harvard University conferred the degree of Doctor of Laws upon President Hayes, Senator Bayard, and Attorney General Devens. "Uncommonly well bestowed," said the *Springfield Republican*. The morning *Sun* on the twenty-seventh took note of the impending event by printing the President's picture on its front page: the forehead was branded "FRAUD."

---

[5] Hayes Memorial Libr., Fremont, Ohio. The letter was written in Washington; the date appears to be the fourteenth, but might be the sixteenth. William O. Bartlett, a lawyer, worked for the *Sun* from 1868 to his death thirteen years later.

[6] Italics in the original.

Among Bradley's papers was a letter from John Livingston of the Erie Railway Shareholders' Committee of New York City, dated February 12, urging "Dont fear such stuff; you are saving the liberty of 40 millions." On February 20 Livingston wrote that he *knew* that Dana was at Tilden's house on February 10, and that the inference was that Tilden had inspired the "inflammatory, incendiary article" of the twelfth. That statement, too, is to be treated with great caution.

George M. Robeson (1829—97), Secretary of the Navy in the Grant Cabinet, was returning to the New Jersey bar, and friends were giving a dinner in his honor. Robeson's administration of his department had been severely criticized for extravagance and allegations of corruption. Justice Bradley, a family friend over many years, in declining an invitation, wrote in a short note on June 22 that "Mr. Robeson has been so persistently maligned by a reckless and dishonest press that his friends do well to show their continued confidence"; he hoped the occasion would be "a marked rebuke to the public slanders which have been heaped upon him."

The *Sun* on July 6 made Bradley's letter the basis for a long article:

> It is not often that a Judge of the Supreme Court throws down his robes and enters the partisan arena, like a bully in a prize ring. But since Grant appointed Bradley and Strong to reverse the decree which Chief Justice Chase had pronounced in regard to legal tenders, and that stopped the first great step toward the resumption of specie payments, that tribunal has greatly fallen in public estimation.

Continuing, "Everybody knows that the Pennsylvania Railroad and other corporations connected with it were unduly instrumental in bringing about that change, which struck a blow at the integrity of the Court." It "was necessary to choose two instruments about whose course there could be no doubt." Strong had so decided on the Pennsylvania bench, and was supported by "the controlling spirits of the Pennsylvania road." "Joe Bradley was counsel to the railroad ring in New Jersey . . . . A sharp practitioner, shrewd, cool, and alert, he suited the book of the corporations then seeking to escape from their legal indebtedness by packing the Supreme Court to reverse its own decision."

> When the time came round for the Court to render a new judgment, Strong and Bradley were faithful to the conditions upon which they were appointed. Chase was overruled and the Supreme Court was dishonored. Like the fraud written on the brow of Hayes, no subsequent acts, however good, could blot out that indelible stigma.
>
> The two blackened Judges were members of the Electoral Commission, and they delivered over the Presidency, just as they had foresworn themselves in the legal tender case, being operated upon by the same corrupt influences in both instances. Bradley, especially, will be known in history as the infamous eighth man who, without scruple and without shame, cast his vote every time to uphold the frauds of the Returning Boards, and violently contradicted his own positions to maintain that corrupt conspiracy.

With those antecedents, the editorial concluded, "it was only natural that Joe Bradley, who owes to Robeson the gown he wears," should defend him from criticism. Their cases were alike: "The 'reckless and dishonest press' regard them both in the same light, and the country shares that opinion without regard to party."

The *Sun* had twisted and falsified the facts in much the same way that Senator Joseph R. McCarthy seventy-odd years later discredited many faithful public servants. A full account of the circumstances exonerates Strong and Bradley in respect to their appointment and in the decision of the *Legal Tender Cases*, as may be seen in the *Harvard Law Review* of April and May, 1941.[7] Some of the same ground was covered in chapter 14 of Volume VI on "The Legal Tender Cases."

On the same day as the *Sun*'s article—July 6—the *Newark Daily Journal*, a Democratic organ published by William B. Guild, used Bradley's note on the Robeson dinner to launch its own attack. Bradley was now in Washington, weary from the demands of the past year, and in no mood to shake off such goading treatment. On July 10 he wrote to his good friend, Thomas T. Kinney, publisher of the *Newark Daily Advertiser*:

> Somebody, (Keasby[8] I think) has sent me a copy of Guild's paper of Friday last containing outrageous abuse of me, pretended to be founded on a note I wrote in reply to the invitation to the Robeson dinner—following in this regard, the Sun of the same day. Guild, at least, deserves a swingleing[9] for his blackguardism. The Sun is designedly abusive. . . . to say that I have interfered in politics is a lie. The dinner, as I understood it, was given by Robeson's personal friends. If it had a political significance, I was not to know that, and to charge *me* with mingling in politics, who have abstained from every thing of the kind, and have ignored every thing of the kind ever since I was on the bench—*me*, who sit by the side of a Judge that is in the inmost counsels of the Democratic party at all times![10] It is base and slanderous! . . .
>
> I don't know but it would make more ado to say a word on the subject and I would not have you do it without consulting other friends. But the scoundrel deserves to be put under the pump. . . .
>
> I may be altogether mistaken in the propriety of writing the letter [about the Robeson dinner]. It seems I was as to its prudence.
>
> Yours very truly
> Joseph P. Bradley

[7] Charles Fairman, "Mr. Justice Bradley's Appointment to the Supreme Court and the Legal Tender Cases," 54:977–1034, 1128–55, where a mass of letters and other materials is set out.

[8] Anthony Q. Keasbey, a Yale graduate of 1843, practicing for some years with Cortlandt T. Parker, and United States Attorney from 1861 to 1886.

[9] The beating of flax with a wooden swingle; in his boyhood Bradley had been used to the process of making linen cloth.

[10] Justice Field. From the resignation of Nelson in 1872 to the resignation of Davis in March 1877, Bradley had been seated at the right end of the bench, with Field on his left.

[Turning over the page:]

> The truth is that this is all an outcrop of the deep malignity and revenge excited by my decision on the Electoral Commission. They *mean* to crush me if they can. Old [Jere. S.] Black sounded the horn in the North American Review.[11] Dana followed—and Guild barked in unison—and so will the whole Democratic press. They want to make a victim of me—by way of political capital. And I believe the leaders, if they could find the least scintilla of a ground, just or unjust, would move to have me impeached. It has been threatened. It has been hinted. They want to get possession of the Bench. It is not a favorable time now, it is true—but they could wreak a delicious revenge at all events.
>
> You see I write under some excitement. I think I have occasion for excitement.[12]

We arrest the stream of denunciation to relate what in the meantime Justice Bradley had been doing.

Even as the Electoral Commission was adjourning, the Supreme Court resumed business up to its adjournment on May 7, 1877. For the following five months each Justice would attend courts of his circuit and take his vacation.

Justice Bradley set out on May 9 for Savannah. On the sixteenth he started for Tallahassee, where the State was engaged in litigation with the Jacksonville, Pensacola & Mobile R.R., whose president, Milton S. Littlefield, was an accomplished rogue who had already left a trail of corruption in North Carolina.[13] After a trial, on Tuesday, May 22, Bradley delivered his opinion, and started back to Savannah, where he held court from May 24 through the twenty-eighth. Then to Atlanta, then Montgomery, then to Mobile, where he held court from June 4 through the nineteenth, disposing of a consolidation of important cases. Homeward bound, he reached Washington on the night of June 21.

Next day he wrote to his favorite sister, in Illinois:

> I have just returned from the South, . . . working all the time very hard, and completing my work as I went. Ever since the fore part of last October I have been under constant pressure of toil. . . .
>
> But good bye. I am getting sad, and you are getting sadder by my writing. Time is carrying us to that bourne whence there is no

---

[11] Jere. S. Black, "The Electoral Conspiracy," *No. Amer. Rev.*, 256: 1–34 (July–Aug. 1877).

[12] It is a pleasure to acknowledge my indebtedness to Dr. Don C. Skemer, Keeper of the Manuscripts in the New Jersey Historical Society, for supplying this letter from the Kinney papers; the article from the *Newark Daily Advertiser* of August 27, soon to be quoted; and for other information pertinent to this chapter.

[13] This is the subject of Jonathan W. Daniels' *Prince of Carpetbaggers* (Philadelphia: Lippincott Co., 1958).

returning however perfectly and completely our work is done; and thank God, there is no appeal. . . .

We start for Stowe in a few days and stay till October. . . .

The family did reach their place of vacation at Stowe, Vermont, but Bradley was twice delayed by counsel who requested him to hear their respective cases, with the result that, as he wrote in his diary,

I staid in Washington most of the month [of July]—very warm—could do very little.

He reached Stowe on July 27. But then on August 6 counsel in the case of the Jacksonville, Pensacola & Mobile called, with the result that Bradley returned to Washington where, as the diary records, on August 9, "12 M. had hearing & delivered opinion in the Florida case."

Again on August 13 he "Started for Stowe," where soon he was "Computing the height of Church Steeple." Mathematical calculations such as this were among Bradley's favorite relaxations.

The *Sun* on August 4, 1877, published what it called "An Interesting Historical Fact":

After the argument upon the Florida case . . . Justice Bradley wrote out his opinion and his decision in full. He completed it at about 6 o'clock in the evening on the day before the judgment of the Commission was to be announced, and read it to Judge Clifford and Judge Field . . . . It contained first, an argument, and secondly, a conclusion. The argument was precisely the same as that which appears in the published document, but Judge Bradley's conclusion was that the votes of the Tilden electors in Florida were the only votes which ought to be counted as coming from that State.

This was the character of the paper when Judge Bradley finished it, and when he communicated it to his colleagues. During the whole of that night Judge Bradley's house in Washington was surrounded by carriages of visitors who came to see him . . . .

When the Commission assembled the next morning, and when the judgment was declared, Judge Bradley gave his vote in favor of counting the votes of the Hayes electors in Florida! The argument he did not deliver at the time, but when it came to be printed subsequently it was found to be precisely the same as the argument which he had originally drawn up and on which he had based his first conclusion in favor of the Tilden electors.

What was the source of this story? How could it be known that Bradley completed the opinion at about six o'clock? Under what circumstances did the three Justices meet? Who saw those carriages surrounding Bradley's house? The *Sun* gave no explanation.

For a critical understanding, the course of events over five days should be recalled.

MON., FEB. 5. *Argument by Evarts and O'Conor concluded. Recess. Closed.* Voted to adjourn to permit study. Adjournment at 3:45.

TUE., FEB. 6. *Closed.* Sat. 12 M to 7:45. Senators, then Representatives, except Payne, gave opinions.

WED., FEB. 7. *Closed.* Sat. from 10 A.M. to 3:45. Payne spoke. Then the Justices: Field; Strong; Miller; Bradley, who at the close of his opinion announced that he desired argument on ineligibility; Clifford.

At 3 P.M. Vote on receiving no evidence not submitted to Joint Session: 8 yeas, 7 nays.

Then vote on hearing evidence on eligibility of Humphreys: 8 yeas (Bradley + Democrats) to 7 nays.

Result to be communicated to counsel; they should be ready to proceed tomorrow.

Adjournment at 3:45. [People awaiting outside now learned the result.][14]

THURS., FEB. 8. Met at 11 A.M. *Evidence and argument by counsel on the ineligibility.* Session closed at 4:50. Voted to adjourn to 10 A.M. tomorrow.

FRI., FEB. 9. *Closed.* After debate, it was voted, 8 to 7, that Hayes electors were those chosen in accord with the Constitution.

At 6:05. Recess for one hour while Edmunds, Bradley, and Miller framed report to Joint Session.

On reassembling, report adopted, 8 to 7.

Injunction of secrecy removed.

Adjournment at 8:05.

Now, to try to fit the "Interesting Historical Fact" into the inexorable facts of the record. The "judgment of the Commission" can only mean the decision at 3 P.M. on Wednesday to receive no extrinsic evidence. But the story that Bradley completed his opinion at about 6 P.M. on the previous evening is contradicted by the fact that he was listening to Commissioners' arguments until 7:45 that evening. From 5:05 to 5:55 Hunton was speaking, and we know that Bradley was listening and taking notes.[15] Presumably all the Commissioners hurried to dinner after the adjournment. If Bradley read his opinion to Clifford and Field after dinner, where did they meet? At Bradley's home, 201 I Street at the corner of New Jersey Avenue? We are told that the house was surrounded by carriages; if so, that would be a most inconvenient place for this unusual meeting. Did Bradley and Clifford go to Field's home, at 21 First Street, East, facing the Capitol? Or did Bradley and Field go to Clifford's rooms

---

[14] Part Two at p. 110.   [15] Ibid., at p. 85.

at the National Hotel? That would be a conspicuous place for their confidential meeting. Perhaps a meeting at the Capitol? The Justices had no chambers there, but they could go to the Conference Room.

Why would Bradley want Clifford and Field to know if he purposed to vote for Tilden? So that they, especially Field, could spread the news in advance? What good would he have seen in that? If his state of mind was such that he might switch before he had to vote, that would be all the more reason why he would not have compromised his freedom of action.

Then according to the *Sun*, the "argument" that had served to support Tilden "was precisely the same as that which appears in the published document." An interchangeable opinion would be a novelty. The document has been quoted in full[16]; that it would not support a decision for Tilden must be obvious. Garfield recorded in his diary the tenor of the opinion as it was heard by the Commissioners:

> It was ten minutes before it became evident that he was against the authority to hear extrinsic evidence. His opinion was clear and strong. Near the close he surprised us all by holding that we could hear testimony as to the eligibility of Humphreys.[17]

The opinion as "printed subsequently" runs to six pages; at two-thirds down the second page one reads:

> It seems to be clear, therefore, that Congress cannot institute a scrutiny into the appointment of electors by a State.

After that point the opinion could not have supported Tilden. Apparently Dana completely misunderstood a report of "surprise" at the close of Bradley's opinion, standing the bulk of the opinion on its head.

The story in the *Sun* fell apart at every point. This suggests that Dana and associates cared little about accuracy. Iago had it right: a trifle light as air would suffice to cause a suspicious mind to believe an untruth.[18]

After the Commission on March 2 had completed its work, Justice Field returned to his circuit in an agitated state of mind. For a year he had been pouring out to District Judge Matthew P. Deady of Oregon his apprehension and then his indignation over the course of events. On April 2, 1877, he sent his opinions in the cases from Florida and Oregon:

---

[16] Ibid., at pp. 95–106.
[17] Ibid., at p. 95.

[18] *Othello*, III, iii, 324. Supra, Part Two at p. 107.

The decision of the Commission, not to enquire into the correctness of the action of the Canvassing Boards of Louisiana and Florida was a great shock to the country. It is the first time, I believe, that it has ever been held by any respectable body of jurists, that a fraud was protected from exposure by a certificate by its authors. I shall have much to say to you during the summer of the proceedings before that Tribunal and of its action. The President, who owes his seat to the success of a gigantic conspiracy and fraud, is not finding his place a bed of roses. It is right that it should be so. He is evidently a very weak man, and hardly knows what to do. . . .

My brother Dudley did good service in Congress during the short time he was there. Although the Press of the Republican side never ceased to misrepresent and villify him, he paid no attention to their attacks. They all arose from vexation at his terrible cross-examination of the scoundrels of the Louisiana Canvassing Board. . . .[19]

When the *Sun* of August 4 reached San Francisco, reporters besieged Field for comment on the "Interesting Historical Fact." The earliest account was that he denied that Bradley had *read* any opinion in advance of delivery in the Commission, with implication that otherwise the story was essentially true. It seems that this exaggerated the import of Field's response.[20] At any rate the account as telegraphed to the East was taken as confirmation of the story.

The *Newark Daily Advertiser* on Monday evening, August 27, published this dispatch from San Francisco:

A few days ago the *Daily Exchange* published a reply from Justice Field . . . to an article recently published in New York, charging Justice Bradley with having read an opinion to Justices Field and Clifford to the effect that the electoral vote of Florida ought to be given to Tilden . . . and reversing his conclusion without alteration of the premises or arguments. A number of attempts have been made by representatives of the press to "interview" Justice Field on the subject, but he has uniformly refused to say anything, and in most cases has declined to see them altogether. The *Exchange* to-day publishes an interview with Justice Field. According to the statement of the reporter he at first objected to giving any statement whatever, but finally said, after some reflection, and speaking with great deliberation, "Well, sir; all

---

[19] Letters of Field to Deady in the Oregon Historical Society at Portland. The concluding sentences refer to David Dudley Field's action as a member of the House Select Committee on the Powers, Duties and Privileges of the House in the Counting of the Electoral Votes, an inquiry carried on concurrently with the proceedings of the Electoral Commission.

[20] Generalization based on three editorials from San Francisco newspapers preserved in Justice Bradley's Scrapbook: the *Chronicle* and the *Morning Call* of August 28, and the *Alta California* of September 7.

that I care to say . . . is that Justice Bradley read (with peculiar emphasis on the word read) no opinion to me in advance of the formal submission of the opinions to the Commission. Beyond that, I think it would be improper for me to say anything. If I should enter upon the subject, I should probably say a great deal more than I wish to say." . . .

In the course of some further conversation, Justice Field urged his preference not to be dragged into the controversy at all. He said he regretted that his name had been used, as he was associated with Justice Bradley on the bench . . . and it would be exceedingly unpleasant were their social relations disturbed by such controversy. . . . [It should be borne in mind that these quotations, even when within quotation marks, were the words of the reporter.]

Immediately after the long quotation from the *Exchange*, the *Advertiser* said that it must suppose that Justice Field would not by innuendo assert what he could not prove. "In studying the report we see that Justice Field places particular emphasis on the word 'read,' and says that Justice Bradley did not *read* to him any opinion in the Louisiana case, but leaves it implied that Bradley did say something incompatible with his final written opinion . . . ."

In the course of the editorial, the writer (doubtless Kinney, the publisher) said *Louisiana* when he should have said *Florida*; the "matter of history" about to be recounted occurred during the consideration of the case from Florida, as Justice Bradley states in his letter written at Stowe on September 2.[21] The lapse was very unfortunate, notably because it gave the *Sun* ground for misrepresentation in an editorial of September 1, "Judge Bradley Heard From," the second of two soon to be quoted.

The *Newark Adverstiser*'s long article of August 27 continued:

Judge Field never saw, knew, or heard Judge Bradley's opinion until he heard it read, not before him and Judge Clifford, but before the full Electoral Tribunal when Bradley gave the casting vote.

It is just as well that the full fact should be known as a matter of history. . . .

The morning before the opinion was given, Senator Edmunds had guessed out Judge Bradley's decision, but he did not know it. . . . At the session next day, Senator Edmunds whispered to Judge Bradley that as the opinion he was to give was to be decisive it ought to be in writing. The argument had not then been closed. Bradley accepted the suggestion and sitting at his place dashed down the decision on paper within an hour, in the presence and during the debate of his colleagues. . . .

---

[21] Infra, p. 135.

It is agreeable to this statement that on February 7 Bradley took virtually no notes on the speeches being made. On Payne there was nothing. On Justice Strong's opinion, only three citations to cases. And on Justice Miller, the "bundle of evidence handed into the house & sent to us cannot be regarded as *in the case.*"

The *Sun* was quick to take advantage of the dispatch from the *Exchange*, provoked by the *Sun's* article of August 4. On August 29 it resumed its attack in "The Case of Judge Joseph P. Bradley"·

> The Hon. Stephen J. Field of the United States Supreme Court has made some additions to what was previously revealed respecting Judge Bradley's decision on the Florida electors.
>
> This statement was in substance [and here its story of the fourth was repeated, without mention of Justice Clifford].
>
> These facts are all substantially reaffirmed or tacitly admitted by Judge Field, who has made an explanation upon the subject for a reporter of the *Daily Exchange*, a San Francisco paper.
>
> [The story of the carriages surrounding the Bradley home throughout the night was repeated.]
>
> Of course this subject will be investigated by the House of Representatives, and it is not improbable that such an investigation may lead to the impeachment of Judge Bradley.

Four days later, on Saturday, September 1, the *Sun* exploited its second windfall, the *Advertiser's* use of *Louisiana* for *Florida*:

> Judge Bradley Heard From
>
> An explanation has at last been offered in behalf of Judge Bradley respecting his alleged misconduct as a member of the Electoral Commission. It is found in the columns of the *Newark Daily Advertiser*, a journal with which he is known to maintain relations of unusual intimacy, and is in the following language:
>
> [Here is quoted at length the passage in the *Advertiser's* comments of August 27 where, after quoting the dispatch from San Francisco, it spoke of *Louisiana, meaning Florida*: "It is just as well that the full fact should be known as a matter of history," and told about Senator Edmunds, etc.]
>
> It will be noted that Judge Bradley evades the charge made against him. He takes up the Louisiana case, saying that he "had already decided in the Florida case that he could not go behind the returns of the State officials." Now it happens that the opinion which he communicated to Judge Field the evening before the judgment of the Commission was made up, but which he changed between evening and morning, was the opinion in the Florida case, and not in the Louisiana case; and when he turns away to talk of the latter, instead of talking of the former, he says nothing to the point, and, in fact, only admits

that the Florida case is the one in which he has reasons for not desiring to explain himself.

That there may be no misunderstanding we will once more repeat the facts as they have come to our knowledge. [The *Sun* reiterates its allegations.]

This is the case against Judge Bradley, and, as we have said, the narrative respecting the subsequent action of the tribunal on the Louisiana question does nothing to relieve him from the perilous attitude in which he has placed himself by his conduct in this affair.

On September 5 the *Advertiser* published a letter from Justice Bradley:

Stowe, Vt., Sept. 2, 1877.

EDITOR OF THE *Advertiser:*—I perceive that the New York *Sun* has reiterated its charge that after preparing a written opinion in favor of the Tilden electors in the Florida case, submitted to the Electoral Commission, I changed my views during the night preceding the vote, in consequence of pressure brought to bear upon me by Republican politicians and Pacific Railroad men, whose carriages, it is said, surrounded my house during the evening. This, I believe, is the important point of the charge. Whether I wrote one opinion, or twenty, in my private examination of the subject, is of little consequence, and of no concern to anybody, if the opinion which I finally gave was the fair result of my deliberations, without influence from outside parties. The above slander was published some time since, but I never saw it until recently, and deemed it too absurd to need refutation. But as it is categorically repeated, perhaps I ought to notice it. The same story about carriages of leading Republicans, and others, congregating at my house, was circulated at Washington at the same time, and came to the ears of my family, only to raise a smile of contempt. The whole thing is a falsehood. Not a single visitor called at my house that evening; and during the whole sitting of the Commission, I had no private discussion whatever on the subjects at issue with any person interested on the Republican side, and but very few words with any person. Indeed, I sedulously sought to avoid all discussion outside the Commission itself. The allegation that I read an opinion to Judges Clifford and Field is entirely untrue. I read no opinion to either of them, and have no recollection of expressing any. If I did, it could only have been suggestively, or in a hypothetical manner, and not intended as a committal of my final judgment or action. The question was one of grave importance, and, to me, of much difficulty and embarrassment. I earnestly endeavored to come to a right decision, free from all political or other extraneous considerations. In my private examination of the principal question (about going behind the returns), I wrote and re-wrote the arguments and considerations on both sides as they occurred to me, sometimes being inclined to one view of the subject, and sometimes to

135

the other. But finally I threw aside these lucubrations, and, as you have rightly stated, wrote out the short opinion which I read in the Florida case during the sitting of the Commission. This opinion expresses the honest conclusion to which I had arrived, and which, after a full consideration of the whole matter, seemed to me the only satisfactory solution of the question. And I may add, that the more I have reflected on it since, the more satisfied have I become that it was right. At all events, it was the result of my own reflections and consideration, without any suggestion from any quarter, except the arguments adduced by counsel in the public discussion, and by the members of the Commission in its private consultations.

As for the insinuations contained in a recent article, published in a prominent periodical by a noted politician,[22] implying that the case was decided in consequence of a political conspiracy, I can only say (and from the peculiar position I occupied on the Commission I am able positively to say) that it is utterly devoid of truth, at least, so far as the action of the Commission itself was concerned. In that article the writer couples my name with the names of those whom he supposes obnoxious to public odium. The decencies of public expression, if nothing more, might well have deterred so able a writer from making imputations which he did not know to be well founded.

Yours respectfully,
Joseph P. Bradley

On the next day the *Sun* responded in an editorial. "Justice Jo Bradley has felt the necessity of coming before the country with a letter in respect to the part he played in the Electoral Commission Fraud. It is a strange piece of work for a man in his senses. . . . Jo Bradley confesses, though we cannot tell how often he changed his mind respecting the nature of the confession he ought to make. Thus he admits the truth and accuracy of the fundamental features of the charge brought home to him by the *Sun*." It called for an investigation looking to impeachment.

In an adjacent column was printed the letter to the *Advertiser* captioned "Justice Bradley's Confession," with subtitles: "How Aliunde Jo Changed From Side to Side—How He Wrote and Rewrote Contradictory Opinions—He Virtually Admits the Charges of the *Sun*—A Farrago About the Electoral Commission Fraud."

Apropos of his letter Bradley wrote this note:

The abuse heaped upon me by the Democratic press, and especially the New York *Sun*, for the part I took in the Electoral Commission . . . is almost beyond conception. Malignant falsehoods of the most aggravated character were constantly published. I bore these things in silence until it was stated that Judge Field had said, in con-

---

[22] See note 11.

versation, that I had changed my mind during the sitting of the Commission, and that I had first written an opinion in favor of Tilden, and had read it to him and Judge Clifford. When this story appeared the Judge was in California and I was spending my vacation at Stowe, Vt. I immediately wrote to him, calling his attention to these charges. He replied, denying that he used the expressions attributed to him, and had said nothing derogatory to my honor or integrity.

Starting with its wholly untenable "Interesting Historical Fact" of August 4, the *Sun* had achieved a great success in a little over a month. Its method was disclosed in its editorial of September 1: "the facts are worth telling and we dare to assert them without any other authorization than our challenge that we cannot be contradicted."

RETROSPECTIONS OF JOHN BIGELOW

JOHN BIGELOW (1817–1911) was Tilden's devoted companion throughout the electoral controversy, and later his biographer. He had been an editorial writer for the *New York Evening Post*, consul general at Paris throughout the Civil War, and always a traveler and observer. His *Retrospections on an Active Life* was published in five volumes in 1909–13.[23] Comments from his diary show the profound suspicion that prevailed in the Tilden camp.

On February 8, it will be recalled, John P. Stockton had written to Tilden with a message from Robert Gilchrist and himself, after they had called on Justice Bradley.[24]

In his diary for February 9 Bigelow wrote:

Senator Stockton came in in the evening. He knows Justice Bradley well, having been a long time associated with him as counsel for the Camden & Amboy RR. He says he is not particular about the means with which he compasses his ends.[25]

It would be of great interest to know what Stockton actually said; the purpose of his call may be judged by his letter of the previous day to Tilden: to talk about a brief to be submitted to the Commission. Bigelow was quick to think evil of anyone who stood in the way of installing Tilden.

---

[23] New York: Doubleday, Page & Co.

[24] Part Two at p. 111.

[25] *Retrospections*, Vol. 5, 298. A footnote identified Stockton as "P. J.

Stockton." The name was John Potter Stockton. Bigelow's writing was sometimes hasty and lax. See *Dictionary of American Biography*.

[26] Letter of May 27, 1865. Morgan Papers, New York State Library.

To suppose that Stockton entertained the view of Bradley that Bigelow imputed would be passing strange in the light of the relations of the two men. Stockton had been elected to the Senate by a plurality of the joint sessions of the New Jersey legislature in 1865. That joint meeting had adopted a rule that a *majority* would be requisite to an election. There were 81 members of the joint session; but when a deadlock had been produced by a little band of extremists, a majority of 41 voted to amend the rule so as to elect by a *plurality*. The two principal candidates had agreed to this change. Then Stockton was elected by 40 votes to 37 for his opponent.

Bradley wrote to Senator Edwin D. Morgan of New York, Republican, informing him of the circumstances, and urging that the move to deny Stockton a seat be defeated. "I am no Stocktonite, and would have been very glad if we could have elected Ten Eyck or any other Republican, but I very much doubt the policy of the mentioned move. In the first place, I do not think that it would be right in point of law. . . . My own opinion is that as the plurality rule was agreed to by a majority, the election is valid."[26]

Stockton was seated when the Senate met on December 4, 1865; a protest signed by 37 members of the state legislature was referred to the Judiciary Committee.

On March 22, 1866, Senator Trumbull reported a resolution from the Judiciary Committee (only one member disagreeing) that Stockton had been duly elected. After two days of debate that was adopted by vote of 21 to 20. But then Lot Morrill of Maine directed that his name be called. He had been paired on this question with Senator William Wright of New Jersey, who had been absent for several months; he had given the absentee notice, and now broke the pair and voted against Stockton. Thereupon Stockton gave his vote in his own favor, making a majority of 22 to 21.[27]

After extended debate on this action, on March 26, Stockton asked leave to withdraw his vote, and promised that he would not again vote on the question. On March 27 it was voted by 23 to 20 that Stockton had not been duly elected to the Senate.[28]

In 1868 Stockton was elected a Senator and served for the term from March 4, 1869. Bradley was nominated to be a Justice on February 7, 1870. Senators needed assurance that he was a sound Republican; there was major opposition by Cameron of Pennsylvania (who was concerned for the interests of the Pennsylvania Railroad) and from some carpetbaggers. In these circumstances Stockton's support must be guarded. Thus,

---

[26] Letter of May 27, 1865. Morgan Papers, New York State Library.

[27] Cong. Globe, 39–1, 1564, 1601, 1602.

[28] Ibid., 1677, 1679.

"I say . . . that you have been considered at the head of the bar since I have been at it, but you are an *extreme politician* in your views." When the vote on confirmation came, Stockton would have the Democrats in their seats, ready to vote to confirm.[29]

No reason is known why Stockton would say what Bigelow wrote in his second sentence. (After Stockton's action in the Senate in March 1866 one might say that *he* had not been sensitive about voting to seat himself in the Senate.) A possible explanation of the diary entry is ventured. To Bigelow, a member of the Electoral Commission who did not at once recognize Tilden's right to the office would be deficient in moral perception. As Stockton would know, such sweeping talk as Jere. Black had addressed to the Commission would only repel Bradley, who would, however, pay close attention to a refined point, such as the effect of constitutional ineligibility, or of the quo warranto proceedings in Florida's circuit court. Presumably Stockton, from his letter, had sought to impress upon Tilden the discriminating quality of Bradley's mind. It may be that to Bigelow this would be translated as "not particular about the means . . . ," although in fact it would show great particularity.

Bigelow's next entry, still for Friday, February 9, was:

> On Thursday Tilden told me a man had called to say that the Commission was for sale. When I expressed an incredulous sort of astonishment he said that one of the justices (Republican) was ready to give his vote to Tilden for $200,000. I asked which one. He thought he would not tell me that at present. I told him it was improbable, for the judges were all well paid and had life terms of their office. He said the justice in question is reported to be embarrassed from old engagements and obligations. As Bradley is the youngest appointment it would look as though he was most likely to be the man, though I did not try again to ascertain. Tilden said the Florida returning board was offered him and for the same money. "That," he said, "seems to be the standard figure."

That shows an eager readiness to believe that one of the three Republican Justices was soliciting a bribe, and that Bradley was "most likely to be the man."

Incidentally, did Bigelow know that the justices were "well paid"? From 1855 through the war and until 1871 the pay was $6,000; then for two years, $8,000. In 1873, in a general raising of salaries, it went to $10,000, where it remained to 1903. The Chief Justice received an additional $500.[30] The Justice assigned to the Pacific Coast (Field), received $1,000 for travel; the others received no such allowance. The railroads

---

[29] VI, 734, 737.

[30] VI, 68n.

offered passes, which appear generally to have been accepted. When Bradley went on his circuit, however, he would sometimes record in his diary the amount of fares paid on the way. When he went on the Court he sold all his railroad stock to Frelinghuysen. Although Bigelow could not have been convinced, this was an honest man.

On February 10, 1877, Tilden's nephew, William T. Pelton, at Washington, sent a message to Bigelow:

> It's of vital importance you see Jno. A. C. Gray, and as an old and tried friend advise him to see that Justice Bradley *does right*. Mr. Gray can do this. It is probably best that he come here on Sunday night *at latest*.[31]

To explain one must touch upon a complicated controversy. In July 1870, a stockholder in the Memphis, El Paso, & Pacific R.R., a bondholder of the road, and trustees under a land grant mortgage by the road, sued for an injunction to restrain the officers of the company, and for the appointment of a receiver of the road. Their allegation was that the officers were wasting the assets by fraudulent management. Cortlandt Parker of Newark represented the plaintiffs. The suit was brought at Newark before Bradley as Circuit Justice for the District of Western Texas. Due notice, it appeared, had been given to the company, a Texas corporation.

John A. C. Gray,[32] a New York lawyer, was appointed receiver. After surveying the condition of the company he made his report to the Justice.[33] The company, it appeared, had practiced enormous frauds on

---

[31] *Retrospections*, V, 299–300.

[32] John Alexander Clinton Gray (who used the name John Clinton Gray) graduated from Harvard Law School in 1866. John Alfred Davenport was a classmate. (So too was Oliver Wendell Holmes, Jr.) Gray and Davenport practiced in partnership in New York City.

On January 22, 1888, Gray was appointed to the Court of Appeals to fill a vacancy, and as Democratic candidate was elected to the place in November 1888. After he had reached the age of seventy his term ended on December 31, 1913.

[33] Forbes *et al.* v. Memphis, El Paso & Pacific RR., Fed. Case No. 4,926 (May 1872).

Objection was later made that Bradley had acted outside his circuit. This was not unlawful, and might be needful. Prior to the Act of April 10, 1869, to amend the judicial system, 16 Stat.

44, it was possible to make the application only to a District Judge or to a Circuit Justice. The former might be absent, and the latter normally made the rounds of his circuit only once in two years. It was common practice to go to the Circuit Justice wherever he might be found. After 1869 there would also be a Circuit Judge, but even so there might be need to resort to the Circuit Justice.

In the Second Session of the 42d Congress, in April 1872, S. 473, a bill to further the administration of justice, contained a provision.

That no justice of the Supreme Court shall hear or allow any application for an injunction or restraining order except within the circuit to which he is allotted, or at such place outside of the circuit as the parties in writing may stipulate.

Senator Carpenter in charge of the bill

Senator Thomas W. Ferry
President pro tem. of the Senate
(Library of Congress)

Governor Lafayette Grover of Oregon
(Oregon Historical Society)

Representative Nathaniel P. Banks
Republican Objector to Certificate from Oregon
(Brady-Handy photo. Library of Congress)

Senator Henry L. Dawes
(Library of Congress)

Joseph P. Bradley, Stephen J. Field, Samuel F. Miller, Nathan Clifford, Morrison R. Waite, Noah H. Swayne, David Davis, William Strong, Ward Hunt

Supreme Court, 1874–1877
(Library of Congress)

Alphonso Taft
(Library of Congress)

James G. Blaine
(Library of Congress)

Henry B. Anthony
(Brady-Handy photo. Library of Congress)

Lot M. Morrill
(Library of Congress)

Charles A. Dana
(Library of Congress)

John Bigelow
(Brady-Handy photo. Library of Congress)

James M. Wells
(Library of Congress)

William P. Kellogg
(Library of Congress)

Zachariah Chandler
(Library of Congress)

Simon Cameron
(Library of Congress)

Roscoe Conkling
(Library of Congress)

Samuel S. Cox
(Library of Congress)

Justice David Davis
(Library of Congress)

Justice William B. Woods
(Library of Congress)

Judge Walter Q. Gresham
(Library of Congress)

Judge Matthew P. Deady
(Oregon Historical Society)

Rear (from left): Stanley Matthews; Horace Gray; John M. Harlan; Samuel Blatchford. *Front:* Joseph P. Bradley; Samuel F. Miller; Morrison R. Waite, Stephen J. Field, Lucius Q. C. Lamar.
Supreme Court Shortly Before Waite's Death in 1888
(Library of Congress)

Charles Francis Adams
Minister to Great Britain, 1861–1868
(Library of Congress)

Judge William McKennan
Circuit Judge for the Third Circuit, 1869–1891
(Library of Congress)

George Harding
Distinguished Patent Lawyer
(Library of Congress)

European investors. "A more utterly fraudulent concern, a more empty bubble of speculation," said Bradley, "is rarely to be met with in this highly speculating and fraudulent age." The receiver advised the sale of the franchises and property of the company to a railroad incorporated in Texas with purpose and means to build along the projected line to the Pacific.

Petitioners sought to intervene, their purpose being to prevent confirmation of the report. They contended that there had been conspiracy on the part of those who brought the suit, and collusion with the receiver. Bradley, J., heard the allegations, found them groundless, and denied the petition.

The Justice authorized the sale as recommended by the receiver. Presently the property was acquired by the Texas & Pacific Railroad Company, an enterprise headed by Thomas A. Scott, formerly vice president of the Pennsylvania Railroad. Texas & Pacific promoters were active in soliciting support from Congress.

Charges of conspiracy in the take-over remained, and found a supporter in Dana's *Sun*.

This explanation enables one to understand what the injudicious Mr. Pelton had in mind in the message quoted above: an assumption that the Memphis, El Paso & Pacific receivership would weigh heavily on Bradley's conscience, and that a reminder by the receiver would make the Justice *do right*.[34]

Bigelow wrote in his diary what he did in pursuit of Pelton's request:

---

said that, absent such a provision, "a man from Maine may give notice that application will be made before Judge Clifford here in Washington. There is no necessity for this." Or a plaintiff in Oregon might give notice to his opponent to appear in Washington to have that cause heard before Judge Field.

Frelinghuysen moved to strike that clause.

If there are any officers in the United States that do not require to be hampered by statutory law for fear they may do something wrong, they are the justices of the Supreme Court. There is no evil complained of, there is no abuse of this power . . . .

Senator Stockton, his Democratic colleague, said at once, "I agree entirely . . . ."

Carpenter replied, "if there should occur a case, for instance, which Justice Bradley thought he ought to hear, does

anybody believe he would not take the train and go over to his circuit to hear it?"

The motion to strike was defeated without a record vote. Cong. Globe, 42–2, 2490, April 17, 1872. The clause appeared in the Act of June 1, 1872, 17 Stat. 197, qualified, however, by the words, "except when it cannot be heard by the circuit judge of the circuit or the district judge of the district." It became a part of Sec. 719, Rev. Stat.

Note that this applied only to injunctions: as theretofore, many civil matters were heard by agreement before a Justice wherever he might be; *e.g.*, before Justice Bradley in Washington in July and August, 1877. Supra, p. 129.

[34] C. Vann Woodward, *Reunion and Reaction* (Boston: Little, Brown & Co., 1951), 157–60.

The *Sun* attacked Bradley in this matter in February and October, 1875. On

Monday, February 13, 1877. . . . I called at Gray's house on Sunday but he was at Garrison. Telegraphed to let me see him as soon as possible. Saw him at his house this morning at ten. He did not think Bradley would allow him to talk about the business of the Commission. Was willing to go to Washington, if he could do any good; would be glad for the interests of the country, as things now looked, to have Tilden counted in. Would not go without seeing Cortlandt [*sic*] Parker. He went to Newark for the purpose, and at half-past two I met him at his son's office. Parker thinks it would irritate Bradley to talk with him about his duty as commissioner; would not therefore undertake it; and, if he did, could not recommend him to decide differently from the judgment in the Florida case, having published a letter taking the same ground, which Gray lent me to read.

In short, Gray and Parker both believed that Bradley would not allow anyone to approach him on his performance as a member of the Commission. These were experienced lawyers who had an appreciation of proper judicial conduct.[35]

While Gray and Bigelow were conversing, the former, as Bigelow wrote in his diary, recalled having been with President Grant shortly after the Court in 1870 held the Legal Tender Act of 1862 invalid as applied to preexisting debts. Gray had an interest in railroad property that would be adversely affected if obligations must be discharged in gold. Grant

---

October 12 Parker wrote to the Justice: he had started to write "a communication to defend you," but as he wrote he doubted the wisdom of making a reply. He had consulted persons in whose judgment he had confidence. "The opinion was unanimous to let it alone. Attentive reading led all to ask how what was alleged, even if true, went to prove anything wrong." He indicated what he believed to be the personal interest of the lawyers concerned in the attacks. "Dana personally favors these people in their attacks for two reasons, first because his paper feeds on libel, second, because he hates Tom Scott." "The thing is especially provoking because I have always felt that I and Gray merited laurels not abuse for this business of the M. & El Paso. The gravamen of Dana's men is that we acted in the North, and did not delay proceedings by going to Texas. Pray, why should we? Had we gone there, there would have been accusation founded on that." He invited Bradley's views. On October 13 Davenport wrote, evidently in Gray's absence:

We have greatly regretted the unparalleled articles in the Sun; but have not felt at liberty so far at least as you are concerned, to even *seem* to concede them to be of sufficient consequence for notice or reply. They carry their own refutation, so far as the Receivership is concerned, and are evidently and simply—dirt. The Sun not only invites, but entreats, reply—and thus far we have abstained from doing what it most wishes.

However he and Gray were "entirely at your disposal" if Bradley or his friends thought that silence was mistaken. Bradley Papers, N.J. Hist. Soc.

[35] Like Frelinghuysen, Parker was a classmate and friend of Bradley's; in this relation, however, the bond was not so strong. Parker had aspired to appointment to the Court in 1870, as he related to Bradley in congratulating him on his success. In 1884–85 Parker was President of the American Bar Association.

said in effect, "Give yourself no trouble about that; that decision will be reversed." Bigelow's entry continues:

> And so it was. Bradley was appointed very shortly after that interview. The President, therefore, must have had an opinion from him before he was named as judge. How natural to select such a man to cast the decisive vote in this presidential question.

That was the only explanation that Bigelow could imagine. In truth, neither Bradley nor Strong, nominated in the same message, gave any promise of what they would do: their conduct already showed their opinion in favor of the validity of the Legal Tender Act.[36]

Bigelow recorded the following item in his diary for Tuesday, February 20:

> While in New York, Tilden showed me an anonymous letter in which it was stated that Justice Bradley, whose decisions in the Electoral Commission have so disappointed the Democrats, received $100,000 as the price for his labors for Hayes before he took his seat.[37]

Such an anonymous letter seemed "strong as proofs of Holy Writ."

The *Sun* had attacked the transactions whereby the Texas & Pacific succeeded to the property of the Memphis, El Paso & Pacific, two years before the Electoral Commission was at work. In all its efforts to discredit Bradley as a member of that body it had made no use of the receivership as a basis for attack, down to February 20, 1877. At that moment the Commission was about to receive the case from Oregon, the last serious chance for a Democratic success. On that day the *Sun* made a maximum effort. The first column on page one bore the headline, "CONSUMMATING THE FRAUD." Then on the editorial page, in column one, was an article seeking to discredit "Senator Edmunds of Vermont, who did more than any other man to secure the passage of the Electoral Bill, and thus became a connecting link between J. Madison Wells[38] and Justice Joe Bradley in the process of counting in a Fraudulent President."

In column six one read:

> DURELL, BRADLEY, MILLER, AND STRONG are the four judges to whom the country is indebted for a Fraudulent President. Durell who started the work, has disappeared in disgrace.[39]

---

[36] See note 7.

[37] *Retrospections*, V, 300–01.

[38] Chairman of the Returning Board of Louisiana.

[39] Edward H. Durell, District Judge for Louisiana from 1863 until in 1874 he resigned to avoid impeachment. His order on December 5, 1872, barring entrance to the State House, resulted in William Pitt Kellogg's gaining power as Governor. From that came the disorder in the government made evident in the election of 1876.

In the seventh column was a dispatch from Washington, headed "WHO IS THE FIFTH JUDGE?" It answered, John A. C. Gray of New York, assisted by Colonel Tom Scott and Cortlandt Parker. "When at the private solicitation of Parker . . . Bradley assumed jurisdiction at Newark of the suits purporting to have been brought in Texas, . . . fraudulent and corrupt and collusive as they were, . . . he ceased to be his own man . . . . How was he ever to recover his independence? . . . If John A. C. Gray were to take any one of several little bundles of papers, neatly tied with red tape, and open them before Mr. Knott's Committee,[40] Joe Bradley would doubtless be impeached in five hours, and before the 4th of March he might be hurled from the highest place to the lowest depths ever reached by an American Judge. But Mr. Gray has not chosen to use his power that way. It would not be well for Col. Scott's Texas-Pacific scheme to have Mr. Tilden in the White House, and so Mr. Gray has allowed Mr. Justice Joe Bradley to go on and seat Hayes. . . ."

In its rancor and in the reiteration of its accusation, this is in the *Sun*'s editorial style in dealing with Bradley; but the fact that it came from Washington, and by reason of some of its details, it seems likely that some financial interest at war with Texas & Pacific participated in composing the article.

If the purpose of the *Sun*'s issue of February 20 was to win the one essential electoral vote for Tilden, the hope was vain from the start; at the least it gave vent to Dana's frustration.

It would go too far afield, and require time not now available, to inquire whether this accusation by the *Sun* was any more meritorious than its others. The Memphis, El Paso & Pacific receivership was not news; it had not affected Hewitt's statement that he had personally known Justice Bradley as a man of the highest integrity, and that he felt that this confidence was shared by Tilden. If Dana really knew anything that would cause this or any other federal Judge to be "hurled to the lowest depths" he should have imparted his knowledge to that branch of government that has power to impeach. The House had been under Democratic control since the 44th Congress met on December 6, 1875, yet Dana had held his voice until a fortnight before the end of the final session.

JAMES M. SCOVEL

NEITHER HEWITT in his "Secret History" nor Bigelow took note of this letter in the Tilden papers:

---

[40] J. Proctor Knott of Kentucky was chairman of the Special Committee on the Rights and Privileges of the House of Representatives in Relation to Counting the Electoral Vote.

Part Three: *"Immense Gratuitous and Unfounded Abuse"*

Camden N J Feby 10, 77

My dear Mr Tilden

I send you a letter about Bradley. At that interview (Tuesday 30 January) Bradley told me at his own House that the Commission would decide in favor of Tilden.

Robeson, Halsey[41] and the whole Cabinet will "Bull doze" Bradley if they can. His heart is *right* if they don't seduce him from the path of Justice. It is worth while to bring every honest influence on him that can be brought.

He is intensely ambitious: very sensitive to public opinion. I know him as well as if I was inside of him. But you are the older and abler soldier than I am.

Surely the Hayes villany can not be consummated. May God defend the *right*.

Sincerely,
James M. Scovel[42]

Scovel was a Senator in the New Jersey legislature. He wrote after the decision in the Florida case, and asserts what Bradley "at his own house" told him. He tells how intimate he is with the Justice, and credits him with an inclination to do right, from which he might be seduced. This is a first-hand report, and might seem strongly to support Hewitt's "Secret History."

Dr. Alexander C. Flick, without identifying and apparently without knowing the identity of the writer of the letter, whom he cites as "Scoville," gave the letter full faith and credit in his biography of Tilden.[43] After quoting Bigelow on Bradley; and Nevins' *Hewitt* and the "mysterious change" in opinion induced by Frelinghuysen and Robeson, with Mrs. Bradley's prayer; and what Justice Field saw as Bradley's "change of views"; and the anonymous letter alleging the acceptance of a bribe of $100,000; and finally that Bradley "told J. M. Scoville [*sic*] that the 'commission would decide in favor of Tilden,' " Flick concludes that "The simplest explanation of Bradley's action is that his judicial impartiality was submerged in partisanship and his vote was what his party expected."[44]

---

[41] George A. Halsey of Newark, a Representative in Congress, 1867–69 and 1871–73; in 1874 unsuccessful as Republican candidate for Governor.

[42] Scovel was sending a number of messages to Tilden, by telegraph and in writing. On February 26 there was a telegram urging resistance to the decisions of the Electoral Commission.

In a paragraph of a letter of April 20 he wrote that

[The People] had begun to fear that you might be indifferent to the monstrous wrong and injustice perpetrated by Joe Bradley & his fellow conspirators.

S. J. Tilden Papers, Manuscripts and Archives Division, N.Y. Public Library; Astor, Lenox and Tilden Foundations.

[43] *Samuel Jones Tilden: A Study in Political Sagacity* (New York: Dodd, Mead & Co., 1939).

[44] At 390–91.

It would have been prudent to examine the letter with critical attention. The statement is said to have been made on January 30. That was one day before the Commission first met: would Bradley have made such a statement? The alleged intimacy is striking. If one appointed to the Supreme Court was so ambitious, what more did he seek?

James M. Scovel was in the practice of giving unsought advice to Presidents and other public figures. In the *Index to the Abraham Lincoln Papers* in the Library of Congress 28 communications are noted, the latest of which caused Lincoln to instruct Stanton that, in case Scovel was drafted, "let him be discharged . . . ." In the Andrew Johnson Papers there are 8 entries; in the Garfield Papers the count is 33.

Scovel also wrote to Senator Charles Sumner. On February 9, 1870, two days after Bradley and Strong had been nominated to be Justices, Scovel wrote to Sumner that the "nomination of Jos. P Bradley is not one 'fit to be confirmed.' "

> As a *man* Bradley will do: also as a gentleman. As a Lawyer he *will not do*—because he is *heart, mind & soul,* Camden & Amboy. *Now* to you I need not say another word. . . . His confirmation will put the last screw into the coffin of Republicanism. His politics are *Camden & Amboy* & we can never tell whether he is for a Democratic or Republican candidate for Governor. No man whose *business* is buying members of legislatures & paying *cash for* them is fit for the Supreme Bench. . . .[45]

On March 6 and again on April 19, 1870, Scovel had written to Bradley in the guise of a friend claiming that he has used his influence with Sumner in Bradley's behalf. Bradley endorsed the claim with the comment, "The fellow did & said all he could agt me to Sumner." Sumner voted to confirm Bradley, which suggests the value he put on Scovel's advice.

By 1872 Scovel had become a Liberal Republican, taking a prominent part in a meeting in January of that year where he called for a resolution that "It is time to stop . . . the packing of the Supreme Court to relieve rich corporations . . . ."[46]

In 1876–77 Scovel was an ardent follower of Tilden. Hence the letter quoted above, written on February 10, 1877. One should have been

---

[45] This is in the Sumner Papers, Harvard University Library.

[46]Ann. Cyc., 1872, 552. That plank did not appear in the platform in May. Ibid., 777.

Scovel was one of a "little band of extremists" mentioned above who in the joint session of the New Jersey legislature in 1865 prevented either of the candidates for Senator from receiving a *majority* of the vote. Then Stockton was elected by a *plurality*. A group of New Jersey legislators, Scovel at their head, filed the objection to Stockton being seated. In the outcome Stockton was unseated. Supra, p. 138.

Then in April 1866 the legislature attempted to elect a replacement; Scovel, suspicious of it at the outset, and with more extensive acquaintance one knows that it was false.

For seven years Bradley had known what was inside Scovel: that he was untruthful and treacherous. The Justice would have had no dealings with him.

CLOSING SOME ACCOUNTS

WHEN THE DEMOCRATS chose Jere. S. Black to be one of counsel before the Commission it was an exercise of poor judgment. He declared that "I hope to God that nobody here, even on the other side, will attempt to deny, that Congress . . . has the verifying power . . . to inquire whether this is a forgery or not . . . ."[47] It should have been evident that such browbeating would win no votes from "the other side," but could not fail to repel. He was given no more work until in the South Carolina case, where all was surely lost and no harm could result from his "insulting" speech.

When Hayes was in office Black took his appeal to the country in the *North American Review* for July–August 1877.[48] Here he was free to choose his theme and proceed without contradiction. The Civil War started, he wrote, when individual rights were "most wantonly . . . assailed by the abolitionists." After the war "the ultra-abolitionists . . . had a two-thirds majority in Congress"; by their Reconstruction Act "all the rights which our forefathers . . . shed their blood to maintain, were insultingly overborne." Then came the carpetbaggers, "who professed to be the special friends and protectors of the African race; yet they permitted them to be slaughtered with quiet unconcern . . . ." "The story of four thousand murders is part of the *Great Fraud*, and was fabricated to serve as an excuse . . . . The heads of the Administration at Washington may properly be called its creators . . . . The theory was, that murder and violence . . . gave them a paramount claim to the perpetual continuance of . . . disorderly rule, and therefore the votes of a popular majority against them . . . for Governor or President ought not to be counted." "Then the *Returning Board* was invented." "Its object was not to *return*, but to *suppress*, the votes of the qualified electors . . . ."

---

now president of the Senate, prevented that body from joining the lower house, unless, it seems, he himself was to be chosen. *The Nation*, reporting the situation, concluded, "but he did not succeed in filling it himself, and was expelled from the Union League of Camden, and has utterly destroyed all future chances of preferment with the Republican party . . . ." 2:418 and 450, Apr. 5 and 12, 1866.

[47]Proc., 98.

[48]See note 11.

And now a pseudo-President had been placed in power. "All that once ennobled the Nation seemed to be buried in this deep grave dug by the Returning Board and filled up by the Electoral Commission." Those who had profited "drank deep potations to the defeat of Tilden's big majority, while Bradley and Kellogg, Chandler and Packard, Wells, and the two mulattoes,[49] were 'in their flowing cups freshly remembered.' "[50]

> If the majority of the Commission could but have realized their responsibility to God and man, if they could only have understood that in a free country liberty and law are inseparable, they would have been enrolled among our greatest benefactors, for they would have added strength and grandeur to our institutions. But they could not come up to the height of the great subject. . . .

In the following issue of the *North American Review,* in September–October, E. W. Stoughton replied in "The 'Electoral Conspiracy' Exploded"[51] with a reasoned argument that concluded "that the nation has not been betrayed, and that the Great Fraud of 1876 was but the figment of a disordered mind."

PELTON AND THE CIPHER TELEGRAMS

FURTHER NOTICE should be taken of William Tilden Pelton, who with Bigelow's aid endeavored to make Justice Bradley "do right." Pelton failed to do as much for himself.

In response to public demand for more information about frauds, the House of Representatives in May 1878 created an investigating committee under the chairmanship of Clarkson N. Potter of New York. The inquiry was proceeding with some embarrassment to Republicans but no startling revelations until on October 7, 1878, the *New York Tribune* announced its impending publication of "THE CIPHER TELEGRAMS." It explained how telegrams sent and received on the part of the Democratic

---

[49]William P. Kellogg, recently Governor of Louisiana, now Senator. Chandler: probably meaning William E., active in inspiring Republican claims in the Southern States; possibly referring to Senator Zach Chandler, chairman of the Republican National Committee. Stephen B. Packard was Republican claimant to the office of Governor of Louisiana, whom Grant refused to support. Wells, chairman of the Louisiana Returning Board. The "two mulattoes" were members.

[50]*King Henry V,* IV, iii, 55. Henry is foretelling the honor that will be done to those who fight with him at Agincourt. Black was exceedingly well acquainted with Shakespeare.

[51]256:193–234.

party had come into the *Tribune*'s hands, and how the several codes had been broken. There was a key to the principal figures: Pelton was "Denmark"; Manton Marble, until recently publisher of the *New York World*, was "Moses."

On October 8 "THE FLORIDA CIPHER TELEGRAMS" with translations and explanations were published. Much that passed was little more than might be expected in the period of canvassing the vote, until on December 2, 1876, Marble at Tallahassee telegraphed to Pelton, addressed at Tilden's home,

> Have just received a proposition to hand over at any hour required Tilden decision of Board and certificate of Governor for $200,000.

There was an immediate reply, unsigned:

> Proposition too high.

Then on December 5 Marble telegraphed:

> Proposition failed. Finished yesterday. Tell Tilden to saddle Blackstone [resort to legal proceedings].

On the day after the *Tribune*'s revelations Hewitt was quoted as saying, "I never knew anything about these dispatches."

On October 16 the *Tribune* published more dispatches to "SHOW HOW MR. TILDEN'S REPRESENTATIVES TRIED TO BUY THE VOTE OF SOUTH CAROLINA." Smith W. Weed, Tilden's private secretary, went to Columbia, where on November 14, 1876, he sent this message to Henry Havemeyer (who seems to have been assistant to Pelton):

> Nothing definite yet, but working. Things mixed here. Our party claims Hampton party are trading off Tilden. I don't believe it. . . . Shall I increase to $50,000 if required, to make sure? . . .

Wade Hampton, Democratic candidate for Governor, was more popular than Tilden or than any lesser candidates. Apparently local supporters of Tilden were fearful of arrangements of a vote for Hayes electors in exchange of a vote for Hampton.

"Denmark" replied on the same day:

> You can go to fifty if necessary. Perhaps use future prospects for some part, but you must see that trading is not done. . . . When do you think you can reach conclusion? Keep me advised. . . .

Weed made a long reply on the fifteenth:

> Careful examination certified copies from 21 out of 32 counties, and estimates of balance, show Hampton elected by about 1,400 majority, and Tilden and Democratic State officers behind Hampton from 1,800 to 2,000. Shall have full returns and know exactly to-night . . . .

The situation was complicated because at that moment a suit was pending in the State Supreme Court wherein Democratic citizens sought a writ of prohibition to restrain the Board of State Canvassers [members all Republicans] from doing more than merely to cumulate the figures sent up by local canvassing boards.

On the sixteenth "Denmark" telegraphed,

> Try and make portion payable after votes are [cast], and the other portion after final result. . . .

Weed was telegraphing that same day,

> Board late last night demanded 75,000 for giving us two or three electors. The intercepter will want something besides think ten [thousand]. What shall I do? Get no aid from Hampton party, who, to say the least, are indifferent.

The reply from New York was,

> . . . Should be willing to accept, believe, if Chamberlain and Board unite to prevent trading and expense was made dependent on final success of Tilden in March. . . .

Chamberlain was the Republican candidate for Governor.

On November 18 Weed telegraphed:

> Majority of board have been secured! Cost is 80,000 to be sent as follows: One parcel of 65,000 dollars, one of 10,000, and one of 5,000; all to be five hundred or one thousand bills; notes to be deposited as parties accept and given up upon vote of land of Hampton [i.e., State of South Carolina] being given to Tilden's friends. . . . Do this at once, and have cash ready to reach Baltimore Sunday night. Telegraph decisively whether it will be done. W.

Apparently an encouraging answer was received, for later that day (the eighteenth) Weed sent the following message to Havemeyer:

Shall leave to-night for B. Meet me yourself if prudent. Returning Board say they will do it, sure, and it's worth trying, but result doubtful to my mind. Must get definite answer before 8 o'clock. Statement of vote by Returning Board shows on face Hayes majority [of] 800; one of Tilden's [electors] within 280 of their lowest. Errors can change. W.

Pelton met Weed at Baltimore but he came empty-handed. The two went to New York, apparently to secure funds. The statutory term of the Returning Board, however, was ten days, expiring on November 22. When the bribe was not forthcoming the board certified that the seven Hayes electors had received the majority of the popular vote. Thereupon it went out of business.

Pelton's attempt corruptly to gain an electoral vote in Oregon was a small affair and came to naught. Cipher dispatches in connection with Louisiana were not produced.

The Potter Committee to investigate election frauds could not, of course, neglect this new and most unwelcome development. A subcommittee under the chairmanship of Representative Hunton was sent to New York City, where it held its sessions in the Fifth Avenue Hotel from Wednesday, February 5, 1879, through Saturday. Thomas B. Reed of Maine (later the Speaker) and Frank Hiscock of upstate New York were the minority members, who subjected each witness to a relentless cross-examination. The *Tribune* had published and sold a pamphlet of the telegrams, far more numerous than the few quoted above, and the substantial accuracy of the translations was admitted by the witnesses.

Weed was examined on Wednesday afternoon, and in the evening Major Edward Cooper told of a brief meeting with Pelton at the entry to Tilden's house, just as Pelton was starting for Baltimore; there had been an indefinite mention of sending money. When the request for $60,000 or $70,000 came next day, Cooper showed it to Tilden, who directed that Pelton be called back.

Pelton was questioned all day Thursday, leaving him thoroughly defenseless, and Manton Marble was given the same treatment on Friday.

Tilden appeared on Saturday, accompanied by his brother, also by Bigelow who had attended all the hearings. He swore that he had known nothing of the dealings by Pelton, Weed, and Marble. He was described as appearing ill, with trembling hands and feeble voice. Occasionally he would speak decisively and strike the table, as when he declared his belief that the Returning Board had been bought by the Republicans. Reed and Hiscock pursued that matter until the witness admitted that he had nothing but hearsay to support his opinion.

The effect of Tilden's appearance seemed to be in accord with an unkind characterization in the House a few days earlier, that he was a simple-hearted old man who found himself surrounded by friends, relations, conspirators, and a nephew.[52]

When the Potter Committee made its report it dwelt on the popular majorities for Tilden electors; in Louisiana, "*the returns, as made and forwarded by the Republican election officers to the Returning Board, disclosed a majority* of 6,405 *for the Tilden electors* . . . ." [Italics in original].[53]

But over against that should be set the conclusion of the minority of the committee:

> We are not aware that anything has been found more significant of wrong than the notorious circular of the Democratic campaign committee of 1876, in which they advise the parade of the Democratic clubs on horseback and their marching as organized bodies to "the central rendezvous" for the purpose of *impressing the negroes with a sense of their united strength,* the recommendation of systematic warning to the negroes that "*we have the means to carry them and mean to use them,*" and the like. To ignore this, as the majority have done, forces us to conclude that the time has not yet come when a fair review of the case and a just judgment in regard thereto are possible. [Italics in original.][54]

JUSTICE FIELD

ON SUNDAY, FEBRUARY 4, 1877, "Judge Field called." So Bradley noted in his diary. (Field may have made one other call during the proceedings of the Electoral Commission.[55]) The Florida case was under consideration. Brother David Dudley Field had presented the Democrats' objections on Friday; counsel had been heard on Saturday.

It was inconsiderate for Field to call. Bradley bore the responsibility for deciding whether Tilden or Hayes would be the next President: he was entitled to do his deliberating in privacy, free from unsolicited comment. But Field was exceedingly persistent, and insensitive. Bradley, however, did not permit any "extended discussion."

Field was, as Bradley had written to Kinney, "in the inmost counsels of the Democratic party at all times"; to Hewitt and his associates

---

[52] Hale of Maine, Cong. Rec., 45–3, 610. Jan. 21, 1879. The friends tended soon to fall apart, divided by mutal suspicions and conflicting afterthoughts about how the dispute should have been handled.

[53] H. Rep. No. 140, 45th Cong., 3d Sess., 27.

[54] Ibid., 92.

[55] Letter to Henry B. Dawson on October 28, 1882, where he recalled that "on one or two occasions Judge Field . . . called at my house on a Sunday." Infra, pp. 194–95.

he was their standard of rectitude in all that concerned the Electoral Commission.

The experience of others induced a different estimate. Recall this item in Volume VI[56]: Orville H. Browning of Illinois, who practiced before the Supreme Court, recorded in his diary for February 14, 1866, that

> Just after 3 P.M. Judge Davis of the Supreme Court sent for me to meet him at the room of the Clerk of the Sup. Court . . . . I went over. He wanted to talk with me about a motion I had entered and argued some three weeks ago to set down for argument [two cases] . . . .
>
> Judge Davis told me of the scene in the Consultation room, and then told me to beware of Judge Field—that he was a d m d rascal and dmd rouge [rogue], and to be very cautious about what I said before him.

Justice Davis was honest, warmhearted, uncomplicated; he was known by all to be trustworthy. Field was deficient in those qualities.

In 1874 Walter Q. Gresham (1832–95), the able and conscientious District Judge for Indiana, went to California for recuperation. This was at the urging of Davis, his Circuit Justice. In the course of a letter of September 15 to Davis he wrote[57]:

> I called on Judge Field a few days ago at San Francisco, and found him well and agreeable. . . .
>
> I am astonished to hear so many grave [?] men express themselves as having no confidence in the integrity of Judge Field—and that seems to be the opinion of lawyers as well as others. A very sensible good man, who is on the bench here [San Jose], Judge Belden—told me a few days ago that he was satisfied that Judge F. was a dishonest man, & that the Bar of the State so regarded him. Isn't that awful? There must be something wrong in the Judge's make up else his neighbors would have more respect for him. Everybody here seems to have an exalted opinion of the Judge's learning and ability.

To qualify the speaker as a witness: David Belden (1832–88) came from Connecticut to Marysville, California, about 1853. (That was Field's place of residence until 1857.) Belden moved to Nevada City, about forty miles distant, read law, and was admitted to the bar in 1856. Soon he was the county judge; later he was a state senator. Presently he removed to San Jose, about forty-five miles south of San Francisco. There he served as District Judge, then (under the constitution of 1879) as Judge

---

[56] VI, 137–38, n. 22.   [57] Davis Papers, Ill. State Hist. Soc.

of the Superior Court. A Democrat before the war, he became a strong Unionist.

In this account where hearsay and anonymous statements have by Tilden's friends and by historians been unquestioningly accepted, let it be made plain at once that *it is not believed that Field ever took money for his judicial action.* First, on the ground that this was not in his character; moreover, Brother Cyrus was rich, David Dudley was affluent, and they would have supplied his needs. But "honesty" and "integrity" refer to a larger standard, including candor, absolute fairness, complete disinterestedness in the discharge of a trust. There will be occasion to judge how well Field met that standard.

For instance, a letter Field wrote to Tilden on December 11, 1877. On returning to the East, Field had called on Tilden in New York.[58] The Judge had expressed himself on Bradley's part in the Electoral Commission; after returning to Washington he wrote:

> I did not forget . . . the promise I made to send you a copy I have of Judge Bradley's letter explaining his action on the Electoral Commission,[59] but for several days I could not find it. Having found it I enclose it to you, and also an extract from an article, which appeared in the Newark Daily Advertiser about the same time, and to which the Judge evidently refers in his letter.[60]
> The language of the letter justifies some of the comments of the Press upon the change of views which the Judge experienced shortly before the vote was taken in the Florida case.

We gave Field the benefit of a favorable construction when he was quoted by a reporter for the San Francisco *Exchange*: perhaps he had been misrepresented. But here in his letter he chooses his words. When read critically it is a remarkable production. Without actually affirming it, he treats it as a fact that Bradley changed his views shortly before the vote on Florida. Now in San Francisco Field asserted that Bradley had not read any opinion to him in advance of delivery before the Commission. Did he know Bradley's view or views before *oral* communication? Field did not so assert, and Bradley flatly denied.[61] Field could not know the

---

[58] Tilden Papers, New York Public Library.

[59] That is, the letter written at Stowe on September 2. Supra, p. 135.

[60] An extract, that is, from the *Advertiser* of August 27 repeating the dispatch about the San Francisco *Exchange*, and the statement that Bradley at Edmunds' suggestion put in writing what he was going to hold in the Florida case, which Bradley affirmed in his letter of September 2. Supra, p. 136.

[61] "I read no opinion to either of them [Clifford or Field], and have no recollection of expressing any. If I did, it could only have been suggestively, or in a hypothetical manner, and not intended as a committal of my final judgment or action. . . ." Letter of September 2.

uncommunicated thoughts in Bradley's mind. He would never have been so unlawyerlike as to declare, I know it because I read it in the newspapers. No, the letter is disingenuous: Field was not saying it himself, only that *Bradley's letter justifies* the comments in the press, etc.

Field could be utterly unreasonable when some strong desire was crossed.[62] After the Electorial Commission he became imbued with a desire to attain the Democratic nomination for the Presidency in 1880. His state of mind when Bradley's vote denied the Presidency to Tilden is foreshadowed and aptly described in Field's own opinion for the Court in a case in 1872.[63]

> . . . Controversies involving not merely great pecuniary interests, but the liberty and character of the parties, and, consequently, exciting the deepest feelings, are being constantly determined in those [superior] courts, in which there is great conflict in the evidence and great doubt as to the law which should govern their decision. It is this class of cases which imposes upon the judge the severest labor, and often create in his mind a painful sense of responsibility. Yet it is precisely in this class of cases that the losing party feels most keenly the decision against him, and most readily accepts anything but the soundness of the decision in explanation of the action of the judge. Just in proportion to the strength of his convictions of the correctness of his own view of the case is he apt to complain of the judgment against him, and from complaints of the judgment to pass to the ascription of improper motives to the judge. When the controversy involves questions affecting large amounts of property or relates to a matter of general public concern, or touches the interests of numerous parties, the disappointment occasioned by an adverse decision, often finds vent in imputations of this character, and from the imperfection of human nature this is hardly a subject of wonder. . . .

---

[62] Recall his abuse of Chief Justice Waite when in 1875 he was not assigned the writing of the Court's opinion in United States v. Union Pacific R.R., VII, 593–95.

[63] Bradley v. Fisher, 13 Wall. 335, 348 (1872). Joseph H. Bradley had been counsel to John H. Surratt on his trial in the Criminal Court for the District of Columbia for the murder of President Lincoln. At the conclusion of the trial (in which the jury disagreed) Bradley accosted Judge Fisher, who had presided, as he descended from the bench and threatened to chastise him for supposed discourtesy. For this Bradley was disbarred from practice before the Criminal Court. Thereupon Bradley sued the Judge for damages; from denial of relief below, error was brought to the Supreme Court. Field, J., speaking for the Court, held that the Judge of a superior court is not liable to a civil action for his conduct in the exercise of his jurisdiction, even where it is alleged that he acted maliciously. Because, as Field wrote, "Few persons sufficiently irritated to institute an action against a judge for his judicial acts would hesitate to ascribe any character to the acts which would be essential to the maintaining of the action."

Field was a Judge of strong mind and unusual power; but to an extraordinary degree he brought imperfections of human nature to the work of the Court.

In 1878 on the eighth anniversary of his coming to office Bradley wrote to his sister, "They have been eight years of hard work and poor pay, and immense gratuitous and unfounded abuse. Public life, in this country is a gauntlet through which one passes subject to be struck at by every villain that chooses to do it."

REPRESENTATIVE SAMUEL S. COX

IT WAS INEVITABLE that there would be little understanding of the constitutional issue in the electoral dispute. The dispassionate discussion in the Senate in 1875 and 1876 had seemed too dull to be noticed in the press,[64] and after 1876 no Democrat mentioned it. To Professor Nevins who in 1935 spoke from the point of view of Hewitt in 1877, "a very simple issue of principle" was at stake: the "shining equities" lay with the majority of the popular vote, while on the other side was "a mere disputed punctilio of State Rights."[65] When the Supplementary Enforcement Act of February 21, 1871, was being debated in Congress, Democrats were resentful of federal supervisors of elections for Representatives in Congress. Representative S. S. Cox of New York declared that it would be "an inquisitorial nuisance," a "blow at local independence and self-government."[66] At that moment New York City was under notorious misgovernment administered by William Marcy Tweed, master of municipal corruption with his crowd of obedient lesser Democrats. (Shortly afterwards Tilden attained distinction by putting Tweed behind bars and causing other miscreants to flee the country.) In 1877 when Democrats saw corruption in the Republican regimes in Southern States in respect of the choice of Presidential electors they were demanding federal inquiry and correction. And when the Electoral Commission denied relief, Representative Cox was indignant, as he related in his *Three Decades of Federal Legislation.*[67]

He described Justice Bradley at the moment of decision in the Florida case:

> All eyes are turned to the Jerseyman. . . . Would he save the Supreme Court from the threatened disgrace? . . . Would his party bias bend his judgment on a question involving the most stupendous consequences

---

[64] In the Prologue.
[65] Nevins, *Hewitt*, 323, 370, 372.
[66] Cong. Globe, 41–3, App. 127–32. Feb. 15, 1871.

[67] Providence: J. A. & R. A. Reid, 1886.

ever within the jurisdiction of a court? Pale and trembling, Judge Bradley unfolds his manuscript. He begins to read. He is impressed, apparently, with a sense of the overwhelming responsibility resting upon his conscience and conduct. As he reads, Democratic hopes grow bright and brighter. Justice will dawn at last with auroral splendor. . . . The drift of his argument leads to but one conclusion. . . . Florida's vote, as we all know, belongs to Tilden. Change! The wind suddenly veers, and Mr. Justice Bradley accomplishes a dextrous *non sequitur*. He closes with the assurance that his vote must be given to the counting of Florida for Hayes. . . .

The Democrats of the Commission felt the humiliation of this departure from constitutional methods. . . . Sadder, but wiser men, were the Democrat "seven" when they marched out of the Supreme Court room that memorable afternoon. The chivalric Bayard . . . bore the mien of one whose illusions had been rudely dispelled. . . .[68]

In all essentials that was wrong. The opinion made no dextrous shift in its conclusion, as might be seen by turning to the *Proceedings*. It was Florida's *nunc pro tunc* expedients that were "departures from constitutional methods" of electing a President. The story of Bradley's switch in opinion goes back to the *Sun*'s "Interesting Historical Fact" of August 4, 1877, and was untrue. Bradley's opinion was in accord with Bayard's own views as expressed in the debates prior to the election; if Bayard felt humiliation it should have been for his own apostasy; but he had forecast that on March 25, 1876, when at the close of the debates he admitted that he and his political friends—and Morton and his friends—might not be able "to look at facts imbued with all the color of party feeling, yet decide them as though we were entirely indifferent to the result of our decision."[69]

Ben Perley Poore, newspaper correspondent and compiler of the *Congressional Directory*, published in 1886 *Perley's Reminiscences of Sixty Years in the National Metropolis*, reprinting articles that had appeared in the weekly *Boston Budget*. This contained the story that Justice Bradley had originally written an opinion in the Florida case favoring the Tilden electors and had submitted it to two of his colleagues, but had afterwards changed it to favor Hayes.

Justice Bradley wrote to Poore on March 24, 1887, noting that he had repeated "a slanderous newspaper article respecting me," and affirming in detail that "The whole story is a fabrication, absolutely false in all its particulars, without any ground of truth whatever . . . ." He was "indignant" at the re-publication.

---

[68] At 653–54. Cox bore a sobriquet, "Sunset" Cox, derived from his glowing description of a sunset in the *Ohio* *Statesman* of May 10, 1853. See D.A.B.

[69] Supra, p. 36.

On the twenty-eighth Poore replied to express regret: he would publish a retraction in the *Boston Budget*, and had instructed the publishers of his book to cancel the objectionable matter and substitute another sentence. An unequivocal retraction appeared in the *Budget* on April 10, 1887.

On May 29 the author died. The evil "Perley" did lived after him; the correction was interred in the *Boston Budget*.

The defamation of Bradley by Dana's *Sun* for his participation in the Electoral Commission began on February 1, 1877, increased in bitterness, and was continued when it served only to nourish Dana's enmity. All this emptied into the stream of rumor.

PART FOUR

Nevins' Hewitt
and the "Secret History"

"The spontaneous tendency of man is to yield assent to affirmations, and to reproduce them, without even clearly distinguishing them from the results of his own observation. In everyday life do we not accept indiscriminately, without any kind of verification, hearsay reports, anonymous and unguaranteed statements, "documents" of indifferent or inferior authority? It takes a special reason to induce us to take the trouble to examine into the origin and value of a document on the history of yesterday; otherwise, if there is no outrageous improbability in it, and as long as it is not contradicted, we swallow it whole, we pin our faith to it, we hawk it about, and, if need be, embellish it in the process. . . ."

Introduction aux études historiques by Charles V. Langlois and Charles Seignobos, Professors at the Sorbonne (Paris: Librairie Hachette, 1898). Translation by G. G. Berry as *Introduction to the Study of History* (New York: Henry Holt & Co., 1909), 69.

FOR THE EXCERPT ABOVE I make a personal explanation. I began graduate study in 1919–20 at the University of Illinois under Professor Evarts B. Greene, head of the Department of History and a fine scholar. He drew the attention of his seminar to the introduction for beginners by Professors Langlois and Seignobos. When more than half a century later I came to the Electoral Commission and saw that I must deal critically with Professor Nevins' biography of Hewitt insofar as it relied upon Hewitt's "Secret History" of the disputed election, my mind flashed back to Langlois and Seignobos, where I found their warning against reliance upon hearsay, unconfirmed statements, and improbability. Those were precisely the ingredients of the "Secret History" as supported by Professor Nevins.

Late in the biography, at page 543, the author relates that

As the years passed, in telling his stories [Hewitt] sometimes indulged in a pardonable tinge of dramatization or exaggeration, a product of his enkindling imagination. Like Sir Walter Scott, he liked to dress up an old anecdote with cocked hat and walking stick. This exaggeration, late in life, sometimes crept into even a public speech. Once in particular, shortly before his death, some overdrawn statements about his "secret mission" from Minister Dayton to Minister Adams in 1862, which Charles Francis Adams, Jr., at once disproved, caused him much vexation. But in conversation allowance could be made for it, and it merely added to the charm of his abounding vitality.

Responding to my request, James H. Hutson, Chief of the Manuscript Division of the Library of Congress, found a full account in the *Proceedings of the Massachusetts Historical Society* for October 1903.[1]

Queen Victoria had died on January 22, 1901, in the eighty-second year of her age and the sixty-fourth of her reign, the vestige of a memorable era. The Chamber of Commerce of the State of New York took notice of the passing at its monthly meeting on February 7. Among the speakers was Abram S. Hewitt, himself in his seventy-ninth year. Here is his story:

He referred to occasions where the Queen had shown her kindly feeling for the United States,

and as to one of these, I am, I suppose the only living witness, and this explains why I accepted the invitation of your President to appear here and do what I have grown very reluctant to do—make an address upon any public occasion. It happened that in 1862 I was sent by the Government on a confidential mission to England and France. In the course of my work I had the most intimate relations with Minister Charles Francis Adams and with Judge Dayton, who was the Minister to France. One afternoon I received a message from Judge Dayton asking me to come to the Embassy, where he asked me if I could leave for London that night. I told him I could if the matter were important. He said a piece of information had just come to his notice which he could not trust to the telegraph or even to the post. That he wished a special messenger to go to Mr. Adams and report to him what had happened. I told him I would go, and then he said, "I have just received information from a confidential source that the Emperor Napoleon III has proposed to the British Government to recognize the Confederacy at once. I am sure that Mr. Adams has no knowledge of the fact. I want you to proceed to London to-night, see him as early as possible in the morning, and communicate the information to him." I went to London. I saw Mr. Adams very early the next morning, as soon as he was visible, and I told him what Judge Dayton had said. I found that

---

[1] 2d Series, XVII.

Mr. Adams had already an intimation from some source that the recognition was impending. However, he said he would call upon Lord John Russell, the Minister for Foreign Affairs, and ascertain what was proposed to be done. He made the call and I waited for his return. He told me that he had seen Lord John Russell and had asked him distinctly whether any proposition had been received for the recognition of the Confederacy. He received an evasive reply. It was evident to him that something of a very serious nature was on foot. But Lord John Russell declined to communicate any definite information on the subject. He told me that he then said to Lord John Russell, "I desire an audience with the Queen." Lord John Russell replied that it was not usual for Ministers to have an audience with the Queen; that all communications must pass through the Foreign Office. I believe—perhaps General Wilson will correct me if I am wrong—that there is a usage by which only Ambassadors can demand an interview with the Sovereign, and that Ministers—at that time we had no Ambassadors—that Ministers had no such right, but that it might be accorded as a matter of courtesy. Mr. Adams said he told Lord John Russell that he hoped he would arrange it; but at any rate he was going to Windsor that day in person, and would send a request asking the Queen to hear him personally. He went to Windsor. Whether Lord John Russell made any communication or not, I do not know. Mr. Adams saw the Queen in the presence of Prince Albert; told her why he had come, and he said to her: "If there is any foundation for this information which I have received, I appeal to your Majesty to prevent so great a wrong, which will result in universal war, for I can assure your Majesty that the American people are prepared to fight the whole world rather than give up the Union." (Applause.) He said that the Queen, in the most gracious manner, replied, "Mr. Adams, give yourself no concern. My Government will not recognize the Confederacy." (Applause.)

Now, this may be a very inappropriate course of remark for this occasion, but I am anxious to leave these facts preserved in the records of the Chamber of Commerce. I think it is very likely that the despatch of Mr. Adams to Secretary Seward contains the information which I have given you here, but I have never seen it, and I do not know that it has ever been published.

NOTE: Prince Albert had died on December 14, 1861.

Charles Francis Adams, Jr., writes of his astonishment when he read of Hewitt's speech:

It is almost needless to say that when I the next morning read the abstract of Mr. Hewitt's remarks in the report of the proceedings of the Chamber of Commerce, I was greatly surprised. I thought myself tolerably familiar with what had taken place in London during the period in question, but I had never before heard even a whisper of any such masterful stroke of diplomacy as here described. The vagueness of the reminiscence, of course, at once attracted my notice. No details of time or place were given. The statements made bore no connection with recognized events. Accordingly, I at once wrote to Mr. Hewitt, with whom I had an acquaintance of long standing,—and for whom I entertained great personal respect,—asking him to give me approximately the date of the occurrences he had described. I wished to verify them by reference to Mr. Adams's diary and papers. Under date of February 19, 1901, I got a reply, from which I quote the following:—

"Of course the language quoted by me is entirely from memory, and probably expresses the impression left upon my mind of what was said to me by your father rather than his exact words. As to time, my impression is that it must have been as early as the month of July. No doubt, as your father kept a diary, you will have little difficulty in fixing the time of his audience with the Queen, but my recollection is that it occurred about the time when the Confederate cruisers were on the stocks at Birkenhead. Your father asked me to examine these vessels, and I went to the shipyard [Lairds'] and with considerable difficulty got admittance. One of the ships was the 'Alabama,' but I am not sure whether she had any name at the time or not.

"After you have made your investigation I shall be glad to be apprised of what information you have secured on the subject."

Mr. Adams continued:

The correspondence here closed. I refrained from complying with Mr. Hewitt's request that he should be "apprised of what information [I] secured on the subject," for a very slight examination satisfied me that, beyond peradventure, the story was in the main but the hallucination of an old man. Indeed, so far as the historian of the future was concerned, it hardly merited attention. It was so very vague and hung together so loosely, it set not only established usage but probability so utterly aside,—showing an almost equal disregard of English constitutional law and of Court etiquette,—that it could have been accepted by no writer of even average care. Nevertheless, coming directly and in a way so aggressive, from Mr. Hewitt, it excited my curiosity. Where and what was the residuum of fact? Presumably there must be some, be it more or less, could I but find it out.

After this search for some residuum of historical fact he wrote that

In the case of Mr. Hewitt I have been obliged at last to conclude that in every part the incident was imaginary.

This, and my reasons for it, I did not of course care to impart to Mr. Hewitt. He was an old man; and that mentally he was failing scarcely needed to be said. Why occasion him mortification? So I filed away the copies he sent me of the proceedings at the Chamber of

Commerce meeting, and deferred all further investigation until he should have passed away. This occurred on the morning of Sunday, 18th of January last [1903]; and, shortly after, I left the country. . . .

On returning and making further comparison with known facts, Adams was

forced to conclude that the whole account of that dramatic Windsor morning call with its royal though strangely autocratic if informal assurances of peace and good-will, was a pure figment of the imagination,—"such stuff as dreams are made on." In this case the analysis yields positively no residuum whatever of historical fact.

If Professor Nevins had stated frankly the story of the "Secret Mission" *before* telling about the "Secret History" at pages 320 and following, readers, and especially historians, would have been put on notice: if Hewitt's mind was unreliable in his seventy-ninth year, there was reason to doubt his credibility six years earlier when he rewrote and amplified his recollection of the great controversy nineteen years before.

Notwithstanding this shaky background Nevins appears to have had absolute confidence in Hewitt's story. And in his own mind he had a firm view of the meaning of the election:

No one could deny that a preponderance of the American people preferred Tilden for the Presidency. His majority over all exceeded 157,000, his plurality over Hayes 250,000; if we exclude the illiterate and ignorant negroes of the South, these margins would be increased by an additional quarter million and more. Yet the shining equities of the situation, the undeniable verdict of the electorate, received not the slightest consideration. This was political war, and in war all is fair. Any weapon was proper if it had the appearance of legality, and the great object was not to give the country the President it voted for, but to fight out the battle till every ruse, every technicality, every bluff, had been exhausted.[2]

To be sure, the Fifteenth Amendment in force since March 1870 had declared that

The right of citizens of the United States to vote shall not be denied or abridged by the United States or by any State on account of race, color, or previous condition of servitude.

---

[2] Allan Nevins, *Abram S. Hewitt, with Some Account of Peter Cooper* (New York: Harper & Brothers, 1935), 322–23.

Even so, "the shining equities of the situation," and "the undeniable verdict of the electorate," should in Nevins' view have been considered—evidently by deciding for Tilden.

THE "SECRET HISTORY"

ABRAM S. HEWITT (1822–1903) of New York, a wealthy iron manufacturer and Representative in Congress, was chairman of the Democratic National Committee in the Election of 1876. Two years later he wrote his secret history of the disputed election, which he rewrote and amplified in 1895. This was incorporated, with supplementary comment, in Professor Nevins' *Abram S. Hewitt* in 1935. Our concern will be with this work as it applies to the Electoral Commission and in particular to the Justices. Hewitt's integrity and public spirit are freely acknowledged. He had devoted his remarkable skill to the campaign for Tilden who, in Nevins' words, was "a willing but laodicean aspirant for the Presidency," a man of "cold disposition, scholarly tastes, and precarious health."[3] Here was something less than an inspiring chief, and Hewitt wished to leave a vindication of his own conduct of the campaign. To the end of his life he believed that he had been more instrumental than any one else in securing acceptance of the Electoral Commission, and he regarded this as one of his chief public services.[4] After the decision there had been no dearth of opinions on how matters might better have been handled. One must doubt that Hewitt wrote on behalf of future scholarship; it is evident that he did not even pay attention to the Journal in the *Proceedings of the Electoral Commission*. The account speaks from a time when rumor passed for fact, and rewriting in 1895 would not have increased the accuracy of his recollection.

We quote from the point where Hewitt wrote that after Justice Davis had been elected a Senator, and Justices Swayne and Hunt had been excluded for what seemed good reasons,[5]

> Practically, therefore, the choice was limited to Justice Bradley, whom I had personally known for many years in New Jersey as a very able lawyer and a man of the highest integrity. The confidence which I felt in him was shared by Mr. Tilden, but in order to make assurance doubly sure I requested a mutual friend of Judge Bradley and myself, the late John G. Stevens of Trenton, N.J.,[6] to confer with Judge Bradley to ascertain whether he felt that he could decide the questions which

---

[3] Ibid., 306–07.
[4] Ibid., 389.
[5] Ibid., 367–68.

[6] John G. Stevens (1820–86) was chief engineer of the Camden & Amboy Railroad, in whose management Bradley had had a significant part.

would come before the Commission without prejudice or party feeling. The report of Mr. Stevens was entirely satisfactory. Judge Bradley was therefore selected with the distinct approval of the Democratic representatives, reinforced by the favorable judgment of Judge Clifford and Judge Field, who assured me that absolute reliance could be placed upon the radical fairness of Judge Bradley. In fact, they both stated that it was absurd to fear that any Justice of the Supreme Court would be governed by partisan feeling or influence, and this was in accordance with the general feeling in Congress and throughout the country.

To this Nevins adds, "Bradley was not a decided partisan."

Four pages later Nevins writes,[7] "Thus the crucial date approached—the date of February 7. The arguments on the questions of receiving detailed evidence as to the actual Florida vote, and of going behind the returns, were concluded late on Monday, February 5. [Actually, at 3:45 p.m.] The Commission withheld its decision until Wednesday. [Actually, there *was* no decision until Wednesday.] All day Tuesday, while it deliberated in secret from ten in the morning until nearly eight o'clock at night, the keenest anxiety prevailed among party leaders as to the stand which it would take. Everyone believed that the fourteen members first named would align themselves seven to seven, and that the decision would rest with Judge Bradley. [This contradicts the statement above that it was absurd to fear that any Justice would be governed by partisan feeling.] As it happened, Judge Bradley had not indicated to the secret session that day how he would vote. There was therefore a moment of extreme tension when, at three o'clock on Wednesday afternoon, Justice Miller offered a motion which in effect declared that the Commission would refuse to go behind the face of the official returns from Florida. . . ."

The Justices had spoken in turn that day: first Field, then Strong, then Miller. Then, as Garfield's diary records, *Bradley began speaking at 2:13*. After him Clifford gave his opinion, Edmunds made some remarks, and at three o'clock the vote was taken.

"Since these returns gave the electoral votes to Hayes, this was the crucial question. It brings us to Bradley's opinion and the dramatic part of Hewitt's narrative":

> The history of this opinion forms an important feature in the final outcome of the electoral count. As stated above, Mr. John G. Stevens was the intimate friend of Judge Bradley. He passed the night previous to the rendition of the judgment in the Florida case at my house. About midnight he returned from a visit to Judge Bradley, and reported to

---

[7] Nevins, *Hewitt*, 368.

General Richard Taylor, who was also staying with me, and to Senator Gibson, who was awaiting his return, that he had just left Judge Bradley after reading his opinion in favor of counting the vote of the Democratic electors of the State of Florida. Such a judgment insured the election of Tilden to the Presidency with three votes to spare above the necessary majority. We parted, therefore, with the assurance that all further doubt as to the Presidency was at rest. . . .

COMMENT: Hewitt ignored the firm restraint within the Court against disclosure of deliberations prior to formal announcement. That Bradley would have disclosed an opinion on a matter before the Commission was simply unbelievable.

An instance of this secrecy in a matter less grave than Hewitt's supposition is presented in connection with *Woodon v. Murdock*, 22 Wallace 351 (1874). The issue was whether the Missouri legislature could release the Missouri Pacific Railroad Company from a debt to the State. The local press published rumors that the Supreme Court had decided in favor of the company. In alarm, Britton A. Hill, counsel for the State, wrote to the Chief Justice to inquire into the accuracy of the rumor. Waite replied: "No such announcement has been made in the case" and "it would be highly improper for me to inform you, or any one else whether a decision has yet been reached." Hill apologized, explaining that he had not sought to learn what was the decision. Waite accepted the apology, but went on to make this statement:

> No one can deprecate more than I do, the idea that the Court, over which I have the honor to preside, can permit its secrets to be divulged. The importance of the cases that come before us, as well as all the proprieties of judicial work, demand that, until our labors as a court are ended, the secrets of the consultation room should be kept inviolate. . . . [T]he implied suspicion of a disregard of this rule, which your letter contained, causes my note in reply.
>
> [W]hile, therefore, I now fully accept your explanation you must permit me to express the hope that, in the future, neither you nor any one will for a moment even, entertain such a suspicion, until we have given better evidence than I think we have already, that we are unmindful of the proprieties of the high position to which we have been called.[8]

Another illustration of the insistence on secrecy in the deliberations of the Court may be seen in the following note by Justice Bradley to John G. Nicolay, Marshal of the Court, in 1872:

---

[8] C. Peter Magrath, *Morrison R. Waite: The Triumph of Character* (New York: Macmillan Co., 1963), 277–78.

Part Four: *Nevins'* Hewitt *and the "Secret History"*

Dear Sir:—

I hope you will take care that no person whatever shall see or handle papers or books left on our desks. We often make *memoranda* which we do not want inspected by counsel or others.—We leave our papers here in confidence that they will be sacred and untouched. It would be very inconvenient to be obliged to lock every thing up. The drawers will not hold some of our documents and papers.

Yours truly
J. P. Bradley

I would suggest that there should always be some person here to see that nothing is touched or examined—when the room's open or accessible to others.[9]

Bradley would have considered any writing he had made on a matter before the Commission to be "sacred"; a disclosure such as Hewitt "remembered" would have been an egregious breach of duty.

We resume Hewitt's account:[10]

I attended the delivery of the judgment the next day [Wednesday, February 7] without the slightest intimation from any quarter that Judge Bradley had changed his mind. In fact, the reading of the opinion until the few concluding paragraphs were reached was strictly in accord with the report of Mr. Stevens.

COMMENT: *The statement could not be true:* the meeting on that day was *closed*. If Hewitt had consulted the record he could have seen that his supposition was erroneous, and the same may be said of his biographer. As the press reported, people waiting outside learned about what had been done only when the doors were opened at 3:45 P.M.

At this point it seems in order to treat it as settled that Stevens saw no opinion by Bradley and that Hewitt did not attend the meeting of the Commission on the morrow. The record was against him, and we know that his secret recollections are highly suspect.

Continuing Hewitt's narrative,

The change was made between midnight and sunrise. Mr. Stevens afterwards informed me that it was due to a visit to Judge Bradley by Senator Frelinghuysen and Secretary Robeson, made after his departure. Their appeals to Judge Bradley were said to have been reinforced by the persuasion of Mrs. Bradley. Whatever the fact may have been, Judge Bradley himself in a subsequent letter addressed to the Newark *Daily Advertiser* admitted that he had written a favorable opinion which on subsequent reflection he saw fit to modify.

---

[9] Nicolay Papers, L.C. | [10] Nevins, *Hewitt,* 371.

For the moment we pass over the story of the nocturnal visit. After stating it Hewitt wrote, "Whatever the fact may have been . . . ." Seemingly he felt some doubt about what was no more than a rumor.

The remainder of the paragraph refers to what Justice Bradley wrote in his letter of September 2 to the *Advertiser:*

> In my private examination of the principal questions . . . I wrote and re-wrote the arguments and considerations on both sides as they occurred to me, sometimes being inclined to one view of the subject, and sometimes to the other. . . .

Each party wanted him to consider *its* side, and could not rightly object if he considered their opponents' as well. That was doing his duty, but Hewitt calls it an "admission."

Nevins followed in a passage that demonstrates his own want of understanding:[11]

> But he [Bradley] explained that he had followed the alleged practice of some jurists in writing out two opinions, thus giving the arguments on both sides, and intending to accept in the end whichever seemed the stronger. In a world where anything is possible, this is possible. But it is certainly hard to believe. If the practise mentioned ever existed, it was excessively rare. There was no need to write out the arguments, for they lay in printed form before the judges. Bradley's quick, clear mind was one of the last on the tribunal to require such aid. Moreover, the vital question of going behind the returns was not complex and did not require elaborate argument—it was a very simple issue of principle. Finally, Bradley's opinion did, as Hewitt writes, include various arguments suggesting an inclination to Tilden's side up to the last few paragraphs. And Stevens' accusation is strongly reenforced by a statement which his colleague on the Commission, Justice Field, shortly sent to Tilden in commenting upon the Newark *Advertiser* letter. "The language of the letter," he wrote, "justified some of the comments of the press upon *the change of views which the judge experienced shortly before the vote was taken in the Florida case.*" [Italics in Nevins' statement.]

Bradley made no allegation of any such practice: the idea was an *invention* by Nevins, who proceeds to heap ridicule on what he had imputed to Bradley.

Then "There was no need to write out the arguments . . . ." That seems to say, copy out what you see in print. No conscientious judge would be so docile. Actually, in the main the substance of a presentation

---

[11] Ibid., 372.

was by oral argument and questioning. Time was short and proceedings moved rapidly. In the published *Proceedings,* a volume of 1,087 pages, the Appendix of Briefs occupied only pages 729 to 816.

To Nevins,

> the vital question of going behind the returns was not complex and did not require elaborate argument—it was a very simple issue of principle. . . .

If Nevins' curiosity had led him to study *Counting Electoral Votes,* he might have learned about the Senate debates in 1875 and 1876, prior to the election. He might have read what Bayard, leading Democrat, had affirmed on February 25, 1875, as his view of the Constitution:[12]

> And nowhere is power given to either House of Congress to pass upon the election, either the manner or the fact, of electors for President and Vice-President; and if the Congress . . . , either one or both Houses, shall assume, under the guise or pretext of telling or counting a vote, to decide the fact of the election of electors who are to form the college . . . , then they will have taken upon themselves an authority for which I, for one, can find no warrant in this charter of limited powers. . . .

Bayard's view was also that of Thurman, Democrat, and of Frelinghuysen, Republican, most thoughtful participants in the debates. It was also the holding of Justice Bradley.

It was only in the light of the election returns that the "states' rights" position of the Democratic party was reversed. In Oregon three Republicans had been chosen as electors: one of them had been a postmaster and his eligibility was questioned. On November 15, 1876, Hewitt as chairman of the Democratic National Committee telegraphed to Governor Grover that the person receiving the next highest number of votes should be counted by the canvassers and certified by the Governor.[13]

> This will force Congress to go behind the certificate, and open the same to get into the merits of all cases, which is not only just, but which will relieve the embarrassment of the situation.

Returning now to Nevins' paragraph: it was bootless to say that various arguments—unspecified—in Bradley's opinion suggested an inclination to Tilden's side.

---

[12] *Counting,* 472.

[13] Part One at p. 43.

Finally, Justice Field's letter of December 11, 1877, to Tilden justifying comments upon Bradley's change of views: that received appropriate censure in Part Three's collection of instances of gratuitous abuse.

In his eagerness to portray Justice Bradley as a vacillating creature, Nevins put in this footnote to page 373:

> Note that O. O. Stealey says in *Forty Years in the Press Gallery*, p. 269: "George F. Edmunds . . . as a member of the Electoral Commission stiffened up Judge Bradley more than once when the latter was wavering."

COMMENT: The title is erroneous: the book is *Twenty Years in the Press Gallery*. The author's first sentence is

> When I first came to Washington, at the short session of the Forty-seventh Congress, the House membership was 323, and the Senate 76. . . .

That session ran from December 4, 1882. Stealey was not present in 1877. At pages 268–69 we find nothing by Stealey, but a brief sketch about Senator Edmunds by F. A. Richardson, a reporter, containing that one sentence about Bradley. No authority is given; no occasion is mentioned where that stiffening occurred. Of what rational value is the sentence? But Professor Nevins lugs it in.

James Ford Rhodes in Volume VII of his *History of the United States* quoted, disapprovingly, a Democratic charge that "when Bradley was wavering, Miller with partisan argument and overbearing disposition" brought Bradley to his point of view.[14] Now Edmunds is added to the story of bringing pressure. To know such a matter one would have had to be very close to the intimacies of the Commission. Even aside from the absence of any authority, one does well to doubt on the ground that however anxious Miller and Edmunds may have been, their own sense of propriety would have restrained them.

The rumor of the nocturnal meeting, repeated by Stevens, which Hewitt had dropped, ["Whatever the fact may have been . . . ."], Nevins picked up and let his imagination take wings.

For comparison one should have one finger inserted at the place in Part Three where Bradley's letter of September 2, 1877 appears, denying the charge that he had changed his view over the night of February 6–7.[15]

---

[14] Volume VII (New York: Macmillan Co., 1906), 282.
An appreciation of Rhodes, businessman-turned-historian, by Dumas Malone may be found in the *Dictionary of American Biography*.

[15] Supra, p. 135.

Part Four: *Nevins' Hewitt and the "Secret History"*

Nevins wrote:

> Stevens' statement indicates that up to midnight on February 6–7, Bradley accepted the Democratic view, but after midnight yielded to other influences. What were these influences? "During the whole sitting of the Commission," Bradley wrote late in 1877, "I had no private discussion whatever on the subjects at issue with any person interested *on the Republican side,* and but very few words with any person. Indeed, I sedulously sought to avoid all discussion *outside of the Commission itself.*" But he does not deny here that he read his opinion to his old friend Stevens, for Stevens was on the Democratic side; nor does his statement carry a denial that he talked with Frelinghuysen after the departure of Stevens, for Frelinghuysen was on the Commission. For thirty years Bradley and Frelinghuysen had been the two leading attorneys at the New Jersey bar, and in perhaps a majority of the highly important cases during that period had been retained either as associates or opponents: there was a long intimacy between them. Hewitt was later told that after midnight Frelinghuysen had rung at Judge Bradley's door; that he had pleaded with Bradley to abandon the Democratic position; and that Mrs. Bradley, a highly religious woman and a strong partisan, had come downstairs in her dressing gown and prayed with her husband. In the end, Bradley had yielded to their argument that, whatever the strict legal equities, it would be a national disaster if the government fell into Democratic hands. Perhaps still other influences were at work. Roscoe Conkling, in his famous assault on the Hayes Administration in the Senate on February 3, 1879, read a letter showing that the Administration had begged a lucrative job for Justice Bradley's son in the New York Custom House, alleging "manifest reasons." The Texas Pacific Railroad lobby, which confessedly feared Tilden and hoped for favors from Hayes, may have instilled additional zeal into some of Bradley's friends. . . . [Italics by Nevins.]

COMMENT: Ignoring Justice Bradley's statement to the contrary, Nevins accepts Stevens' rumor of the post-midnight change of opinion. He repeats the canard that Bradley "read his opinion to his old friend Stevens." Presumably what Bradley had in mind when he wrote "any person" not a Republican was that after he had voted with the Democrats on February 7 to receive evidence on the eligibility of Humphreys, Stockton and Gilchrist had called on him the following morning about submitting a brief on that question, as Stockton informed Tilden.

Certainly Bradley was free to converse with Frelinghuysen, but that did not place him in company with Robeson in the wee hours of the morning. The story of what was said in pleading with the Justice was an invention and a giveaway, for the language is unmistakably Nevins'. The description of Mrs. Bradley, "highly religious" and "a strong partisan," is unsupported. The dressing gown and the prayer could have been known only by a person present in the room. None of the four persons mentioned would have blabbed: then who would have seen? Was there a snoop in the room?

Nevins asks what other influences were at work? Here he treats as present to Bradley's mind in the early hours of February 7, 1877, conditions not then in existence, such as the inauguration of Hayes and the lucrative job in the Custom House. Had Bradley fallen so low that he would have cast his vote for the Florida electors in the hope of receiving a job for his son? But if he was so abandoned in his morals, would he not have foreseen that if he voted for the Tilden electors the hungry Democrats would do still more to reward him?

Did Nevins actually believe that Bradley had sunk so low? Did he suppose that Texas & Pacific lobbyists could instanter make firm the decision to which (according to Nevins) Bradley had already been persuaded by Frelinghuysen and Robeson? Had not Nevins lost touch with reality?

Charles Bradley reached the age of twenty on August 31, 1877. It was just at this moment that the Justice came to Stowe after the trying months of circuit work and the ensuing delay in Washington. The boy did not aspire to enter a profession, and on September 11 set out for New York City in search of a job. Next day the Justice wrote to him:

> I don't know when I have felt more sad than to let you leave me with so little help as you did . . . . I do hope you will be able to find a good place, though it is far from being a promising time for it. I think I shall come down to N York a few days in advance so as to give you some help if I can. . . . Be of good heart, my dear son, and resolve to push your way somehow—and remember that it can only be done by rigid economy and perseverance.
> My blessing be with you—and God's blessing also.[16]

Rhodes' account of the Electoral Commission was notably well informed and objective. He restates Bradley's denial of the story of his changing his opinion and the nocturnal visit, on which Rhodes declares, "Beyond question, every word which Bradley has written concerning this matter may be implicitly believed."[17]

When the Electoral Commission Act of January 29, 1877,[18] was in the course of passage it was supposed that Justice Davis would be the fifth judicial member. Coincidentally, however, Davis was being elected a Senator by the Illinois legislature, whereupon he refused to serve on the Commission. Hewitt, dismayed, supposed that this was a result of Republican intrigue. When in the outcome Hayes had become President, Hewitt declared that

---

[16] Bradley Papers, N.J. Hist. Soc.
[17] VII, 282.

[18] 19 Stat. 227.

If Senator Davis had remained on the bench and acted as the 15th member of the Electoral Commission in lieu of Judge Bradley, the Democratic Party would have owed him a debt of gratitude. As it is, it is due to him, and him alone, that Mr. Tilden was not inaugurated to the office to which he was elected by the people.[19]

Of two pertinent facts Hewitt was uninformed. First, it was due to Pelton, Tilden's nephew, seeking to create a feeling of obligation on the part of Davis, that the Illinois legislature had been induced to act as it did. Second, Davis' reaction to Justice Bradley's judgment in the Commission was that "No good lawyer, not a strict partisan, could decide otherwise."[20]

Professor Nevins' performance did not measure up to the elementary teaching of Langlois and Seignobos: he was wrong in putting faith in Hewitt's "Secret History," and in embellishing it in the process. He detracted from the good name of Justice Bradley. And he led into error younger historians who trusted him.

"SHINING EQUITIES" AND "STRICT LEGAL EQUITIES"

GENERAL FRANCIS CHANNING BARLOW (1834–96), a man of extraordinary merit,[21] was among the Republicans who were sent to Florida to observe the canvassing of the vote. Hewitt wrote what was to be seen:[22]

local returns which on the surface gave Tilden a clear majority; returns canvassed with barefaced partisanship; many Democratic precincts and one whole county thrown out, sometimes on flimsiest pretexts; Republican precincts counted even when open to grave objections; the final

---

[19] Charles C. Tansill, *The Congressional Career of Thomas Francis Bayard, 1869–1885* (Washington, D.C.: Georgetown University Press, 1946), 170 note 99. Hewitt, Ms.

[20] Willard L. King, *Lincoln's Manager, David Davis* (Cambridge, Mass.: Harvard University Press, 1960), 292–93.

[21] (1834–1896). A graduate of Harvard College and a member of the New York bar, he enlisted in the army on April 19, 1861, and next day was married. In 1862 he was severely wounded, and promoted to brigadier general. In 1863, again severely wounded and left for dead, he was nursed back to health by his devoted wife. Back in service, in 1864 his health broke down under the strain of battle, and his wife died. He went on leave and was breveted major general. In April 1865, back on duty in command of a division, he performed distinguished service leading to Lee's surrender at Appomattox, and he was placed in command of a corps.

Back in civil life, he was elected secretary of state of New York in 1865, and filled that post until he became the attorney general, wherein he prosecuted the Tweed Ring.

His last public service was his report on the election in Florida in 1876.

In 1922 the State of New York erected a monument in memory of Barlow on the battlefield of Gettysburg.

[22] Nevins, *Hewitt*, 329.

result, proclaimed December 5, giving Hayes the electoral vote by majorities of which the lowest was 924. General Francis C. Barlow, who concludes that the Tilden electors have majorities of 30 to 55, and urges one of the Republican members of the Board to give Tilden the State; careful later analysis proves almost conclusively that Tilden carried Florida.

Barlow was certainly making a most conscientious review of the situation. But Hewitt omits the following part of Barlow's letter to President Grant:[23]

> I may say here that I have no doubt that in deciding this case the judgment of the canvassing-board was much affected by the example set by the democratic House of Representatives in the election case of Platt against Goode, in which the vote of a whole county giving a large republican majority was rejected for the sole reason that a few unimportant words of attestation upon a county return were omitted although a copy correctly attested and certified was produced. The decision was far more flagrantly wrong than any made in the Florida case . . . .

Platt v. Goode[24] was a protracted controversy, bitter as it was fought out in Virginia and bitter as continued in the House, where the Democratic majority overrode the committee report in which two Democrats had joined with the minority members. In the result John J. Goode, Jr., was on July 28, 1876, confirmed in the seat by a vote of 107 to 95.

Goode served as Solicitor General in the first Cleveland Administration from May 1885 to August 1886.

More immediately of concern in our examination of the Electoral Commission is the companion case of *Abbott v. Frost,* decided in favor of the Democratic challenger on July 14, 1876.[25]

ABBOTT v. FROST

THIS WAS A CONTEST brought by Josiah G. Abbott to gain the seat of Rufus S. Frost, Member-elect to the 44th Congress. The basis of the challenge and the holding of the majority of the Committee on Elections are taken verbatim from the summary in the *Digest of Contested Election Cases in the House of Representatives, 1789–1901.*

---

[23] S. Rep. 611, Part IV, p. 12, 44th Cong. 2d Sess. Feb. 5, 1877.
[24] *Digest of Contested Election*

Cases in the House of Representatives, 1789–1901, 318.
[25] Ibid., 314–18.

Part Four: *Nevins' Hewitt and the "Secret History"*

Contestant charged that the ballots, check list, and return of the Fourth Ward of Chelsea were not returned forthwith by a constable, but were returned the next morning by a policeman; that certain votes cast for him without giving his name in full had not been counted for him, and made general charges of fraud, bribery, and illegal voting.

The law required the officers of election to count the votes, and after making out their returns to seal up the ballots and forward them forthwith by a constable or ward officer to the city clerk's office. The count in the other wards of Chelsea was completed by 9 o'clock in the evening and the election papers regularly forwarded, but in the Fourth Ward the ballots were not returned until after 1 o'clock. The ballots were sealed up and given to a police officer, who carried them to the city clerk's office, and finding it closed, took them into the marshal's office and left them with the captain of the night watch. The next morning at 7 o'clock he received the envelope from the night watchman, found that the seals had not been tampered with, and delivered it to the city clerk. The ballots were afterwards recounted by the board of aldermen, with the ballots of other precincts, and found to agree with the returns regularly forwarded on the night of the election to the city marshal's office.

The committee held that the law had been violated in not returning the ballots forthwith to the city clerk's office, in forwarding them by an officer not authorized by law, and in leaving them for several hours in the custody of an unauthorized person.

The majority of the committee reported that "the provisions of the statute . . . are not merely formal and directory, but vital and essential . . . ." It had been "totally and unblushingly disregarded" in the Fourth Ward.

The minority of the committee held that "The law which was violated was clearly directory, and all that was proved was that the ballots were not returned as promptly as they might have been, were carried by a police officer instead of a constable, and were left sealed with a night watchman because the clerk's office was closed. The fact that the seals were intact showed that the ballots had not been tampered with, and in any case the returns, which were regular and not in any way attacked, were proof of the vote. The fact that the ballots, on being *recounted,* agreed with the returns, was additional proof that they had not been tampered with."

Here we are concerned with the election in the Fourth Congressional District of Massachusetts on November 3, 1874. Frost, Republican, had received a slight majority over Abbott, Democrat. The former, a resident and former mayor of Chelsea, had a large majority there; his opponent's strength lay elsewhere in the district. Frost took his seat and participated in the First Session from December 6, 1875, until Abbott's challenge was decided in July 1876. It was not alleged that Frost was in any way at fault: but Chelsea's Fourth Ward had disregarded the law, and for the *principle* of the thing the seat was awarded to Abbott, although he had received only a minority of the votes actually cast.

Six months later a somewhat comparable problem arose, in the matter of the election of a President. On this the Constitution says nothing about popular votes. Each State shall appoint Presidential electors in such manner as the legislature may direct. At times fixed by federal law the electors are to be appointed, and then are to meet in their States and cast their votes, which shall be transmitted to the seat of government, to be counted at a session of the two Houses. A person receiving a majority of the electoral votes shall be the President.

Tilden, Democrat, had received a majority of the popular vote, but he had not received a majority of the electoral votes cast, certified and transmitted as prescribed by the Constitution. However, the House, which had strained at a gnat to seat Abbott, was now eager to swallow a camel and disregard the Constitution in order to seat Tilden. And in the ensuing dispute over the Presidency, the House chose Abbott, the beneficiary of an exceedingly strict construction of the law, to represent it in presenting its case in the Commission.

On January 12, 1877, the Committee on the Privileges, Powers and Duties of the House reported "That in the counting of the electoral vote, no vote shall be counted against the judgment and determination of the House of Representatives."[26] This was a new pretension, at a moment when the House was disregarding principle.

It was an unwholesome situation. A few weeks later in his Florida opinion Justice Miller affirmed that for one or both Houses of Congress to take control over the process of electing the President would be a "menace to the liberty of the people," and Justice Bradley warned against "the appetite for power . . . if indulged without great prudence."

ABOUT JUSTICE BRADLEY

WE HAVE SEEN how much has been charged in bitterness and degradation about Justice Bradley; it is due to his memory that a true account be set out before our book is closed. This will be in a sort of scrapbook, with items drawn from his "Fragments of an Autobiography" for his children, and notes, letters, and comments by and about him.

Joseph P. Bradley was born March 14, 1813, on a farm in the town of Berne, in Albany County, New York. Berne lay some sixteen miles west of Albany on the Delaware turnpike, a highway cutting in a generally southwesterly direction from the Hudson to the Delaware River. All about

---

[26] Cong. Rec., 44–2, 609.

rose the Helderberg Mountains, while to the east loomed the bright blue masses of the Catskills. Down the steep slopes of the Helderbergs a number of streams fell into the impetuous Foxenkill whose waters finally reached the Hudson. The Foxenkill had engineered the line of the road through the town from east to west, and in Bradley's day turned the saw and grist mills that served the neighborhood. Along its banks stood the few houses comprising the village of Berne, with the post office and— center of Bradley's youthful interest—the town library.

On the paternal side, Bradley's family went back to a colonist who settled in Fairfield, Connecticut, in 1660; his great grandfather migrated to Berne in 1791.[27] His mother's family, the Gardiners, came from Newport, Rhode Island, and settled in New York in 1781. Early marriages were common—Bradley's parents were married at seventeen—and the new household would be set up close to the ancestral roofs. Picture Bradley as the eldest grandchild in a rather closely knit family: listening to recollections of the Indian Wars and the Revolution, imbibing the lessons of the Bible from the ordinary discussion of grandparents and great grandparents, learning geometry and ciphering on the hearth during winter evenings.

At the age of five Bradley went to his first school. Significantly, he could recall by name the twelve men and one woman who held the summer and winter sessions between 1818 and 1827, when he completed the education of a country youth. Among them was Abraham H. Myers, who in 1831 returned to Berne as preacher in the newly erected meeting house. It was in Myers' parsonage that Bradley was to learn the Latin and Greek which were a prerequisite to college. In 1828 Bradley taught his first school, an occupation which he continued, winter and summer, until 1832.

By the age of eleven he was working in the field with scythe and harrow, and driving the plow over hillsides so steep that he could reach the handles only by standing on tiptoes. In 1827 his father bought land of his own, part of which had yet to be brought into cultivation. The forest was cut down and the wood reduced to charcoal which Bradley would cart to town at night over the mountain roads and then peddle by the bushel in the streets. Sometimes there was tanbark to be hauled to the tanneries.

The family practiced an almost moneyless economy, subsisting on the products of the farm. Of course they raised their own breadstuffs— wheat, rye, barley, corn, and buckwheat. Vegetables came from their garden, sugar from the maple trees. They slaughtered their own beef, pork, and mutton, putting by a supply for the winter. The hides yielded

---

[27] Bradley, *Family Notes Respecting the Bradley Family of Fairfield* (Newark: A. Pierson, 1894).

shoes and harness. Linen cloth came from the flax they grew, woolen clothes from the backs of their own sheep. Bradley went to college in a suit spun and sewn on the farm.

In the midst of it all, however [runs the autobiographical sketch] I was an incessant devourer of every mental aliment that could be obtained . . . . Histories and travels I obtained from the Town library of which our uncle, only three or four miles distant, was the keeper. Many and many a Saturday night, when I could get away, would I tramp down to this mecca and during the entire Sunday revel in the intellectual treats which it offered. . . . In my father's collection was an old copy of Moore on Surveying, and Wilson's old book on navigation. These were favorites. I learned the art of practical surveying before I was sixteen, and was frequently employed by the neighbors to settle disputed boundary lines, and to survey their farms. This brought me a little money. My fees were a dollar a day.

When Bradley was about fifteen, a mathematical problem went the round of the country schools, but nobody could "do the sum." It was really a problem in algebra. "Of course we knew nothing of algebra in these mountainous regions. Everything was solved by arithmetical rules." This was a challenge. Bradley struggled with the problem for a year or more, and at last propounded the rule for its solution.[28] It was no small achievement.

Having tried my rule upon various problems of similar character, and finding it correct, I was naturally very much elated. Amongst my country friends, I had one a few years older than myself, who had the good fortune to be a student in the Albany Academy. In my simplicity I sent the problem to him, asking him to propose it there. To my utter surprise and mortification, by the return mail came a letter from him with an algebraical solution by himself which I did not understand, but

---

[28] Bradley's note appended to his own account: "The question may be stated and solved by Algebra, thus: To divide any tract of land, valued in the aggregate at a given price per acre, into two parts of equal value, one of which shall be worth a given sum per acre more than the other? Solution. If the average price of the whole tract per acre be a, and the difference of price per acre of the two parts be b, and the quantity be any number of acres, . . . [and x be the price per acre of one part, so that $x + b$ will be the price per acre of the other], then

$$\frac{a}{x} + \frac{a}{x+b} = 2; \text{ therefore } x^2 - (a-b)\,x = \frac{ab}{2}$$

$$\therefore x = \frac{a-b}{2} \pm \sqrt{\frac{a^2 - 2ab + b^2}{4} + \frac{2ab}{4}}$$

$$\therefore x = \frac{a}{2} + \frac{1}{2}\sqrt{a^2 + b^2} - \frac{b}{2}$$

$$x + b = \frac{a}{2} + \frac{1}{2}\sqrt{a^2 + b^2} + \frac{b}{2}$$

which exactly corresponds with the rule given by me."

which gave the result correctly. I said to myself if Algebra is such a wonderful thing as this, to enable Peter Harrower (who I know does not understand figures better than myself) to solve a question, at once, which has taken me more than a year, I will know something about it. A relative had recently purchased Bonnycastle's Algebra at a book stand in Albany. I heard of it, and walked five miles to borrow it; and hardly ate, drank or slept until I knew that book from beginning to end. This was in December, 1828, whilst I was engaged in teaching my first school.

Now back to Bradley on the farm:

> At length, in December 1831, an event occurred which changed the whole current of my existence, and determined my future destiny.
>
> Whilst my father and I were threshing out the buckwheat crop one day in the month of October or November of that year, the desire for an education became so vehement that I broke out in a way I had never done before to my poor father. I told him that my life was being wasted. That what I was doing amounted to nothing. That I felt that I *must* have an education. He said, "I cannot afford to give you an education." I said, I did not expect him to do it; but if he would let me go (I was then over 18) I would somehow obtain an education myself; and I would fully make up to him the loss of my unexpired time before coming of age. . . . He finally consented to my proposition, only stipulating that I should help him get in the balance of the Fall crop. He further gave me a small amount of money (about twenty dollars) to start with. Now what do you suppose was my magnificent plan? It was this. I would go to New York (without a letter of intro-duction, or a personal acquaintance); I would get a clerkship; I would return to Albany, enter the academy and conquer an education! That was my plan!

When Bradley appeared at the Albany wharf to start for New York, the boat was pulling out ahead of time, the gangplank was up and the distance was too great to jump. The river was freezing. It was announced that another boat would leave next morning. That night the river froze solid.

> What an escape was this! . . . I returned to the modest hotel where I had lodged, and having a little money in my pocket, concluded that I would spend a few days in Albany and look around a little there for an opportunity of employment that might turn up. But I suspect that my search in this direction was not very active, as I remember that most of my time was spent in listening to the debates of the Assembly and in poring over coveted volumes in the State Library. . . . I remem-ber that the Revised Statutes were under consideration [by the legis-

lature], and John C. Spencer[29] was frequently on the floor to explain various alterations and improvements which the reviser proposed. I was greatly charmed by his clear logic and elegant diction. It was my first initiation into the mysteries of law. In the library I was greatly attracted by an old black letter edition of Chaucer and by the elegant essays of Sir William Temple. Junius also held me entranced for hours at a time. . . . At the hotel I met an old broken down gentleman . . . who had enjoyed the benefit of a liberal education, and had seen better days. He took quite an interest in me, and taught me how to read. That is to say, he gave me an idea of the advantages of proper elocution. Having Junius in my hand, he asked me to read one of the stinging letters to Sir Wm. Draper, which I did. Then he read the same letter himself, and I was surprised at the point and force and beauty which, by proper intonation and emphasis, he brought out. It seemed like a different composition when he read it. . . .

When at last Bradley alighted from the stage at Berne, he encountered the new "dominie" of the Reformed Dutch Church. This proved to be Mr. Myers, the teacher "who had always predicted that I would turn out something above the common run of country boys." The teacher recalled an episode that, in Bradley's mind, always seemed a portent. The teacher had once asked, "Would you rather be a Judge or a King?" Bradley had replied, "A Judge, because he judges the King." The outcome of this reunion was that the dominie took the boy under his roof and prepared him for college.

Looking back at these early events, how strange they appear! Had I gone to Albany a day sooner, or had I arrived at the wharf ten minutes earlier, I should have gone to New York, I should have missed . . . the opportunity to prepare for College. The whole course of my life would have been different. . . .

---

[29] John C. Spencer (1788–1855) was appointed by Governor Clinton to the commission to revise the statutes, vice Henry Wheaton, resigned. His colleagues were John Duer and Benjamin F. Butler of New York. This work became the Revision of 1829. In 1844 Spencer was nominated by President Tyler to be a Justice of the Supreme Court, but the nomination was rejected by a Senate dominated by Spencer's political enemies.

In a letter of January 17, 1889, to William Allen Butler, Bradley wrote:

"I regret not to be able to attend the presentation of the portraits of John Duer, Benjamin F. Butler and John C. Spencer to the Bar Association of New York City. . . . I have always had the highest admiration for those able and accomplished jurists, and owe them personally a large debt of gratitude. [He recounts the episode of his visit to Albany.] His [Mr. Spencer's] fluent and accurate speech, and far reaching views made a deep impression upon me and gave me the first stimulus in the direction of legal studies. . . ."

BRADLEY AT RUTGERS

I entered Rutgers College, in the Freshman Class, in September, 1833. The college year then consisted of three terms. . . . After remaining in the Freshman Class two terms . . . I was examined for promotion, and entered the Sophomore Class. In this class I found Frederick T. Frelinghuysen . . . and Cortland and John Parker, who became my intimate friends and exercised a permanent influence upon my subsequent life. I went [to college] under the . . . auspices [of the Reformed Dutch Church] intending, at first, to study theology; but subsequently abandoned it for the law. The inability to return to the Church fund, at once, what I had received from it (the whole amounting to about $250), gave me great distress. I endeavored, in after times, to make up to the Church and the college as many fold as I was able, of what I had received. . . .

At the college, as before, I was a very hard student. I do not remember ever to have entered a professor's room without being ready to answer any question that could fairly be put on the lesson of the day. Besides the regular studies, I also mastered a vast amount of other reading; and soon commenced writing for the press. In mathematics I stood the acknowledged head of the college. . . . Having concluded to abandon the study of theology, I availed myself in March, 1836, (being then in the Senior Class) of an offer to take the academy for boys at Millstone; the faculty having promised, in consideration of my proficiency, to recommend me for a degree at the ensuing commencement with the rest of my class. . . .

College life was centered in the Philoclean and Peithessophian literary societies. Bradley and the friends just named were leaders in the former. The Society's weekly program included declamations, essays, and finally a debate. What to do with the surplus revenue (in 1836 there still was such a thing)—whether the Presidential term should be longer than four years—whether it was justifiable for citizens of the United States to espouse the cause of Texas—whether Texan independence should be recognized—were all debated. Congress was found to be without authority to abolish slavery in the District of Columbia. "Should a State be permitted to secede from the Union?" was decided in the negative. "Is it probable that the present form of government in the United States will last a hundred years?" was the topic for November 28, 1834. "After several eloquent appeals from the members," the Society adopted a profession of faith, though the negative debaters had presented a better case.

During Bradley's senior year a great constitutional struggle shook the little world of Rutgers. The incident began with the adoption in the Philoclean Society of a resolution expressing "the greatest contempt [for] the practice lately become common of carrying tales to the Faculty of the bad conduct of individuals.'' It ended two months later when, ''out of deference to the opinion of the Board of Trustees that the Resolutions of the Society . . . were 'dangerous to the government of the college,' '' the Society, by a majority of only two, voted to rescind, ''at the same time reserving to itself the right to express any opinion not in conflict with the laws and regulations of the college.''

Bradley represented the Society in arguing its case before the Faculty and in taking an appeal to the Board of Trustees. The entire cause was conducted in the spirit of the great struggles for constitutional liberty in the late eighteenth century. Here is a typical passage from the solemn protest:

> . . . For be assured, that we shall always make it a point to observe the strictest subordination to lawful rule, but at the same time can NEVER consent to relinquish those rights which NATURE has given us and which we *never* voluntarily conveyed away.

Joe Bradley was a desperately serious young man. His commonplace books are replete with entries such as this pledge of Sobriety:

> I hereby declare . . . that I will not, by any means, or on any account whatever, except it be from absolute necessity, call at any of the public houses of this city for the purpose of getting refreshment, refectory, or trash of any kind except oysters, during my collegiate course. . . .

In his ''Thoughts on Commencement'' he concluded:

> Oh, God, be my help, & lead me where it is proper I should go, & make me what it is proper I should be: above all make me humble and contented with my lot.

AT THE BAR

FRELINGHUYSEN AND CORTLANDT PARKER read law with the former's uncle,[30] in Newark. When Parker learned that Archer Gifford, a lawyer and the Collector of the Port of Newark, was seeking a clerk, Bradley's

---

[30] Theodore Frelinghuysen (1787–1862), attorney general of New Jersey (1817–29), United States Senator (1829–35), Chancellor of the University of the City of New York, President of Rutgers College, unsuccessful candidate for Vice President on the Clay ticket in 1844. One of the most respected figures of his day.

name was at once urged. He could keep alive on the pay, and read law in Gifford's office. Frelinghuysen wrote, urging him to come:

> Mr. Gifford is a nice man and you would do well by him. . . . Cort and I are mighty hard students, it would be a great advantage to you if you could be present at some of our examinations.

Bradley accepted, and on November 3, 1836, entered upon the clerkship and his legal studies. He was largely his own teacher:

> I adopted my own course of study and frequently had mutual examinations with Frelinghuysen. Of course we mastered Blackstone, and Kent. Sellon's Practice I studied with the New Jersey Statute book and reports constantly in my hand, so as to know how the English practice and pleadings were modified by New Jersey legislation and usages. Stephen's first Edition of Pleading I had by heart. Mitford's Equity Pleading was also thoroughly mastered. Chitty's first two chapters on the parties to, and on the forms of actions were also carefully studied. Old Chief Baron Gilbert's little work on Evidence I not only studied and re-studied, but made a careful analysis and index of the work. Chitty on Bills and Contracts were largely read, and many of the articles in Bacon's Abridgement. I never read any other work on real estate systematically through besides Blackstone; but in reading every chapter of Blackstone, I had constantly in hand either Cruise's Digest, Coke on Littleton, or the Statutes and Reports of New Jersey. The result was that when we were examined for Attorney's license in November 1839, I had no difficulty in answering all questions propounded on that occasion, so momentous to every student of law.
>
> [In 1840] I received a proposal from John P. Jackson Esq. to enter into partnership with him in Newark. He was secretary and attorney of The New Jersey Railroad and Transportation Company, and practically the Superintendent of the road. Being unable to attend to all his engagements, he desired the association of some young man who would do the professional work required by his law business, and share with him the emoluments. This was exactly what I desired. . . . He guaranteed me five hundred dollars a year, and our partnership commenced. . . . The cases which . . . came into my hands, soon brought me into notice; and from that day forth I never lacked employment in my profession. My connection with railroad cases took its origin from that partnership, and brought me to the notice of other institutions— the Camden and Amboy, the Morris and Essex Companies,—from which I afterwards received frequent employment.

In 1844 Bradley was married to Mary, the youngest daughter of Joseph C. Hornblower, Chief Justice of New Jersey. Home life was as he had pictured it: a growing family; evenings and Sundays given to good reading and serious conversation; a refuge from the world's striving. It was Mary Bradley who made this happiness; she devoted herself to a husband who never learned to be patient. Professional success made increasing demands. In 1857 Bradley's account was: "My days are filled with toil and anxiety. Of business I have as much as I can do, and more. . . . The Spirit life, I fear, is not as prosperous as the worldly life. . . ."

In 1845, just as the earliest life insurance companies in the United States were getting started, the Mutual Benefit Company was established at Newark. For twelve years, 1851–63, Bradley served as its mathematician. There were novel actuarial problems to solve, but his command of mathematics was adequate to their solution.

Although he had a general practice, Bradley's most important client was Camden & Amboy. He was drawn into the management as well as the legal work, being made secretary of the board and member of the executive committee. "Camden & Amboy" was a hateful name throughout the land, for it represented a monopoly in transportation across New Jersey and a privilege accorded to the Stevens and Stockton families by a docile and managed legislature. When the Civil War came, and greater facilities were demanded for movement between New York and Washington, powerful rival interests sought a federal right of way across New Jersey. Bradley was kept busy before Congressional committees and in the courts warding off this threat. The Pennsylvania Railroad, seeking access to New York, was obliged to depend upon the New Jersey facilities. In 1871, the Pennsylvania company leased the New Jersey properties for 999 years. This had been in the offing when Bradley was appointed to the Supreme Court in 1870.

ON THE BENCH: MIND AND CHARACTER

THE NEW JUSTICE came to his office free from attachment to the interests of railroad corporations. Evidence may be seen in his opinion for the Court in *Railroad Co. v. Lockwood*[31] in 1873 where, refusing to follow the wavering opinions of the courts of New York, it laid down very strongly the proposition that public policy forbids the enforcement of a common carrier's stipulation for exemption from liability for negligence.

> Is it true that the public interest is not affected by individual contracts of the kind referred to? Is not the whole business community affected by holding such contracts valid? If held valid, the advantageous position of the companies exercising the business of common carrier is

---

[31] 17 Wall. 357.

such that it places it in their power to change the law of common carriers in effect, by introducing new rules of obligation.

The carrier and his customer do not stand on a footing of equality. The latter is only one individual in a million.

In like spirit with *Lockwood* was Bradley's "Outline of my views on the subject of the Granger Cases." At issue was the validity of an Illinois statute fixing rates for the storage of grain, and statutes of Iowa, Wisconsin, and Minnesota for its transportation.[32]

The "Outline" declared that

> The fundamental principle which governs the main question is this: that wherever a particular employment, or a business establishment becomes a matter of public consequence so as to affect the whole public and to become a "common charge," it is subject to legislative regulation and control. Whatever affects the community at large ought to be subject to such regulation, otherwise the very object of legislative power—the consulting of the general good—would be subverted.

Evidently Justice Bradley kept working at notes about the basis for sustaining the regulatory laws. There is a five-page memorandum, headed "Granger Cases," much cut up with insertions and deletions—obviously an early effort. The twenty-three-page final "Outline" is written more smoothly, being the culmination of continued revision; the broken sequences in numbering, moreover, show that the pages were in part assembled from earlier drafts.

Challenges to decisions sustaining the laws were argued before the Supreme Court between October 25, 1875, and January 18, 1876. *Munn v. Illinois*[33] was the last to be heard, and the last word to be uttered was by John N. Jewett, an enemy of innovation:

"The Dartmouth College case," he recalled,[34] "decided a question of vast importance to one class of private property only"—rights founded upon a charter of incorporation. "The rule which it established adverse to the pretensions of legislative power in the States, has successfully held in check all the efforts of radical politicians and crazy communists, who have, from time to time, sought to make capital for themselves by the

---

[32] Discussed in Charles Fairman, "The So-Called Granger Cases, Lord Hale, and Justice Bradley," *Stan. L. Rev.*, 5:587, July 1953.

[33] 94 U.S. 113 (1877).

[34] The Dartmouth College Case, 4 Wheat. 518 (1818), had held that the charter granted to Dartmouth College by the Crown in 1769 was within the

protection of the Constitution's provision against the impairment of a contract. In the Charles River Bridge Case, 11 Pet. 420 (1837), however, it was held that franchises from a State were to be strictly construed in favor of the public; corporations have only such powers as were explicitly granted.

overthrow of the financial interests and credit of the country." What Jewett now sought from the Court was a decision conceived in the same spirit, that would put private rights generally beyond the "vacillating influences of political power" and the "petty strife and confusion of party politics."

On November 18, 1876, the Justices were polled among themselves: seven would sustain the statutes, Field and Strong would dissent.

At about this time Bradley passed his "Outline" to the Chief Justice, who was going to speak for the Court.

The Electoral Commission Act of January 29, 1877, as we know, called for the participation of Justices Clifford, Miller, Field, and Strong, who on the following day elected Bradley as the fifth Justice. For an indefinite period the Court was inactive. Waite was working on his opinions.

The Electoral Commission met on January 31, 1877, and continued until it adjourned sine die on March 2. The Court met on March 1 and announced its decisions sustaining all the statutes. Waite's principal opinion in *Munn v. Illinois* was a memorable production; in the estimation of Professor Frankfurter,

> Judged by any standards of ultimate importance, his ruling in that case places it among the dozen most important decisions in our constitutional law. . . .[35]

Waite returned Bradley's "Outline" with this acknowledgment:

> With many thanks
> M R W
> Had it not been for the within I could never have won your approbation
> of my own
>
> MRW

So Bradley had made a substantial contribution to the wise construction of the Constitution, but this was unknown to the public.

Now recall that in the meantime, in the Florida case before the Electoral Commission, according to Nevins' story, Bradley had written an opinion in favor of Tilden, had permitted Hewitt's emissary to read it, and then after midnight had yielded to the urging of Frelinghuysen and Robeson, aided by the prayers of Mrs. Bradley, and switched his opinion to favor Hayes; perhaps, Nevins suggests, he was influenced to make this great change in the outcome of the presidential election by the prospect

---

[35] *The Commerce Clause under Marshall, Taney and Waite* (Chapel Hill: University of North Carolina Press, 1937), 83.

of getting a "lucrative job" for his son. On Nevins' word this story has been widely believed by the American people.

One of the most protracted suits in American history—the litigation of Mrs. Myra Gaines over her father's will—came before Bradley from time to time on the circuit. Among his papers I found this note, evidently written by him to be copied by his daughter Caroline (Carrie), who had accompanied him to New Orleans:

Dear Mrs Gaines
> Father thinks that situated as he is in reference to the courts in Louisiana, I ought not to receive presents from you; that it would expose both him and you to misconstruction. With kindest regards therefore you must allow me to return the basket and flowers. Father is very particular about these things—it is so easy to be misjudged by the world.

By Section 610 of the Revised Statutes it was the duty of each Justice to attend the Circuit Court in each district of his circuit at least once in every two years. Bradley set forth in May 1870 to hold his first court at Galveston.

The impression he left is preserved in the words of the leader of the local bar, William P. Ballinger, who wrote to his brother-in-law, Justice Miller:

> Justice Bradley held court here nearly three weeks. . . . [H]e did a great deal of business, holding court several days until nearly dark. He was a new dispensation to us—contrasting very strongly with our manner of judges for a long time past. I like him extremely—and that was the sentiment of the Bar. He is a thorough ready lawyer, and the most complete *business man* I have ever seen on the bench—becomes the perfect master of the case, down to its minutiae, with a facility and dexterity very admirable. His anxiety to get through here rendered him a little impatient in some instances; but he seemed ready to admit any mistake into which he might fall, and commanded the utmost confidence of the bar. We were unprepared—didn't expect him to do anything—and I was conscious that the Bar didn't show to good advantage, professionally, before him; but still I think, he was pleased with its deportment and judged favorably of its ability.

From the beginning of his study for the bar Bradley had tested the common law by comparison with other legal systems. Thus when he presided over the Fifth or Southern Circuit, he proved completely competent to deal with the civil law of Louisiana and with the legal problems peculiar to the territories formerly under the Spanish Crown. In the words of one of the most accurately informed members of the Texas bar, Justice

187

Bradley "become very much interested in our intricate system of land titles and principally in our Spanish and Mexican grants. He acquired the reputation here in Texas of being one of the greatest trial judges that ever tried cases in the state, and this reputation extended especially to land suits."[36] A student of analytical or comparative jurisprudence would find more instruction in Justice Bradley's opinions than in those of any of his contemporaries on the Court.

In 1871 Bradley attended the Eastern districts of his circuit, and had this experience as reported in a letter to his daughter Carrie:

> I started to go to church at Savannah, the first Sunday I was there, and not being able to walk the distance, took the horse car. I requested the driver to put me down at Broad Street, (in which the best Presbyterian preaching was to be had); but the stupid fool, (who makes me mad every time I think of him since) put me out at Broughton Street, which had nothing but an Episcopal Church in it. . . . This accident had such an effect on my temper, that I have not made the attempt to go to church since. . . .

Four weeks had passed, but the Justice's Sabbath anger had kept him from going to church! Bradley couldn't abide stupid errors, in himself or in others. Mrs. Bradley devoted her life to protecting the Justice from irritation.

In retrospect Cortlandt Parker recalled that "He was amusingly petulant—naturally eccentric; and he had stimulated eccentricity by its indulgence throughout his life."[37]

One may see eccentricity in Bradley's opinion in *Bradwell v. Illinois,* where the State Supreme Court had denied admission to the bar to Myra Bradwell solely on ground of her sex. Resort to the Supreme Court brought a ruling that no federal right had been denied. Bradley concurred in the rejection for a quite different reason:

> The paramount destiny and mission of woman are to fulfill the noble and benign offices of wife and mother. This is the law of the Creator. . . .[38]

---

[36] Letter of Charles L. Black, Sr., to the author.

[37] Lecture, "Mr. Justice Bradley," read before the Historical Society of New Jersey, January 24, 1893, at p. 17.

[38] 16 Wall. 130 (1873).

On January 15, 1864, Bradley wrote to his daughter Caroline, who was then nineteen years old:

My daughter, I wish very much to see you, by your education fit yourself for life—so that if need be you can take care of yourself. I know that the practices of society offer but little opportunity for a woman to earn her bread alone, and occupy an independent position; but the times are gradually improving in that respect, and I hope to live to see the day when an industrious woman can earn a

In fact Myra Bradwell (1831–94) was well equipped for the law. In 1868 she had established the *Chicago Legal News,* well edited and especially useful for its prompt publication of Illinois statutes and supreme court decisions. On March 12, 1872, the legislature enacted that no person should be debarred from any profession on account of sex.[39] Myra Bradwell made no move to qualify under this statute. Years later, however, the Illinois court on its own motion, and on the basis of the original application, directed that a license to practice law be issued to her.

On March 28, 1892, on the motion of Attorney General W. H. H. Miller, Myra Bradwell was admitted to the bar of the Supreme Court. Considerately, this was not done until two months after the death of Justice Bradley.

Section 714 of the Revised Statutes provided that any federal Judge, resigning after age seventy years with at least ten years of service, would be entitled to his then salary for life. Bradley came within that provision on March 14, 1883. Upon Strong's resignation in December 1880 Bradley had been assigned to the Third Circuit.

In 1884 a rumor was circulating that Justice Bradley intended to retire. On January 27, 1885, Circuit Judge William McKennan and District Judge William Butler of the Eastern District of Pennsylvania wrote to him assuring him that age had not diminished his mental vigor and expressing their hope that he would not consider retiring. Two days later the Justice wrote:

My dear friends:—

I have received your very kind letter expostulating against my resigning my seat on the Bench. All the newspaper talk on the subject is the *purest fiction*. I have never spoken to a soul in relation to the matter, one way or the other, except to evade it, as best I could when it was broached by others. No one has asked me to resign or even hinted that I should do so: on the contrary whoever has spoken about it at all has expressed the hope that I would not resign. My brethren on the Bench here agree with you, that I ought not; intimating that Judge Strong made a great mistake in doing so.

How soon that idea may enter my head I cannot tell; it has not seriously done so yet. My health is good,—better than usual; and, if the respect manifested by my associates for my views on cases, and

---

livelihood, as well and as honorably as an industrious man; and the best preparation for it is to acquire a thorough education—especially in the practical branches . . . .
In his opinion in *Bradwell v. Illinois* Bradley had expressed his "heartiest concurrence" in "the humane movements . . . for woman's advancement" but not in occupations for which her "proper timidity and delicacy" were unsuited.

[39] Act of Mar. 22, 1872, Laws of 1871–72, p. 578.

questions of law, is to be regarded as evidence of much weight, my faculties have not greatly deteriorated.

Thanking you for your kindness, I am sincerely yours,

Jos. P. Bradley.

When Bradley was receiving this assurance of the continuing vigor and accuracy of his mind he was approaching the age of seventy-two, approximately that of Hewitt when he rewrote and amplified his "Secret History" of the Electoral Commission, based on unreliable recollection and false rumor.

In Cortlandt Parker's appreciation of his deceased friend the following is uniquely significant:[40]

> I am free to say that it has not ever happened to me to meet a man informed on so many subjects entirely foreign to his profession, and informed not slightly or passably, but deeply—as it seemed, thoroughly on them all. Literature, solid or light, in poetry or prose; science; art; history, ancient and modern; political economy; hieroglyphics; modern languages, studied that he might acquaint himself with great authors in their own tongues; the Hebrew and kindred tongues, that he might perfect himself in biblical study; mathematics, in knowledge of which he was excelled by few—all these were constantly subjects of his study.

The most persuasive support of that statement is found in the *Catalogue of the Library of Joseph P. Bradley,* printed for the auction to be held in New York on April 25 to 29, 1892. It is a document of 132 pages listing 1,707 items. An item might consist of a single volume, or a set of many volumes. No more can be attempted here than to suggest the breadth of the collection and the amazing erudition it represents.

On page 12 one begins with *Biblia Hebraica,* the scriptures in Hebrew; then comes a *Polyglot* of Hebrew, Greek, Latin and German versions. Continuing one comes to Cranmer's Bible, presently to Luther's, then a Dutch version, and a Bible in Arabic—57 items in all. There are moreover numerous commentaries and ecclesiastical histories. Then there are other sacred books—the Book of Mormon, the Koran, those of the Parsees, and the teachings of Confucius.

Auxiliary to this literature were the dictionaries and comparative grammars to enable one to move from one language to another—to Latin, German, Greek, Hebrew, from Chaldee to Hebrew, Gothic to Anglo-Saxon, dictionaries to Zeng, Sanskrit, and to Slovenian.

One item is singled out for notice: Calepini, Ambrosh, *Dictionarium Octolingue* in two volumes, printed in 1681. Albrogio Calepini

---

[40] Parker, Lecture, n. 37, at p. 11.

(1435–1511), an Italian monk, had devoted his life to compiling a polyglot dictionary.

Classics of antiquity were included, notably Homer, Herodotus, Thucydides, Plato, Aristotle, Plutarch.

Showing Bradley's interest in the restoration of antiquities were the works of Heinrich Schliemann (1828–90), author of several volumes with maps on work being done at the sites of Troy and Mycenae. (By a happy coincidence, as this passage was being written in our text, a six-part British series, *In Search of the Trojan War,* was being shown on public television, and abundant acknowledgment was made of the labors of Schliemann.)

The library contained a mass of magazines; the *Atlantic Monthly,* 69 volumes; *Century Magazine,* 21; *Eclectic Magazine,* 117; *Edinburgh Review,* 123; *Harper's Monthly,* 84; *London Quarterly Review,* 39, and the *Westminster Review,* 34 volumes.

There was a substantial collection of works on American history and biography: Bancroft's *History of the United States* and *History of the Constitution;* Peter Force's *American Archives;* and *American State Papers* are examples. Also works on or by distinguished leaders: Washington, Franklin, John Adams, Jefferson, Madison, John Jay, John Quincy Adams, and Henry Clay. Pathfinders were represented by the *Travels of Lewis and Clark,* Frémont's *Expeditions,* and the *Account* of Zebulon Pike. There were several reports by Arctic explorers.

On July 9, 1877, Bradley wrote to his daughter Carrie, chiefly about books. The Electoral Commission was in the past; he had attended his circuit, and now he was detained in Washington to hear some matters "in chambers." He had read two serious novels by Charles Reade, and found them "very good." He had cast his eye over Harpers' list of novels, "all of which have been since the death of Walter Scott, and . . . the question arose in my mind, What is all this fiction worth, and what effect is it going to have on the English and American mind? It must displace a vast amount of better reading—history, poetry, and the works of such immortal authors as Shakespeare, Milton, Dryden, Addison, Johnson and Burke; to say nothing of Macaulay and the modern essayists. . . ."

From this comment one may judge the scope of the collection of works of literature.

We shift to science and mathematics. One notes Archimedes' *Opera,* an edition published in London in 1675; then Tycho Brahe (1546–1611), the Danish astronomer whose *Opera Omnia* was published in Frankfurt in 1648. Also Pierre S. Laplace (1749–1827), author of the *Traité de Méchanique Célest,* 4 vols., Paris 1799. William Chauvenet (1820–70), a French youth and Yale graduate whose *Manual of Spherical and Practical Astronomy,* 2 vols., 1864, was hailed as "the most complete treatise on trigonometry in the English language."

Last of all we notice Bonnycastle's *Algebra,* which Bradley had devoured so eagerly when he was fifteen years old.

Among scientific works by university professors we notice from Yale the books on *Geology* and *Mineralogy* by James D. Dana, and from Harvard, Asa Gray's *Lessons in Botany,* Agassiz' *Structure of Animal Life,* and Josiah P. Cooke's *The New Chemistry.*

Bradley's interest in a somewhat special branch of science is shown by Thomas Ewbanks' *Hydraulics and Mechanics,* the work of a self-educated inventor who served as Commissioner of Patents from 1849 to 1852. A. A. Humphreys and H. L. Abbot were Army topographical engineers whose *Report upon the Physics and Hydraulics of the Mississippi River; the Protection of the Alluvial Region against Overflow* (1861) was a valuable contribution to a continuing problem. Rossiter W. Raymond, an honor graduate of Brooklyn Polytechnic Institute, became editor of the *American Journal of Mining.* Bradley owned Raymond's *Mining Statistics West of the Rocky Mountains,* 2 vols. (1870 and 1873), and *A Glossary of Mining and Metallurgical Terms* (1881).

Did the Justice really possess the learning represented in his library? That was put to a test in the following circumstances. On February 22, 1891, Justice Field had been a guest at a dinner where distinguished political figures were present. When Field spoke of the wonderful hydraulic operations in the mines of California it had brought "a smile of incredulity," and Field set out to find confirmation. Having failed in several quarters he turned to Justice Bradley, who promptly made the following answer. The text in full attests to the thoroughness of Bradley's knowledge.[41]

Washington, D.C., March 5, 1891.

Dear Judge Field:

The velocity of water issuing from a pipe is, of course, due to the pressure it receives—natural or artificial. If derived from a natural head of water, it is proportional to the square root of such head or height. If it were not for the resistance from the friction of the pipe and contraction of the vein as it issues from it, the velocity would be eight times the square root of the height in feet, or, more accurately, 8.025 times. The resistance varies according to circumstances. If the water has to be carried a long distance in the pipe, or if the pipe is rough or crooked, it is considerable. Supposing the reservoir near, and the pipe favorably arranged, the velocity will be 75 per cent of the theoretical amount, or six times the square root of the height. Thus, suppose the head to be 450 feet; its square root is 21.2, multiplied by 6, it equals 127.2 feet velocity per second. If the cross-section of the

---

[41] Charles Bradley, ed., *Miscellaneous Writings of the late Hon. Joseph* | *P. Bradley* (Newark: L. J. Hardham, 1902), 352–53.

pipe were equal to one square foot, this velocity would produce a discharge of 127.2 cubic feet per second. A round pipe, 6 inches in diameter, having a cross-section of only .19635 square feet, would discharge only 24.975 (say 25) cubic feet per second.

But this 25 cubic feet issues with a velocity of 127.2 feet. Multiplied together, it shows an effective force, or momentum, of 3,180 cubic feet moving at the rate of 1 foot per second. As each cubic foot of water weighs 62½ pounds, the above result is equivalent to 198,750 pounds, moving 1 foot per second. This is what is meant by foot pounds.

A horse-power is equal to 33,000 foot pounds per minute, or 550 per second. Therefore, dividing 198,750 by 550, we have 461$\frac{4}{11}$ horse-power.

The force of soft substances, when thrown with great velocity, almost exceeds belief. A gun wadding may be made to perforate a plank. An injector has been invented (by a Mr. Jeffards, I believe) for injecting water into a locomotive boiler, in which the pressure often exceeds 100 pounds to the square inch; and yet, by this instrument, a small, swift stream of water is injected into the boiler with perfect ease. I can well believe all that you say with regard to the tremendous force of streams issuing from the pipes of the miners under a large head of water. Of course they would produce instant death if directed against a man standing near, and would probably cut his body in two.

Yours sincerely,
Joseph P. Bradley.

In nine days the Justice would have a birthday and enter upon his seventy-eighth (and final) year. That would be Hewitt's age when in 1901 he told the Chamber of Commerce his fancied tale about his "Secret Mission" to Minister Adams. Two distinguished Americans, but what a difference between the informed and reliable mind of the one and the "enkindling imagination" of the other!

Bradley's diary contains this entry:

> March 14, 1891. 5½ a.m. My birthday. 78 years completed. Unable to work at my table last evening from somnolence I rise early this morning to make up for lost time; as, being conference day, I have many cases to master, & decide. I have now been nearly 21 years on the bench . . . & begin to be pretty tired with the awful hard work of the court. It comes hard to write opinions.

Unable to attend the Rutgers alumni dinner on February 26, 1891, Bradley had responded by letter to the invitation to speak on "The Bench." The essence of his reply lay in this passage:[42]

---

[42] Ibid., 88–89.

Before us, on the Bench, stands the awful Goddess of Justice and Law, watching every word and weighing every decision; if we make a mistake, sending a chill through every vein; if we decide right, rewarding us only with a kindly nod of approval, but leaving us to incur small thanks, and often deep curses, from those whose cases we are called upon to determine. And, how fearful is the abiding consciousness, that, however just our decisions may be, wretchedness, poverty, ruin on one side or the other, may hang on our words. Rejoice, fellow Alumni, for your freedom from such trials. . . .

So far as is known, Bradley's final statement on his opinion in the Florida case before the Electoral Commission was in this letter to Henry B. Dawson, a sententious historian of revisionist views. Bradley's reply was conciliatory:

Washington, Oct. 28th, 1882

Henry B. Dawson Esq.
Dear Sir:—

I admire your out and out spoken manner of expressing your sentiments with regard to the Electoral Commission. But I want to put in a word in my own vindication. So far as I was concerned I took the subject up for consideration as a pure judicial question. I envied the other members who all, seven on one side, and seven on the other, seemed to have no difficulty in reaching a conclusion; whilst to me the questions raised were perplexing and difficult in the highest degree. I gained all the time for examination and reflection which I decently could. I heard every member (in the private conference) express their views at large; and then, in a short opinion, which you find in the book, gave the conclusions to which I had come. I believe Justice Clifford read his opinion after mine; but we all knew what his opinion was. I speak now of the Florida case, which was the first and the test case. The great question was, whether the members of the two houses, when assembled to hear the count of votes for President and Vice President, could go behind the returns, (not of the electors), but of the elections of the electors, and institute a scrutiny into the original elections; or, whether the action of the state authorities on that subject was final. I came to the latter conclusion. So far as I am capable of judging my own motives, I did not allow political, that is, party, considerations to have any weight whatever in forming my conclusion. I know that it is difficult for men of the world to believe this; but I know it, and that is enough for me. And upon a careful review of the whole subject, I am still of the opinion that my conclusion was right. And, moreover, I have had the assurances of eminent democrats that they concurred with me in my opinion.

During the anxious period that the Commission was in session, I allowed no one to approach me upon the subjects under discussion, except on one or two occasions Judge Field, a member of the Commission, called at my house on a Sunday, and adverted to the questions at issue, but we entered into no extended discussion. I received almost every day, after delivering the first opinion, threatening letters of the coarsest and most vengeful character. But I did not feel any great alarm, because I supposed that the dogs which bite do not usually bark.

I have now given you a very brief, but exact, description of my part in that great drama. I have done so because I do not like to be misunderstood and misjudged by those whose opinion I esteem.

But, let it pass. If I have the ill-fortune to be unjustly judged, I am not the first who has been in that predicament. We must take the world as it is, and having done what we conceived to be our duty, trust the rest to a higher power than that [that] rules the ordinary affairs of many in society.

Very truly yours,
Joseph P. Bradley

Justice Bradley died on January 22, 1892, his mind clear to the end.

The Bar of the Supreme Court held memorial proceedings on February 6. George Harding of Pennsylvania reported resolutions, and made remarks that were well informed, based on intimate acquaintance of long standing.[43] On one important point,

> [H]e maintained his judgment in complete suspense until both sides had been fully presented. After argument he retired to his library and examined the records and briefs patiently before arriving at a decision. He was accustomed oftentimes to prepare an outline of an opinion which he laid aside temporarily in order to return to it again after an interval, to criticise his own work and to see if he was still satisfied with the conclusion reached and the reasoning on which it was based. It is known to his associates that not infrequently after preparing this written outline, his own criticism thereon induced him to change his conclusions and rewrite a new opinion adverse to his first draft. These outlines or draft opinions he called his "studies."

Coming to aspersions cast on the Justice for his action in the Electoral Commission,

> He was called to perform an office which was no part of his duty, and which he was certain must expose him to the enmity of one or the other of the two great political parties of the country, he nevertheless patriotically entered upon it and fearlessly performed the duty thrust upon

---

[43] *In Memoriam. Joseph P. Bradley,* a volume containing the Proceedings of the Bar Meeting of the Supreme Court, February 6, 1892. Remarks of George Harding, 17–25.

him. Those nearest to him at the time know that while so acting he refused access to himself to all who sought to advise or to influence him, and decided conscientiously according to the dictates of his judgment. . . . He had reached the summit of his legal ambition. His position was secured for life. He had never been a partisan politician. His most intimate friends and admirers belonged to both political parties. What motive of friendship or reward then existed to swerve his judgment? He placed the reasons for his judgment on record, and few of those who have sought to abuse him have troubled themselves to read or reply thereto, but have contented themselves with impugning his motives. He bore the slanders heaped on him by political rancor with dignity and patience, conscious of their falsity and injustice. I mention all this now because the occurrences are within my recollection and I think they should always be remembered . . . .

Our volume seeks to contribute to that hope.

Index

INDEX